NARRATIVES OF TRAUMA

D0732824

WITHDRAWN
UTSA Libraries

GERMAN MONITOR No. 73
General Editor: Pól Ó Dochartaigh

GDR/German Monitor founded by Ian Wallace in 1979

International Advisory Board

Daniel Azuélos	Université de Picardie-Jules Verne, Amiens
Anna Chiarloni	Università di Torino
Geoffrey V. Davis	TU Aachen
Helen Fehervary	Ohio State University
Gert-Joachim Glaeßner	Humboldt-Universität, Berlin
Gisela Holfter	University of Limerick
Karen Leeder	University of Oxford
Wolfgang Schopf	Archiv der Peter Suhrkamp Stiftung, Johann Wolfgang Goethe-Universität, Frankfurt am Main

NARRATIVES OF TRAUMA

Discourses of German Wartime Suffering in National and International Perspective

Edited by

Helmut Schmitz and Annette Seidel-Arpacı

Amsterdam - New York, NY 2011

Cover image: SLUB Dresden / Deutsche Fotothek / Richard Peter sen.

Cover design: Aart Jan Bergshoeff

The paper on which this book is printed meets the requirements of "ISO 9706:1994, Information and documentation - Paper for documents - Requirements for permanence".

ISBN: 978-90-420-3319-1
E-Book ISBN: 978-90-420-3320-7
©Editions Rodopi B.V., Amsterdam - New York, NY 2011
Printed in the Netherlands

Table of Contents

Library
University of Texas
at San Antonio

Helmut Schmitz and Annette Seidel-Arpacı

Introduction

The emergence since roughly the turn of the millennium of a public debate about German wartime suffering represents the greatest shift in German memory discourse since the screening of the US television series *Holocaust* in 1979, which brought the Holocaust back to the centre of public memory. It is probably not accidental that this shift followed in the footsteps of the institutionalisation of Holocaust memory at the heart of the Berlin Republic, an institutionalisation that for all its controversy put some form of closure on the process of Germany's public soul-searching with respect to the memory of National Socialism.[1]

The debate around cultural representations of German suffering and German victimhood was to a large extent triggered by and fed from a wide variety of textual and visual representations of German suffering in both fictional and non-fictional form. Following the publication of W.G. Sebald's *Luftkrieg und Literatur* in 1999 and the ensuing critical debate about a self-inflicted taboo on German memory of wartime suffering, literary texts like Günter Grass's *Im Krebsgang* (2002), historiographical works like Jörg Friedrich's *Der Brand* (2002) and works of memory like Uwe Timm's *Am Beispiel meines Bruders* (2003) became national bestsellers and TV event movies like *Dresden* or *Die Flucht* attracted record audiences.[2] If it could be said that the 1990s were the decade of Holocaust remembrance in German culture,[3] the ten years after 2000 were very much dominated by the question of how to appropriately remember German wartime suffering. Nor was this a purely German-centred issue. Grass's *Im Krebsgang* and Friedrich's *Der Brand* were translated into several languages, and were widely reviewed and debated outside Germany. *Dresden*, with production costs of over 10 million Euro the most expensive German TV production to date, was explicitly made with an international audience in mind.[4] Although *Der Brand* with its implicit accusation of Bomber Command as war criminals produced a heated response from the UK, on the whole the issue of German-centred memory of wartime suffering received a less controversial reception

in Western Europe than one might have expected. Moreover, this
reception is closely tied to national memory politics in the various
countries.[5] After several decades of a German culture of attrition, it
seemed, the western world was willing to consider the plight of the
ordinary Germans during the Second World War.[6] Things were
different, though, with Germany's Eastern neighbours, particularly
Poland and the Czech Republic. While the question as to what extent
the Allied Bombing Campaign might have been morally questionable
is ultimately an issue of historical interpretation, the story of the flight
from the eastern territories and the ensuing expulsion remains a
politically sensitive issue, particularly since it is tied up with claims
for restitution by the League of Expellees and issues of national
politics and self-image in Poland and the Czech Republic.

Over the last years, a number of academic publications have
critically examined, from a variety of angles, the complex issues and
problems around German self-representation as suffering victims.[7]
However, the majority of publications in the field of German Studies
have engaged with the issues of cultural representations of German
suffering from a contemporary perspective.[8] It would be fair to say
that all theoretical and conceptual arguments regarding the issue of
German suffering from the perspective of contemporary memory
culture, for example the issue of competition with Holocaust memory,
the problematic use of the term 'Opfer' etc. have been comprehensively aired.[9] One consensus that seems to emerge is that, despite a
history of articulation of a sense of victimhood in post-war German
culture, the memories of traumatic suffering had little chance of being
articulated outside a highly politicised and contested field of memory
discourses that were dominated to a large extent by political interests
determined by a Cold War political landscape.[10] Rather than giving a
comprehensive overview over the whole issue, we would like here to
briefly focus on the issue of trauma and taboo that underlies the whole
contemporary discourse of German suffering.

Trauma vs. Mourning

The disciplines that participate in what we call 'memory studies' –
i.e., historiography, psychoanalysis, social anthropology, literary
studies – operate, it seems, with two distinct and largely incompatible
concepts of mourning in relation to the issue of German wartime
suffering. The first, and most widely used, is the Freudian model of

remembering, repeating and working through, a model originating in individual psychology; the second is an implicit model of mourning as a public and performative ritual for the containment of excessive pain and loss, rituals that through symbolic actions inscribe this loss into a meaningful collective, national (or family) narrative.

Robert G. Moeller, for example, asserts that the post-war period is awash with 'ubiquitous [...] forms of commemoration, stories of German loss and suffering' in both East and West Germany.[11] Mourning is precisely the term Moeller uses in this context for the public commemorative rituals of the 1950s, contending that the Germans 'demonstrated a striking ability to mourn' for their own losses.[12] The cities of Pforzheim and Hamburg, for example, held regular commemorative events to remember their destruction, Pforzheim annually and Hamburg every ten years until interest began to wane in 1973 as a result of the generational shift and the student movement.[13]

In contrast, contemporary psychoanalysis, cultural studies and public discourse frequently operate on the assumption that German losses have never been 'properly' mourned, due to either the severe trauma of the war or the instrumentalised and increasingly binary post-war guilt discourse, or both.[14] Propagators of a theory of silence about German suffering by reason of the belated nature of trauma generally follow both Sebald's and the Mitscherlich's assertion of a nexus between guilt, shame, denial and trauma, re-accentuating the Mitscherlichs' thesis about the German 'inability to mourn' the Nazi victims and transferring it onto the Germans themselves.[15]

The return of images of German suffering subsequent to the publication of Sebald's *Luftkrieg und Literatur* has been described in terms both of the return of the repressed and traumatic images and the chance for a 'proper' (i.e. non-instrumentalised) form of mourning. Aleida Assmann perceives the return of images and memories into the mainstream of public discourse as a 'Rückgewinnung deutscher Opfererinnerungen aus ihrer Erstarrung und Verkapselung', arguing that these memories had 'had no chance to be communicated in their humane dimension and shared with empathy in the public sphere', as their inclusion in public memory had been blocked both by right-wing political instrumentalisation of these memories and by the left's resistance to acknowledging them.[16] The argument about a traumatic silence regarding German suffering in the post-war period, however, depends on the incompatibility of trauma and mourning in individual psychology – the symptomatology of trauma simply does not allow for a process of working through, since the traumatic event by its very nature as disruption of the psychic apparatus cannot be 'owned'.[17]

The tension or contradiction between these two forms of assessment regarding the issue of mourning of German losses appears to run along the fault line between a concept of mourning based on collective rites and rituals and one that operates within a framework of mass individual trauma that has not been adequately addressed due to the political instrumentalisation of commemorative discourse in the entire post-war period.

The issue becomes a little clearer if one considers the interconnection between the issue of trauma and the allegation of a discursive taboo on German suffering

A discursive Taboo?

The idea that there is or has been a taboo on representing or discussing German suffering now or at any time in the post-war period has been reiterated with a persistency in the face of all evidence to the contrary that is truly astonishing. The debate about the Allied air war, for example, is not at all – as often maintained – a new one as such;[18] the air war was being discussed anew increasingly since the mid-1990s, and in particular during 1994 and 1995 when Germany began to debate the commemoration of the 50th anniversary of capitulation, particularly the question whether the defeat of or the liberation from National Socialism should be emphasised. The Allied bombing of German cities, in particular the case of Dresden, became one major focus in these debates and was frequently evoked in conjunction with debates about the commemoration of the Holocaust and the question of financial restitution.[19] The frequent 'breaking' of the alleged taboo thus represents not the unearthing of something allegedly forgotten but rather the forgetting of a remembering.[20] While the issue of German victim status has certainly been controversial and part of a contested field of memory culture, a taboo on representations of German suffering did not and does not exist.[21] It would be more accurate to speak of a bifurcation in memory discourse along both the political lines of left and right and along the lines of public and private discourse. Bill Niven convincingly argues that the period of the Cold War resulted in the 'distorted and manipulative representation of themes such as bombing and expulsion' in both East and West

Germany.[22] The end of the Cold War thus presented the possibility of a less politicised discourse on both the Holocaust and German suffering. However, the ensuing institutionalisation of Holocaust memory brought to the fore a second bifurcation within memory discourse, one between public memory and family memory. In their volume *Opa war kein Nazi*, the outcome of a research project on the transmission of memory of the Nazi past in the family, Welzer, Moller and Tschuggnall introduce the distinction between what they refer to as 'Lexikon' and as 'Album.' 'Lexikon' stands for the knowledge about history, as learned, for instance, at school, and it represents the critical, 'worked through' and distanced relationship to National Socialism. 'Album', however, denotes another, an emotionally more important system of reference for the interpretation of the past: family and relations, letters, photographs and personal documents. Welzer et al. found the predominant presence of stories about German suffering, about bombs, war and imprisonment by the victorious forces within family memory whereas the 'Lexikon' focuses largely on issues of responsibility for National Socialism.[23] The important issue for Welzer et al. is the incompatibility between 'Album' and 'Lexikon'. The return of images of German suffering after the turn of the millennium thus represents a complementation of the 'Lexikon' by images from the 'Album'. Not infrequently, though, it appeared as competition, as the public focus on Nazi crimes was seen to de-legitimise German memories of hardship and suffering.

The idea of a discursive and representational taboo on German suffering can thus be described as an ideologeme in the sense of Fredric Jameson's definition of a 'conceptual or belief system, an abstract value, an opinion or prejudice', an 'historically determinate conceptual or semic complex which can project itself variously in the form of a "value system", a "philosophical concept" or in the form of a [...] private/collective fantasy.'[24] The discursive function of the ideologeme of the taboo is thus to legitimate precisely that discourse that the ideologeme alleges is forbidden. This can be observed, for example, in the reception of Sebald's theses in *Luftkrieg und Literatur*.[25] Sebald's assertion of a historical absence in Germany of a debate about the bombings due to an unspoken collective agreement that referred both the Holocaust and the bombings to a past never to be fully assessed was picked up by the German review pages to produce precisely the debate Sebald claimed had been absent.[26]

The idea of a discursive taboo is thus intimately tied to the idea of German post-war trauma and the impossibility of it being fully articulated, either as a result of a causal nexus between guilt, shame and trauma in the immediate post-war period, a self-inflicted silence about suffering that was complicit with the silence about the Holocaust, or as the result of a belated acknowledgement of responsibility for Nazi crimes in which the Germans' own suffering became taboo. In any case, the re-emergence of images of German suffering over the last decade can be described as a shift from a culture focusing on German crimes and responsibilities to a culture focusing on pain, suffering and traumatisation.[27] This cultural shift, described by Aleida Assmann as a transition from a juristic to a therapeutic discourse, marks a change in the younger generations from the judgemental attitude of 1968 to a position of listening and understanding.[28] This more 'inclusive' picture, one that suspends the hitherto mutually exclusive conceptions of Germans as perpetrators and Germans as suffering, however, is always in danger of resorting back to the simplification of hypervalidating one side of the discursive divide. Moreover, this inclusive picture is intimately related to both the emergence of the Holocaust as a global memory phenomenon and the issue of collective identity-building.

The Globalisation of Holocaust Memory and Trauma

The contemporary discourse of German trauma cannot be separated from the emergence of trauma as a central interpretive category for historical experience in the 1990s and the simultaneous rise of the Holocaust to a global model for historical trauma in the 20th century. Over the last two decades, trauma has moved from a psychoanalytical and therapeutic concept denoting individual experience of excessive events to a cultural and collective explanatory model. As Sigrid Weigel has argued, the conflation of individual psychology and collective history in cultural studies and public discourse results in a 'universalisation of trauma' as marker of historical experience *per se*.[29] The problem, however, is not just the universalisation of trauma but that the model for traumatic experience that this universalisation is based on stems directly from the Holocaust, or rather, from Holocaust Studies. The Holocaust thus becomes the universal signifier for traumatic historical experience in the 20th century.[30]

The globalisation of Holocaust memory in the 1990s paradoxically feeds into the emergence of a discourse of German victimhood. Throughout the 1990s the Holocaust is taken up as a central memory marker in a number of European countries, both West and East.[31] Ironically, the European countries' consideration of their own implication in the Holocaust relativises Germany's absolute responsibility at the same time when Germany institutionalises Holocaust memory at the heart of the Berlin Republic. This in turn makes the whole issue of 'German suffering' more palatable to its (West) European neighbours.

The 'Germanness' of 'German suffering'
What does one make of the use of the terms 'German suffering' and 'German victimhood'? The problems are manifold: 'German suffering' in any context of World War II and the Holocaust excludes once again the suffering of German Jews and other persecuted groups, such as Sinti and Roma. Andrei Markovits and Simon Reich argued in 1997 that, due to the historicisation of Auschwitz, Germans not only will be able in the near future to view Germany's suffering as a legitimate part of their collective memory, but that such emphasis on German victimhood would constitute the very re-enactment of collective 'Germanness'.[32] This also implies that even the designation of suffering as 'German' runs the risk of constructing a binary opposition between 'Germans' and those who allegedly made Germans victims (*as* Germans), thus approaching an analogy to Jewish suffering. The acknowledgement that there were also individual Germans (or rather 'German-Germans'?) that suffered is entirely different from the discursive construction of Germans *as* (collective) victims. The 'Germans' who historically suffered were largely, though not exclusively, those of the ideologised Nazi people's community. A contemporary collective re-imagining of 'German suffering' thus runs the danger of dissolving the contemporary collective in the historically ethnicised 'people's community'. At the very least, it re-ethnicises the collective in a similar fashion as the discourse on *Vergangenheits-bewältigung* did in the 1990s.[33]

Moreover, the construction of 'Germans as victims' runs the danger of implicitly operating within the aforementioned model of victimhood originating in the globalisation of Holocaust memory, one in which all 'victims' are innocent. Daniel Fulda's essay on Jörg Friedrich's *Der Brand*, for example, operates with a concept of 'victim' that is essentially passive: 'Opfer ist im Sprachgebrauch des vorliegenden Beitrages, wer Gewalt erleidet.'[34] This is something Daniel Levy and Natan Sznaider have suggested with respect to Japan and an inclusion of the bombing of Hiroshima into the 'Holocaust model':

> [Die Einbettung der Angriffe auf Hiroshima in das Holocaustmodell] bedeutet, dass es in der Zweiten Moderne keine 'schuldigen Opfer' geben kann. Alle Opfer sind unschuldig geworden. Und natürlich ist der jüdische Holocaust hier die Leitfigur. Dass nun alle Opfer unschuldig sind, gehört zu den großen Kosmo-politisierungsmechanismen der Zweiten Moderne. Alle Opfer werden zu Juden. [...].[35]

With regard to public memory it could be argued that German memory discourse is a decidedly 'German-German' one, that is, largely exclusive of 'other' memories of individuals/groups not connected to an implicitly ethnicised German collective. Thus the ethnic/national/political direction of the discourse on German suffering and its potential for stabilising a homogeneously national/ ethnic collective is an integral part of any consideration of discourses of German suffering.[36]

Normalisation?

It could be argued that the shift in German memory discourse to a more inclusive picture that allows for the articulation of German grief and grievance without exculpation from German crimes and responsi-bilities is part of a German 'normalisation', a process that marks the years following German unification in 1990.[37] If nations as 'imagined communities'[38] are construed by, among other things, commemorating their war dead, the shift towards a public representation of Germans as victims is both part of the development of Germany into a 'normal' nation (i.e. one without the particular status afforded by its 20th-century history) and part of collective identity-building in the Berlin Republic. Bill Niven has pointed out that the Second World War is the last historical period Germans in West and East have in common.[39] While representations of Germans as suffering victims are certainly not new and were part and parcel of the cultural logic of the early Federal Republic, the contemporary discourse on German suffering marks the emergence of an acceptable image of German war experience based largely on a collective consensus, an image that unites all Germans. Again, the question arises as to who is constructed as 'German' by this discourse.

The Present Volume
The chapters in the present volume further testify to the absence of a discursive taboo on articulations of 'German suffering' both past and present. The volume explores these articulations across a wide variety of media, from historiography via monuments to public commemorations, literature and film. In addition, it moves beyond the considerations of national debates in looking at the response to and reflection on the discourse on 'German suffering' in other countries, some of which were victims of the Nazis.

The volume starts out with two essays considering historical issues in the context of the discourse of 'German wartime suffering'. Suzanne Brown-Fleming turns her attention to a pivotal yet over-looked figure in the political and religious landscape of occupied post-war Germany: American-born Cardinal Aloisius Muench who served both as liaison for the US-military administration and as papal emissary and whose headquarters were in the American Zone. Brown-Fleming re-reads Muench's 1946 pastoral letter 'One World in Charity' and undertakes a close reading of German Catholic responses which the Cardinal received after the text had migrated across the Atlantic in 1947. These responses show the rejection of responsibility for National Socialism and the Holocaust and give us a glimpse of the very early forms and argumentative patterns of the discourse of 'German wartime suffering'.

Bas von Benda-Beckmann analyses the perspective GDR historians took vis-à-vis the Allied Bombing War. Benda-Beckmann specifically focuses on the work of East German historian Olaf Groehler and his interpretation of the Allied bombing campaign. Groehler developed a position that was critical of both West German interpretations of the Allied bombings as military irrelevant and Anglo-American accounts which he regarded as apologetic. Benda-Beckmann shows that, while Groehler recognised the exculpatory tendencies in both West and East German victim discourse and criticised its production of a 'German victimhood', he nevertheless remained within the parameters of such a discourse by shifting German responsibility onto 'fascist imperialism', or Anglo-American imperialism.

The following section focuses on public memory and mourning in Germany from the 1950s to the present. Nicholas J. Steneck discusses the perception of Germans as victims in relation to civil defence bunkers during WWII. Steneck is interested in how post-war policies in West Germany were influenced and shaped by wartime memories of Nazi civil defence. He comes to the conclusion that memories of bombing and defeat – specifically the failed civil defence – considerably hindered the post-war West German attempts at building a civil defence for the atomic age.

Christian Groh's contribution is a case study of public memory in Pforzheim, one of the cities that was most heavily destroyed in the last days of the war. By reconsidering the local memorial culture of the city, not least through an analysis of speeches given by mayors at the annual remembrance events, Groh provides us with evidence of how the debates about the air war constitute a vehicle to construe a sense of 'German victimhood'.

Jeffrey Luppes continues the investigation into local memory and memorialisation. His chapter examines post-war local monuments erected to commemorate the expulsion of Germans after the war. Luppes comes to the conclusion that – while the larger debate focuses on the 'Centre against Expulsions' in Berlin – the monuments for expellees on the local level generate narratives of German victimhood and contest the memory of the Holocaust.

The last chapter in this section reflects on the more recent construction of a new victim generation of witnesses within the German memory discourse, the 'Kriegskinder'. Michael Heinlein's central thesis is that while Europeanisation and globalisation of collective memories are one of the catalysts for the 'Kriegskinder' discourse, this very transformation of spatial memory coordinates offers an analytical framework to examine the invention and formation of a collective 'Kriegskinder' identity.

The next section deals with visual and literary representation in the context of Holocaust memory and the discourse of 'German wartime suffering'. In her contribution, Cathy Gelbin analyses queer femininity and Holocaust film. Gelbin shows that where earlier Holocaust film tended to associate the queer woman with complicity or relegate her to the narrative margin, lesbian-feminist film has invoked the Holocaust to bring lesbian figures of victimisation and empathy into the discursive centre. However, she clarifies the necessity of strategies of undermining viewer identification, especially in the German context, in order to counter the current tendency to identify with victims and absolve bystanders.

Helmut Schmitz's chapter examines the foundational aspect of trauma narratives in works by Günter Grass, Dieter Forte and Hanns-Josef Ortheil. Starting from the trope of the Holocaust as a traumatic rupture in European civilisation, he argues that the status of traumatic wartime experience in current literature is structurally analogous to and replaces the Holocaust as origin of the present.

The last section explores international perspectives and representations pertaining to the discourse of Germans as victims. Bill Niven undertakes a comparative analysis of this discourse internationally. Contextualising the German discourse with debates about the public memory of both Communism and the Holocaust in Eastern Europe, Niven argues that the German case is closer to Eastern European 'memory struggles' in the post-communist era.

Krijn Thijs's contribution examines Dutch perspectives on Germans as victims and investigates the effect of the German discourse on Holland's own memory. As a victim of Nazi occupation, one would expect Holland to have a rather critical view on German suffering. Thijs argues, however, that Holland's memory discourse cannot accommodate German victim narratives due to its sharp polarisation and the absence of victims at the hands of the Dutch.

In the closing chapter of the volume, Annette Seidel-Arpacı traces representations and constructions of transgenerational German suffering, of German and Israeli identities, and of redemptive queerness in Eytan Fox's film *Walk On Water* (Israel 2004). It shows how notions of gendered/queered national identities intertwine with a search for redemptive narratives, and thereby shape Israeli perspectives on young Germans as traumatised. Fox's film presents this young German generation as having acquired a different access to and sense of fluid gendered identities in stark contrast to an Israeli nationalist hyper-masculinity. Seidel-Arpacı argues that in *Walk On Water* the new 'Germanness' has to be feminised and queered in order to establish the possibility for a common ground between Germans and Israelis after the Holocaust.

The chapters in this volume originate in a conference held at Leeds University in summer 2008 as the conclusion to the 3-year AHRC-funded research project 'From Perpetrators to Victims? Discourses of

"German Wartime Suffering" from 1945 to the Present', which was located at Leeds University 2005-8.

Notes

[1] See Bill Niven, *Facing the Nazi Past. United Germany and the Legacy of the Third Reich*, London: Routledge, 2002, pp. 1-9.

[2] *Im Krebsgang* headed the *SPIEGEL*'s bestseller list for several weeks. *Der Brand* sold over 200,000 copies in hardcover and the paperback edition of 2004 sold 25,000 copies in the first two months. *Dresden* attracted viewing figures in Germany of 12.7 million or 32.6% on its first night of broadcasting on 5 March 2006.

[3] For an assessment of public memory discourses in the 1990s see Niven, *Facing the Nazi Past*. For the field of literature see Helmut Schmitz, *On Their Own Terms. The Legacy of National Socialism in Post-1990 German Fiction*, Birmingham: University of Birmingham Press, 2004 and Stuart Taberner and Karina Berger, eds., *Germans as Victims in the Literature of the Berlin Republic*, Rochester, NY: Camden House, 2009.

[4] See Paul Cooke, '*Dresden* (2006), Teamworx and *Titanic* (1997): German Wartime Suffering as Hollywood Disaster Movie', *German Life and Letters*, 61:2 (2008), 279-94 (here: p. 280).

[5] In the UK, for example, the reception of the issue of German suffering appears to be closely linked to a newspaper's political leaning and its attitude towards European integration. Hence the liberal-left *Guardian* with its pro-EU stance was generally more positively disposed to the notion of German trauma and suffering than the conservative *Daily Telegraph*. See for example Ian Buruma's article 'Germany's unmourned victims', *The Guardian*, 26 November 2002.

[6] Indeed, Dagmar Barnouw's *The War in the Empty Air: Victims, Perpetrators, and Postwar Germans*, Bloomington: Indiana University Press, 2005, and the collection by Wilfried Wilms and William Rasch eds., *Bombs Away! Representing the Air War over Europe and Japan*, Amsterdam: Rodopi, 2006, with their decisively non-judgemental and understanding attitude to the issue of German victimhood discourse could be said to be primarily targeted at a US market and a culture in which the predominant image of Germans is that of goose-stepping Nazis in popular films.

[7] See for example the *German Life and Letters* Special Issue on German Suffering, 57:4 (2004), Laurel Cohen-Pfister, 'The Suffering of the Perpetrators: Unleashing Collective Memory in German Literature of the Twenty-First Century', *Forum for Modern Language Studies*, 41:2 (2005), 123-35, Helmut Schmitz, ed., *A Nation of Victims? Representations of German Wartime Suffering from 1945 to the Present*, Amsterdam: Rodopi, 2006 (German Monitor 67), and Taberner and Berger, eds., *Germans as Victims in the Literary Fiction of the Berlin Republic*.

[8] The essays in Bill Niven's collection *Germans as Victims. Remembering the Past in Contemporary Germany*, Basingstoke: Palgrave Macmillan, 2006, provide an excellent overview over the political as well as the historical field of German suffering. Aleida Assmann's *Der lange Schatten der Vergangenheit. Erinnerungskultur und Geschichtspolitik*, Munich: C.H.Beck, 2006, is a comprehensive attempt to synthesise the whole discourse on (international) memory culture, trauma theory, politics of history and aesthetic representation.

[9] See especially the essays in Niven, *Germans as Victims* and Schmitz's introduction to *A Nation of Victims*, pp. 1-30.

[10] See for example Aleida Assmann, *Der lange Schatten der Vergangenheit*, pp. 169-82 and Niven, *Germans as Victims*, 'Introduction', pp. 1-25. On German self-representation as victims in the post-war period see Robert G. Moeller, *War Stories. The Search for a Usable Past in the Federal Republic of Germany*, Berkeley and Los Angeles: University of California Press, 2001.

[11] Robert G. Moeller, 'The Politics of the Past in the 1950s: Rhetorics of Victimisation in East and West Germany', in: Niven, *Germans as Victims*, pp. 26-42 (here: pp. 27-8).

[12] See Moeller, *War Stories*, p. 174.

[13] See Christian Groh's article in this volume. See also Daniel Fulda, 'Abschied von der Zentralperspektive. Der nicht nur literarische Geschichtsdiskurs im Nachwendedeutschland als Dispositiv für Jörg Friedrichs *Der Brand*', in: Wilms and Rasch, eds., *Bombs Away!*, pp. 45-64 (here: p. 46).

[14] See for example Ian Buruma, *The Wages of Guilt. Memories of War in Germany and Japan*, London: Jonathan Cape, 1994, p. 303: 'But the mourning of the German dead – the soldiers, and the civilians killed by allied bombs or by vengeful Polish, Czech or Slovak neighbours, who drove them from their homes – such mourning was an embarrassing affair, left largely to right-wing nationalists and nostalgic survivors, pining for their lost homelands.' See also Aleida Assmann, *Der lange Schatten der Vergangenheit*; and Susanne Vees-Gulani, *Trauma and Guilt. Literature of Wartime Bombing in Germany*, Berlin and New York: de Gruyter, 2003. Both Assmann and Vees-Gulani argue that mourning and communication of the war experience had been silenced due to the issue of guilt and trauma.

[15] See Assmann, *Der lange Schatten der Vergangenheit*, pp. 108-12; Stuart Taberner, 'Hans-Ulrich Treichel's *Der Verlorene* and the Problem of German Wartime Suffering', *Modern Language Review*, 97:1 (2002), 123-34 (here: p. 126); Wilfried Wilms and William Rasch, 'Introduction', in: Wilms and Rasch, eds., *Bombs Away!*, p. 10; Werner Bohleber, 'Trauma, Trauer und Geschichte', in: Burkhard Liebsch and Jörn Rüsen, eds., *Trauer und Geschichte*, Cologne: Böhlau, 2001, pp. 111-27. Vees-Gulani argues that the 'lack of attention to the topic' [of traumatic experience in the air war], whose psychological consequences 'have not been sufficiently explored in

Germany […] can be explained both by coping mechanisms involving denial and suppression and the complicated issues of German guilt, shame and responsibility'. Gulani, *Trauma and Guilt*, p. 191.

[16] Assmann, *Der lange Schatten der Vergangenheit*, p. 186; and Assmann, 'On the (In)Compatibility of Guilt and Suffering in German Memory', *German Life and Letters*, 59:2 (2006), 187-200 (here: pp. 191-2).

[17] Cathy Caruth describes trauma as a 'breach in the mind's experience of time, self, and the world' and as 'experienced too soon, too unexpectedly, to be fully known and […] therefore not available to consciousness.' See Caruth, *Unclaimed Experience. Trauma, Narrative, and History*, Baltimore and London: Johns Hopkins UP, 1996, p. 4.

[18] Jörg Arnold states in a review of Friedrich's *Der Brand* that a certain strand in the current debate 'feeds off a discourse that emerged during the final years of the war and is grounded in local memory.' Jörg Arnold, 'On Friedrich, *Der Brand:* A Narrative of Loss', review on H-Net German History (3 November 2003), www.h-net.org/reviews (accessed 10 February 2010).

[19] In 2005, on the occasion of the 60th anniversary, the term 'Kriegsende' was commonly adopted in Germany. The fact that 'Kriegsende' has now emerged as the dominant term is telling: it is a compromise that evades any traces of political and moral but also economic responsibility. 'Kriegsende' veils the gap between Germany's enforced capitulation and the celebrations of victory in many parts of the world. Moreover, the Holocaust disappears behind this euphemism of the 'end of the war.'

[20] There remains nevertheless the issue of political culture, memory and temporality: the German constructions of 'victim' and the shifting of responsibility are constantly in progress and re-shaping. Gilad Margalit has described the current state of these developments as 'a conciliatory, non-judgmental attitude reflecting a desire to understand the spell that Nazism cast on Germans, but not to criticize or judge the fairly enthusiastic participation of ordinary Germans in Nazi initiatives.' Following Margalit, 'this mood is reflected as well in the current discourse on the Germans during WWII as victims in the political culture of the Federal Republic.' Gilad Margalit, 'The Downfall of Hitler and the German People', H-Net German film review of *Der Untergang* (7 November 2004), www.h-net.org/reviews (accessed 10 February 2010). Remarkable in the context of a 'forgetting' is here also the terminology: the term 'air war' always refers in German discourse to Allied air raids, never to German bombardments of cities in Poland, Britain and elsewhere.

[21] See Ruth Whittlinger, 'Taboo or Tradition? The "Germans as Victims" Theme in West Germany until the early 1990s', in: Niven, ed., *Germans as Victims*, pp. 62-75.

[22] Niven, ed., *Germans as Victims*, 'Introduction', p. 4.

[23] See Harald Welzer, Sabine Moller and Caroline Tschuggnall, *Opa war kein Nazi. Nationalsozialismus und Holocaust im Familiengedächtnis* Frankfurt/M.: Fischer, 2002, p. 10.

[24] Fredric Jameson, *The Political Unconscious. Narrative as a Socially Symbolic Act,* Ithaca: Cornell University Press, 1981. Quoted from the reprint, London: Routledge, 1989, p. 87 and p. 115.

[25] For a discussion of the politics of translation and English-language reception of *Luftkrieg und Literatur,* see Annette Seidel-Arpacı, 'Lost in Translations? The Discourse of "German Suffering" and W. G. Sebald's *Luftkrieg und Literatur*', in: Schmitz, ed., *A Nation of Victims?,* pp. 161-79.

[26] See Stephan Braese, 'Bombenkrieg und literarische Gegenwart. Zu W.G. Sebald und Dieter Forte', *mittelweg 36,* 11:1 (2002), pp. 4-24.

[27] See Norbert Frei, *1945 und Wir. Das 'dritte Reich' im Bewußtsein der Deutschen,* Munich: C.H. Beck, 2005, p. 10

[28] See Aleida Assmann, 'Stabilisatoren der Erinnerung – Affekt, Symbol, Trauma', in: Jörn Rüsen und Jürgen Straub, (eds), *Die dunkle Spur der Vergangenheit. Psychoanalytische Zugänge zum Geschichtsbewusstsein,* Frankfurt/M.: Suhrkamp, 1998, pp. 31-52.

[29] Sigrid Weigel, 'Telescopage im Unbewussten. Zum Verhältnis von Trauma, Geschichtsbegriff und Literatur', in: Elisabeth Bronfen, Birgit R. Erdle, Sigrid Weigel, eds., *Trauma. Zwischen Psychoanalyse und kulturellem Deutungsmuster,* Cologne, Weimar, Vienna: Böhlau, 1999, pp. 51-94 (here: pp. 53-4).

[30] For a critique of Cathy Caruth see Ruth Leys' investigation into the history of the concept of trauma: Ruth Leys, *Trauma: A Genealogy,* Chicago: University of Chicago Press, 2000, pp. 266-95. See also Michel Heinlein's chapter in this volume.

[31] See Lothar Probst, '"Normalisation" through Europeanisation. The Role of the Holocaust', in: Stuart Taberner and Paul Cooke, eds., *German Culture, Politics and Literature into the Twenty-First Century. Beyond Normalization,* Rochester, NY: Camden House, 2006, pp. 61-74. The UK introduced a Holocaust Memorial Day (on 27 January, the day of the liberation of Auschwitz) in 2001. For a discussion of Holocaust memory in Eastern European states after 1990 see Bill Niven's chapter in this volume.

[32] Andrei Markovits and Simon Reich, *The German Predicament: Memory and Power in the New Europe,* Ithaca: Cornell University Press, 1997.

[33] Dan Diner remarked on the inscription of responsibility for Nazi crimes into the *raison d'être* of the Berlin Republic that it implicitly excludes non-ethnic Germans.

See Diner, 'Gedächtnis und Institution. Über zweierlei Ethnos', in: Diner, *Kreisläufe*, Berlin: Berlin Verlag, 1995, pp. 113-22 (here: pp. 119-20)

[34] Fulda, 'Abschied von der Zentralperspektive', p. 49, footnote 12.

[35] Daniel Levy and Natan Sznaider, *Erinnerung im globalen Zeitalter*, Frankfurt/M.: Suhrkamp, 2001, pp. 215-6.

[36] Samuel Salzborn, for example, points out that the *Zentrum gegen Vertreibungen*, supported by the *Bund der Vertriebenen*, operates with an ethnic concept of Germanness that has its roots in the Nazi people's community. See Salzborn, 'The German Myth of a Victim Nation: (Re-)presenting Germans as Victims in the New Debate on their Flight and Expulsion from Eastern Europe', in: Schmitz, ed., *A Nation of Victims?*, pp. 87-104.

[37] See Stuart Taberner and Paul Cooke, 'Introduction', in: Taberner and Cooke, eds., *German Culture, Politics and Literature into the Twenty-First Century*, pp. 1-15.

[38] See Benedict Anderson, *Imagined Communities*, London: Verso, 1983.

[39] Niven, 'Introduction', *Germans as Victims*, pp. 1-2.

Suzanne Brown-Fleming

'Killing Us in a Slow Way Instead of Doing it with Gas': The German Catholic Discourse of 'Suffering', 1946-59

In January 1946, the first instalment of the pastoral letter 'One World in Charity' appeared in the United States. Its author, American-born Cardinal Aloisius Muench (1889-1962), was a key and heretofore ignored figure in internal German Catholic discussion about the Holocaust, Jews, and Judaism between 1946 and 1959. As papal emissary, he had close ties to the highest political and religious figures in Germany. 'One World' migrated across the Atlantic Ocean to Germany in the early months of 1947. This article examines German Catholic responses to 'One World' as part of the broader pattern of rejection of collective guilt.

In January 1946, the first instalment of the pastoral letter 'One World in Charity' appeared in the United States. It surfaced in occupied Germany one year later. 'One World' called Allied authorities 'other Hitlers in disguise, who would make of [the German] nation a crawling [Bergen-] Belsen.'[1] Only a few criminals perpetrated the inhuman crimes carried out under the Nazi regime, argued 'One World.' Why, then, asked its author, Aloisius Muench, should women and children suffer, because 'some policy makers in top levels revived the Mosaic idea of an eye for an eye?'[2] In Muench's view, presented in his pastoral letter 'One World in Charity', this 'one world' could 'never be built by those who hate, and hating take their inspiration from the hard teaching of an eye for an eye and a tooth for a tooth. It will have to be built by those who believe in Christ's law of love',[3] he wrote in 'One World', juxtaposing the Old Testament laws of Moses and Israel – the laws of Judaism – to those of Christ, of love, of the New Testament, of Christians.

American-born Cardinal Aloisius Muench (1889-1962) was a key and heretofore ignored figure in internal German Catholic discussion about the Holocaust, Jews, and Judaism between 1946 and 1959. He was the most powerful American Catholic figure and influential Vatican representative in occupied Germany and subsequently West Germany during this period. Cardinal Muench held five key positions in Germany between the years 1946 and 1959. He was the Catholic liaison representative between the U.S. Office of Military Government[4] and the German Catholic Church in the American zone of occupied Germany (1946-49), Pope Pius XII's apostolic visitor, or 'emissary', to Germany (1946-47),[5] and later Vatican relief officer in Kronberg, near Frankfurt/Main (1947-49). He was Vatican regent in Kronberg (1949-51),[6] and, later, Vatican nuncio, or papal diplomat, from the nunciature's new seat in the suburb of Bad Godesberg, outside of Bonn (1951-59).[7] As papal emissary, he had close ties to the highest political and religious figures in Germany.

Spanning his stay in Germany between 1946 and 1959, Muench received tens of thousands of letters from German Catholics. Some requested help with immigration to the United States, others wanted help to obtain a revision of their denazification sentence, and still others needed extra rations of food or clothing. A small number wrote in the hopes of commuting their imprisonment for war crimes. Still more hoped to locate lost relatives, or sought the release of family members retained as prisoners of war by American, British, French, or Russian authorities, or wished to fend off restitution claims from Jewish survivors. German Catholics wrote for aid in resisting the requisitioning of their homes by American GIs, or sometimes sent philosophical reactions to Muench's annual pastoral letter. Some penned their political reactions to Allied policies, especially the Potsdam Agreement (1945), or reflected on their social reactions to displaced persons, including Jews.

'I always wished to meet and make the acquaintance of a non-German of good will who holds a position of weight and influence', Elisabeth Baumgart of Selingen told Muench after reading his pastoral letter 'One World in Charity' (1946).[8] At a time when only 'cries of hate' could be heard toward Germans, argued Theodor Lebeda of Limburg in 1947, Muench's pastoral letter calling for charity and mercy toward Germans was a welcome change.[9] Thea Brack, wife of *SS-Oberführer* (and Catholic) Viktor Brack, wrote a letter to Muench seeking his help in obtaining clemency for her husband, who had been tried as a war criminal and convicted for his integral part in the Nazi euthanasia program. In it, Thea Brack referred to Muench as 'the highest Roman Catholic American dignitary in Germany.'[10] Muench's position within the Catholic hierarchy in the United States and in the Vatican, combined with his role as American liaison to the German Catholic Church for U.S. occupation authorities, was the reason for Muench's receipt of such letters. A major theme that emerges in these letters is the denial of any significant level of ideological and practical participation in the National Socialist regime by German Catholics.

'One World' migrated across the Atlantic Ocean to Germany in the early months of 1947. What circulated in Germany was not a reprint of 'One World' as distributed in the diocese of Fargo or United States German-language newspapers, but multiple truncated versions of it. While the multiple circulating versions differed in length, all had four features in common. First, they retained Muench's comments exonerating the majority of Germans of guilt or responsibility; second, they retained also the lengthy passages on the suffering of ethnic Germans and the German civilian population; and, third, the equation of Allied and Nazi so-called 'crimes.' Last, they all omitted Muench's brief references to the Nazi extermination campaign against European Jewry.[11]

Evidence shows that the dissemination of 'One World' in Germany was a grassroots movement among German Catholic clergy and laity, a fact of great importance to the question of how German Catholics understood their own culpability for the Holocaust. According to 'One World', they seemed to have no culpability. In 1952, Father Gabriel Vollmar wrote to Muench, 'how happy I am today to have distributed your wonderful pastoral letter of February 1946.'[12] Monsignor Joseph Kamps kept a borrowed copy obtained from a priest of the *Gesellschaft Jesu* in Beuren, Westphalia.[13] In April 1947, Sister Maura of the Mission for the Poor and Sick (*Missionare der Armen und Kranken*) in Dortmund, read 'One World' while hospitalised in St. Joseph's hospital, Dortmund-Hörde. Struck by it, she asked her fellow nuns 'to pray for Muench every day, so that his great work on behalf of Germans would be supported.' After showing it to her doctor, she ordered it to be copied and distributed in 'academic circles.'[14] Sister Alodia of the *Missionare* told Muench, 'her friends and acquaintances read Muench's pastoral with great interest and wonderment.' The *Missionare* 'had the pastoral copied again, for the poor German people were no longer used to such understanding and deeply shared sympathy.'[15] A Munich schoolteacher claimed she got the pastoral 'from friends who themselves received it from an employee of the military government.'[16] Various translations of 'One World' acquired a life of their own and became something of an underground sensation.

Cardinal Frings of Cologne summarised 'One World's' effects on German Catholics most succinctly in a conversation with Muench: 'no

bishop in the world is so welcome [here] as you.'[17] A number of other
German bishops wrote letters of praise about Muench to the pope.[18] The
Stadtpfarrer of St. Cyriakus in Oberkirch called the pastoral letter
'courageous', showing 'how justifiable it was, that His Holiness Pope
Pius XII named [His] Excellency Muench apostolic visitor to Germany.'
The parish of St. Cyriakus sent deepest thanks, but did not stop there,
mimeographing and circulating five hundred copies of the pastoral
letter.[19] Scores of letters to Muench from German Catholics indicate
widespread knowledge of and support for 'One World', indicating also
the rejection of notions of German guilt or responsibility for Nazi
crimes. 'Daily I express my deepest respect for Your Excellency's
valiant and resolute pastoral letter, a copy of which came into my hands.
It is an apostolic speech which cannot be ignored', Auxiliary Bishop
Höcht of Regensburg wrote to Muench in 1946.[20]

More than anything else, 'One World' was the document that
established Muench's reputation among German Catholics early on.
'Just an hour ago I read your pastoral in the *Tagesspiegel*', wrote
Sudeten expellee Franz Münnich, now of Ostlutter. 'No one feels its
truth like we *Flüchtlinge* (refugees) and *Ausgewiesenen* (ethnic German
expellees)', he insisted.[21] Master builder Franz Grübert residing in Furth
im Wald, an ethnic German expellee from Silesia, elaborated more on
what made it so cheering: it validated his belief that the majority of
Germans now paid for the crimes of the few: 'Again, the great masses,
who had no influence on [Germany's] fate and yet were exposed to its
promises and led astray by it, now suffer for it', objected Grübert, 'and I
am one of these', he added.[22] Elisabeth Baumgart of Selingen, after
thanking Muench for his 'One World', wrote indignantly, 'admittedly,
the Nazis plunged the world into this chaos. But, does that give others
the right to use the same means employed by the Nazis? The Nazis were
not the German people.'[23] H. Mertens, an ethnic German Sudeten
expellee now living in Kreis Hersfeld, claimed to have read an excerpt of
'One World' in *Der Ruf* in September 1947. He too soundly rejected the
idea of 'collective' guilt. A convert to Catholicism in 1936, Mertens
wrote,

> We did not contribute to the many things for which Germans are today reproached.
> We refused to contribute, held high our faith and therefore are not guilty for the many
> things that have so besmirched the German name in the world today.[24]

Barbara Vincenz, teacher in a Koblenz *Volksschule,* obtained a copy of
Muench's pastoral in February 1947. 'Why is one German treated like
the next? There are so many, who wanted nothing to do with Hitler. I
was not in the party, but I am punished. Why don't people like myself
get more to eat', asked Vincenz.[25] Therese Wagner, a teacher in Munich,
read an excerpt from 'One World' in the *Isar Post* in March 1947. 'On
your extended trip through Germany [in winter 1946], you saw our
distress and you know [...] that the majority of the German people were
not susceptible to National Socialism, were against National Socialism',
she told Muench.[26]

A deeply distressing response to 'One World' came from Hedwig
Rohmer of Munich, a teacher in a Munich public school. 'We
understand that other peoples shrink from our deeds, thinking we [are]
all of bad character', acknowledged Rohmer. 'It is deeply humiliating
and depressing, though we did not know anything, most of us, of those
cruel acts and places [revealed after the war's end]', she continued.
'There are real plans to kill millions and millions of Germans', she
insisted, adding:

> We all wish to give satisfaction to those countries suffering from us and to help those
> victims of the past time. But we presume that the idea is of killing us in a slow way
> instead of doing it with gas. Sometimes we think it more merciful to die like them in
> the KZ.[27]

In the eyes of some of its German Catholic readers, 'One World' put
Muench on par with the likes of the famous anti-Nazi bishop von Galen
and even with the Holy Father himself. Master builder Franz Grübert of
Furth im Wald linked 'One World' to speeches by von Galen. 'Reading
your words, my thoughts quickly go back to the now-famous preaching
of Cardinal Count Galen. He, too, was a brave confessor in a godless
state', noted Grübert.[28] Priest Franz Weimar drew a similar connection.
'Yours were the most powerful lines written since the most holy bishop
of Münster against the Nazis some years ago', insisted Weimar.[29] Priest
Franz Schmal of Todtnauberg told Muench that 'One World' embodied
'the spirit of Pope Pius XII.' Schmal wrote, 'I cannot remember an
Episcopal manifesting in such a high degree the very mentality of our
Holy Father.'[30]

Even after making a splash in 1947, the fame of 'One World' and the
reputation it imparted to its author continued to spread. In telling his
friend Muench about a new booklet published by the Neuberg Abbey in

September 1951, Vollmar noted that the last page referred to a word (*Liebe*, translated as 'charity') from the Holy Scripture, a noble tradition that Muench, too, stressed in his 1946 'One World.'[31] Vollmar called Muench's 'One World' a 'heroic act and a document of historical importance [written] in a time of hate' against Germans.[32] In December 1952, Dr. H. Hassenbach wrote Muench to request additional copies of 'One World', noting that 'among the colleagues in his circles, there was a great interest for it.'[33] In another letter dated 1957, former Nazi party member and prison guard Josef Hering of Amberg wrote Muench to complain about his treatment under American internment. He cited a passage from 'One World' to repudiate the behavior of the Americans: 'Let us not become party to the crimes of Hitler, in that we now do what we so harshly judged and fought the Nazis for doing [...] no double-standard should be applied to the law of justice', Hering quoted from 'One World'.[34] When Muench retired from the nunciature in Bad Godesberg in December 1959 to join the College of Cardinals in Rome, he still remained famous for 'One World'. In an article entitled 'Friend and Champion of the Germans', the *Kirchliche Nachrichten Agentur* quoted passages from 'One World' to capture the spirit of Muench.[35]

In their letters to Aloisius Muench, Catholics used a variety of arguments to combat accusations of guilt for Nazism. In late 1947, Muench had a conversation with Monsignor Schwickert about Germans and Nazism. The monsignor told Muench that 'Nazi ideas were still in the German people.' He called Hitler's followers 'bankrupt people, mostly militarists, businessmen or psychopaths, who had no sense of guilt.'[36] In Catholic confessional booths, such Germans revealed 'no consciousness of wrong', said Schwickert. But those that had what Monsignor Schwickert called 'religious pride' remained immune to Nazism, he said.[37] Schwickert's argument equating 'religious pride' with rejection of Nazism is questionable. Due to traditional loyalties to the Catholic Centre Party prior to its dissolution in 1933, as a rule Catholic support for Nazism was weaker than Protestant in the years leading up to 1933.[38] But its weakness relative to Protestantism did not exclude the possibility of Catholic electoral support for Nazism. Oded Heilbronner has examined the expansion of National Socialism in the predominantly Catholic Black Forest-Baar region of southern Baden. As early as 1930, the Nazis won above-average votes and significant support in a number of

Catholic communities in the region, belying the long-held notion that Catholic electoral support for Nazism was non-existent.[39] In his quantitative study of 1,581 men and women involved in Nazi genocide, Michael Mann concludes that among Holocaust perpetrators, a majority came from Catholic regions.[40] Aleksander Lasik's study of Auschwitz SS men showed Catholics as *more* likely to become perpetrators than were their Protestant counterparts. Information about religious persuasion was available for 9% (roughly 630) of the 7,000 SS personnel under study. Of these, a total of 237 (nearly 40%) proclaimed themselves to be Catholic.[41]

Franz Burger of Munich put forth five commonly held beliefs about who was accountable for Nazism. The first was that 'the non-German world met the pre-1933 German regime half-way and thus, through erroneous politics, favoured developments toward Hitler.' This was a common argument that blamed post-World War One diplomacy and the Treaty of Versailles (28 June 1919) for the rise of Nazism. Second, Burger pointed to 'the pre-1933 political parties [who] erroneously carried on a policy leading to mass unemployment and ever greater, more widespread misery.' This argument blamed the ruling Weimar political parties for acquiescing in the economic stipulations of the Treaty of Versailles and for causing rising taxes, unstable currency, and unemployment. Third, Burger noted, 'the Austrian bishops, through solemn demonstration, likewise supported Hitler's *Anschluss*.'

'We submit that all the above-mentioned circles, including those who voted for the law authorising Hitler as the sole power in Germany, are likewise of the chief criminal group', argued Burger in his fourth point. He referred here to the Enabling Law of March 1933, which abolished the democratic Weimar constitution and formed a quasi-legal base for a dictatorship. In his fifth and final point, Burger reminded Muench that Paul von Hindenburg called Hitler to power. 'Therefore all those who voted for Hindenburg should be punished', he wrote.[42] While Burger's arguments had undeniable merit (these factors indeed contributed to the rise of Nazism), they cannot fully explain widespread German acquiescence and cooperation in the face of Nazism, including its anti-Jewish measures.[43]

Another way in which Catholics writing to Muench denied the validity of German guilt and responsibility was by focusing on what they considered to be similarities between Nazism and post-1945

Allied occupation policies. One curate who wrote to Muench complained of 'countless house searches, days-long interrogations, and the bitter taste of exile [...] the same as experienced under the Nazis.'[44] Georg Kretschner of Baden-Baden told Muench,

> Today's world is outraged by those war criminals who committed bestial atrocities [and were] executed by hanging [at Nuremberg]. And yet, the same world remains silent when 200,000 German brothers and sisters in the occupied territory [of] Poland – annexed by the Polish State – are forced into slavery and separated from their families in Germany.[45]

Expelled westward due to the Potsdam accords, Kretschner was originally from Breslau. Germans accused American occupation officials of focusing on the 'little fish' while the 'great criminals' of Nazism escaped punishment. Munich politician Dr. Otto Hipp wrote in a letter to Cardinal Faulhaber, 'the main criminals (Hauptschuldige) and their followers are increasingly forgotten [...] singular personalities and institutions [place] blame for widespread poverty and oppression on those who have not earned it.'[46] Wilhelm Zimmermann of Karlsruhe expressed his opinion that 'Little Nazis were hung while the Big Nazis were allowed to escape.' Zimmermann waited three years before his *Spruchkammer* decision (classifying him as a *Mitläufer*) was handed down, meaning gainful employment was delayed for these three years.[47]

Some Catholics at least acknowledged the wrongful war but still eschewed collective guilt. Catholic canon and *Caritas* employee Felise Book of Borken (Westphalia) told Muench that she realised Germans 'lost the war because we were arrogant and wanted to occupy the entire world. But a great percentage of the German people are as humble as you yourself, and we must suffer all the consequences', Book told the apostolic visitor.[48] When Heinz Krämer of Rüsselsheim (Hesse) wrote to Lucius Clay in Berlin, he admitted it was 'true that this nation was abused by irresponsible subjects [...] Germany's own criminal government [...] to bring disaster to mankind.' But Krämer continued, 'this does not change the fact, however, that the Germans too had to suffer immensely, and faced heaviest mental depression. [And our] situation is not eased by the "hunger cure" lasting over two years now.'[49] Josefa Reiter of Bad Tölz expressed a similar view: 'No one loathes the crimes of our former *Führer* more than we Germans. But the picture of justice and humanity painted by the Allies has not materialised', said Reiter.[50]

Still others fell back on the argument that some Germans 'just followed orders.' Dr. Leisler Kiep of Kronberg, a former admiral in the German Navy, disagreed with the conviction of thirteen I.G. Farben employees as 'war criminals' by United States Military Court IV in Nuremberg (Case Six). Leisler Kiep, brother to Otto Karl Kiep and married to Eugenie (vom Rath) Kiep, ran in the highest circles.[51] Leisler Kiep was on the board of directors at I.G. Farben.[52] After its liquidation in 1950, he was affiliated with one of its largest successor companies, Hoechst.[53] Kiep's son married the daughter of Dr. Fritz Meer, a German chemist who was one of the thirteen men convicted at the 1948 I.G. Farben trial. Leisler Kiep wrote frequent correspondent Muench that he was 'the last person in the world to condone the sins and crimes committed under the Nazi regime.' But, wrote Leisler Kiep,

> these industrialists only did what they were obliged to do, as did their colleagues in other countries, under the orders of their governments [...]. This seems to me to be a question of clemency and that certainly pertains to the Church.[54]

A number of German Catholics told Muench that their own priests advised them to join the Nazi party. Bishop Heinrich Wienken of Meissen (1883-1961) told Muench some priests 'thought they might influence trends, protect livelihoods and families, or channel the Nazi movement into right acts.'[55] August Unseld, *Ortsleiter* of Achsteffen, was one example. In 1937, Unseld decided to resign as *Ortsleiter*. The local pastor, Father Strahl, visited Unseld in his home and begged him not to resign. Otherwise, worried Strahl, an 'unjust and radical man could get it.'[56] Wienken claimed other priests 'feared concentration camps, [were] natural leaders for [presumably anti-Nazi] political activity, or feared communism.' Generally speaking, Wienken told Muench, Catholic priests knew that 'speaking [up against the regime] was not desired.'[57] Whether Wienken meant that speaking up was 'not desired' by the Holy See, by his superiors in the German hierarchy, or by the Nazi regime itself is unclear.

In conclusion, evidence suggests that Cardinal Muench's openly partisan philo-German position provided psychological comfort to many German Catholics. The wild popularity of 'One World' earned then-Bishop Muench a platform from which he might have encouraged a real reckoning with the years 1933 to 1945. Instead, Muench concerned himself with those whose self-congratulatory or self-pitying labelling of themselves as 'victims' or 'resistors' was often questionable. Cardinal Muench is an important figure in any study of German 'selective memory' regarding the Nazi past and in the Catholic Church's failure during this period to confront its own complicity in Nazism's anti-Jewish ideology. He exemplified both of these phenomena perfectly. So long as the cardinal remained *prudent* about maintaining his (and sometimes their) agendas without attracting undue attention or bad publicity to himself or his Church, his superiors granted him the Church's highest honours and titles.

Notes

[1] Aloisius Muench, 'One World in Charity: A Pastoral', p. 7. I thank the librarians of the Aloisius Cardinal Muench Seminary in Fargo, North Dakota, for sending me a copy of the pastoral letter's original edition. A Second Edition version of 'One World' is available in HM 37/93/4, ACUA.

[2] Ibid. Here, Muench quoted the second and third books of the Old Testament, Exodus 21:24 ('eye for eye, tooth for tooth, hand for hand, foot for foot') and Leviticus 24:20 ('fracture for fracture, eye for eye, tooth for tooth').

[3] Muench, 'One World', p. 7.

[4] In November 1943, President Franklin D. Roosevelt assigned the primary role in military government training and personnel to the U.S. Army's War Department. Earlier that year, the Civil Affairs Division was created within the War Department as a staff division limited to the 'planning and supervision of military government wherever needed, anywhere in the world'. Despite the fact that the War Department oversaw the training of military government personnel, the State and Treasury Departments also sought jurisdiction over occupation policies and goals. American occupation presence in Germany had three phases. The first was the wartime military phase, lasting from June 1944 until July 1945, during which military government officers operated out of the War Department's Civil Affairs Division and under the command of either the British-U.S. Combined Command of Supreme Headquarters, Allied Expeditionary Forces (SHAEF) or the Command of United States Forces-European Theater (USFET). The second was the non-wartime military phase, lasting from July 1945 until June 1949, during which military government officers reported to the Office of Military Government-United States Zone (OMGUS). The third was the civilian phase, which followed West German independence, during which military government officers reported to the Office of the High Commission for Germany (HICOG). General Dwight D. Eisenhower, former commander of SHAEF and USFET, was the first military governor of the U.S. zone of occupation under

OMGUS. General Lucius D. Clay was his deputy military governor. In the late fall of 1945, General Joseph T. McNarney replaced Eisenhower, and Clay remained deputy military governor. In March 1947, Clay replaced McNarney as military governor, but in reality, he already played the dominant role in responsibility for military government affairs under both Eisenhower and McNarney. On 18 May 1949, the United States formally announced the agreement to transfer (nonmilitary) responsibility of the occupation from the Army to the State Department. On 6 June 1949, HICOG formally replaced OMGUS. John J. McCloy, formerly Roosevelt's assistant secretary of war, became the first U.S. high commissioner to Germany. See Rebecca Boehling, *A Question of Priorities: Democratic Reforms and Economic Recovery in Postwar Germany*, Providence, RI: Berghahn Books, 1996, pp. 17-19; 43. See also Warren F. Kimball, *Swords or Ploughshares? The Morgenthau Plan for Defeated Nazi Germany 1943-1946*, Philadelphia: Lippincott, 1976. During the U.S occupation of Germany, U.S. forces in Europe had the three following designations: United States Forces-European Theater (USFET), July 1945-March 1947, under General Dwight D. Eisenhower (until November 1945) and subsequently General Joseph T. McNarney (November 1945-March 1947); European Command (EUCOM), March 1947-August 1952, under General Lucius D. Clay (March 1947-May 1949), General Clarence R. Huebner (May-September 1949), and General Thomas T. Handy (September 1949-August 1952); and United States Army in Europe (USAREUR), beginning August 1952, under General Manton S. Eddy (August 1952-April 1953), General Charles R. Bolte (April-September 1953), General William M. Hoge (September 1953-February 1955), General Anthony C. McAuliffe (February 1955-May 1956), and General Henry I. Hodes (May 1956-April 1959). Generals McNarney and Clay also served as U.S. military governors for OMGUS.

[5] An apostolic visitor, also referred to as a 'papal visitor', is a papal representative to a particular church, government, or internationally accredited council. Apostolic visitors differ from other papal legates in that the pope summons them for special emergencies only, and their missions are generally of short duration.

[6] The role of the Vatican regent was in practice that of a nuncio, but due to the Federal Republic of Germany's lack of full autonomy in 1949, no diplomats (and hence no papal nuncio) could, in principle, operate there. This changed in 1951, when the Federal Republic established an independently operating Foreign Ministry and received foreign diplomats for the first time.

[7] The Holy See employs its own ambassadors, called nuncios, to represent the pope to hundreds of civil governments. Nuncios hold the rank of ambassador and also hold the honorary title 'dean of diplomatic corps' in nation-states adhering to the Congress of Vienna (1815). In each nation-state, nuncios operate from their nunciature, or diplomatic headquarters.

[8] Letter from Elisabeth Baumgart, Selingen, to Muench, Kronberg, 24 July 1947. HM 37/20/10, ACUA.

[9] Letter from Theodor Lebeda, Limburg, to Muench, Kronberg, 7 October 1947. HM 37/116/15, ACUA.

[10] Letter from Thea Brack, Reichenbach am Heuberg, to Muench, Kronberg, 24 September 1947. HM 37/128/3, ACUA. A copy of Muench's reply is not available.

[11] As noted, Muench alluded to the Holocaust two times and to Jews specifically once in 'One World'. In brief, these references were: 'extermination of millions of persons due to theories of race inferiority;' 'Hitler's cruel policies of extermination of what he called inferior races and peoples', and '[American] horror when the Nazis proclaimed the doctrine of racial guilt against all the Jews'.

[12] Letter from Vollmar, Bonn, to Muench, Bad Godesberg, 23 April 1952. HM 37/90/3, ACUA.

[13] Letter from Monsignor Joseph Kamps, Beuren, to Muench, Kronberg, 25 January 1948. HM 37/92/5, ACUA.

[14] Letter from Sister Maura, Dortmund, to Muench, Kronberg, 3 April 1947. HM 37/37/6, ACUA. Her letter does not clarify who actually copied the letter.

[15] Letter from Sister Alodia, Dortmund, to Muench, Kronberg, 18 April 1947. HM 37/37/1, ACUA.

[16] Letter from Hedwig Rohmer, Munich, to Muench, Kronberg, 14 January 1947. HM 37/9/2, ACUA.

[17] Muench Diary entry dated 21 January 1947.

[18] Letter from Muench, Kronberg, to his sister Terry Muench, Milwaukee, 18 February 1947. HM 37/32/2, ACUA.

[19] Letter from *Stadtpfarrer* Ruh to Muench, 6 September 1947.

[20] Letter from *Weihbischof* (Auxiliary Bishop) Höcht, Regensburg, to Muench, Kronberg, 1946. HM 37/142/6, ACUA.

[21] Letter from Franz Münnich, Ostlutter, to Muench, Kronberg, 26 April 1947. HM 37/20/9, ACUA.

[22] Letter from Franz Grübert, Furth, to Muench, Kronberg, 2 January 1947. HM 37/83/1, ACUA.

[23] Letter from Elisabeth Baumgart to Muench, 24 July 1947.

[24] Letter from H. Mertens, Hersfeld, to Muench, Kronberg, 26 September 1947. HM 37/128/3, ACUA.

[25] Letter from Barbara Vincenz, Koblenz, to Muench, Kronberg, 5 February 1947. HM 37/20/9, ACUA.

[26] Letter from Therese Wagner, Munich, to Muench, Kronberg, 5 March 1947. HM 37/20/9, ACUA.

[27] Letter from Hedwig Rohmer, Munich, to Muench, Kronberg, 14 January 1947. Two copies, one in German and one translated copy, exist in the collection. See HM 37/9/2 and 55/3, ACUA.

[28] Letter from Gruebert to Muench, 2 January 1947.

[29] Letter from Father Franz Weimar to Muench, Kronberg, 11 October 1947. HM 37/53/7, ACUA.

[30] Letter from Father Franz Schmal, Todtnauberg, to Muench, Kronberg, 18 April 1947. HM 37/92/3, ACUA.

[31] Letter from Vollmar to Muench, 3 December 1951. HM 37/96/8, ACUA.

[32] Letter from Vollmar to Muench, 23 April 1952. HM 37/90/3, ACUA.

[33] Letter from H. Hassenbach, Frankfurt/Main, to Muench, Kronberg, 22 December 1952. HM 37/21/8, ACUA.

[34] Letter from Joseph Hering, Amberg, to Muench, Bad Godesberg, 1 August 1957. HM 37/131/4, ACUA.

[35] 'Freund und Anwalt der Deutschen', *Kirchliche Nachrichten Agentur (KNA) Beilage.* HM 37/45/2, ACUA.

[36] Muench Diary entry dated 10 December 1947, Vol.7, pp. 18-19.

[37] Ibid.

[38] In Catholic farming areas, the Nazi party rarely gained so much as ten percent of the vote, due to the fact that in Catholic regions, the NSDAP faced opposition from the Church, Catholic parties (the Centre Party, or, in Bavaria, the Bavarian People's Party), and local Catholic notables and press. See Richard F. Hamilton, 'The Rise of Nazism: A Case Study and Review of Interpretations – Kiel, 1928-1933', *German Studies Review* XXVI/1 (2003), 43-62. See also Martin Broszat, et al., *Bayern in der NS-Zeit*, 6 vols. Munich: Oldenbourg, 1977-83.

[39] See Oded Heilbronner, *Catholicism, Political Culture, and the Countryside: A Social History of the Nazi Party in South Germany*, Ann Arbor, MI: University of Michigan Press, 1998.

[40] Mann relied upon Fritz Bauer, ed., *Justiz und NS-Verbrechen: Sammlung deutscher Stafurteilte wegen national-sozialistischer Tötungsverbrechen 1945-1966*, Amsterdam: Amsterdam University Press, 1968-81, 22 volumes, among other sources. For his discussion of religion as a factor in likelihood to become a perpetrator, see Michael Mann, 'Were the Perpetrators of Genocide Ordinary Men or Real Nazis? Results from Fifteen Hundred Biographies', *Holocaust and Genocide Studies*, 14:3 (2000), 347-9.

[41] In 1940, the total SS staff members in Auschwitz did not exceed 500. On 15 January 1945, one day before the camp's evacuation, the number of SS personnel reached its peak of 4,481 SS men and 71 SS women supervisors. Throughout the camp's entire history, a total of 6,800 SS men and about 200 SS women supervisors (total population under study) served in the camp. See Aleksander Lasik, 'Historical-sociological Profile of the Auschwitz SS', in: Israel Gutman and Michael Berenbaum, eds., *Anatomy of the Auschwitz Death Camp*, Bloomington: Indiana University Press in association with the United States Holocaust Memorial Museum, 1994, p. 274 and pp. 279-80.

[42] Letter from Franz Burger, Munich, to Muench, Kronberg, November 1946. HM 37/125/9, ACUA.

[43] See Robert Gellately's *Backing Hitler: Consent and Coercion in Nazi Germany*, Oxford: Oxford University Press, 2001. Gellately debunks the myth of acquiescence due solely to the regime's terror methods.

[44] Letter from unnamed curate in Wies, to Muench, Kronberg, 18 December 1950. HM 37/81/8, ACUA.

[45] Letter from Georg Kretschner, Baden-Baden, to Muench, Bad Godesberg, 11 June 1951. HM 37/21/7.

[46] Letter from Hipp to Faulhaber, 28 June 1948.

[47] Letter from Wilhelm Zimmermann, Karlsruhe, to Pope Pius XII, Rome, 18 October 1955. The letter arrived at the Bad Godesberg nunciature, and Muench was to forward it to the Vatican.

[48] Letter from Felise Book, Borken, to Muench, Kronberg, 25 September 1947. HM 37/83/1, ACUA.

[49] Letter from Heinz Krämer, Rüsselsheim, to Lucius Clay, Berlin, 1 September 1947. In folder #1 (document #65), Box #116 (AG 000.1 through AG 000.3: Religion, January-June 1947), Office of the Adjutant General: General Correspondence and

Other Records (Decimal File) 1945-1949 (hereafter OAG-GC), Records of the Executive Office (hereafter REO), RG 260-OMGUS, NARA.

[50] Letter from Josefa Reiter, Bad Tölz, to Muench, Kronberg, 9 February 1947. HM 37/69/6, ACUA.

[51] Otto Karl Kiep (1886-1944) was a high-ranking German diplomat who withdrew from active service in 1933 due to ideological differences with Nazism. In 1939, he joined the Foreign Division of the *Wehrmacht* High Command. He was arrested and executed by the Gestapo in July 1944 for his contacts with opposition circles in the *Abwehr* (Wehrmacht Intelligence). Eugenie Kiep (born vom Rath) was related to Ernst vom Rath (1909-38), famous for his death at the hands of Herschel Grynszpan on 7 November 1938. Grynspan mistook vom Rath, legation secretary for the German embassy in Paris, for the ambassador.

[52] Muench Diary entry dated 20-21 March 1957, Vol.21, p. 263.

[53] Letter from Kiep, Kronberg, to Muench, Bad Godesberg, 16 February 1954. HM 37/22/3, ACUA.

[54] Letter from Dr. Leisler Kiep, Kronberg, to Muench, Bad Godesberg, 17 December 1953. HM 37/15/8, ACUA.

[55] Muench Diary entry dated 6 August 1946, Vol.4, p. 39.

[56] Letter from Maria Unseld (sister to August Unseld), New York, to Muench, Kronberg, 26 September 1947. HM 37/14/7, ACUA.

[57] Muench Diary entry dated 6 August 1946, Vol.4, p. 39.

Bas von Benda-Beckmann

Imperialist Air War.
East German academic Research and Memory Politics reflected in the Work of Olaf Groehler

This chapter analyses the work of GDR historians on the air war and the Allied bombing campaign, particularly the work of Olaf Groehler, the leading GDR expert on the air war. The chapter situates Groehler's work within official GDR memory politics and explores Groehler's work as an attempt to distance himself from both the dominant SED narrative as well as West German apologetic tendencies. It argues, however, that Groehler ultimately remained within the parameters of a GDR 'victim discourse' by shifting German responsibility onto 'fascist imperialism', or Anglo-American imperialism.

Introduction

This chapter will explore the ways in which historians from the GDR interpreted the Allied bombings. Particular attention will be given to the work of East German historian Olaf Groehler. Arguably, Groehler's work can be seen, due to his extensive efforts, knowledge and archival research, as the only real academic approach to the Allied bombings in the GDR.[1] Groehler was considered to be the leading academic expert on the subject of the air war in the GDR, and contemporary researchers still value his work. His work provokes the question, to what extent a distinctive academic 'Marxist' interpretation of the Allied bombings was developed in East Germany and how this perspective is to be valued. What historical causes and backgrounds were thought to be of importance in the air war strategy and practice of the Western Allies? To what extent did East German academic research ascribe certain political and moral meanings to this history? How did this perspective relate to GDR popular memory culture, to SED-propaganda and to the official politics of the past? To be able to give a proper answer to these questions it should be made clear that there are a few overlapping problems when regarding the East German academic historical perspective on the Allied air war. Therefore, two relevant layers that surround Groehler's position will be analysed.

First, some of the key aspects of East German memory politics shall be illustrated. This is particularly important for placing the later and more sophisticated academic research of Olaf Groehler in a proper discursive context. Secondly, the specific character of the East German historical discipline will be addressed. Acknowledging that academic historians operated within the strict limits of censorship and of what Martin Sabrow has labelled 'das Diktat des Konsenses',[2] the question arises in which respects GDR historians actually managed to develop a serious academic perspective on this subject. What space did GDR memory politics leave for a more sophisticated and less politically and morally loaded perspective?

Considering his role as a prominent GDR historian Groehler's perspective on the Allied bombings has often been regarded as a mere extension of official SED memory politics. This perspective was dominant in the West German reception of Groehler's work before and shortly after 1989 and recently has been represented by historians writing critically on GDR memory culture.[3] On the other hand, the recent renewed attention paid to the Allied bombings has also led to a re-evaluation of Groehler's work.[4] Academic experts working in the field have especially recognised *Bombenkrieg gegen Deutschland* as an important and valuable historical account.[5]

A closer analysis of Groehler's work shows that these seemingly contradictory interpretations both are partly valid and not necessarily incompatible. Rather than asking difficult questions about his academic and personal integrity, Groehler's perspective on the bombing war will be analysed in the light of official GDR memory politics. Should his work be regarded as a more elaborate repetition of the official view or did his work collide with official memory politics? Since on a few important matters the latter seems to be the case, the additional question is: to what extent was Groehler's perspective different and how is this to be explained? Can one even go as far as to say that Groehler created a specifically East German academic narrative? Or was it possible to provide the official memory politics with historical argumentation and documentation?

Official memory politics and the Allied 'terror-bombing' of Dresden
From the end of the 1940s the public remembrance of the bombing of Dresden spread out throughout the GDR and subsequently the official interpretation of the event changed dramatically. With the interpreta-

tion of the historical event becoming more and more aggressive and anti-Western in character, the scale on which the bombing of Dresden was publicly remembered was growing. Whereas in the first years after the war the bombings had been presented as consequences of failed air protection and the aggressive war of the Nazi State, now the actual 'perpetrators' of the bombing were identified. In 1948 an article in the *Sächsische Volkszeitung* stated for the first time that it was 'Anglo-American airplanes' that had dropped their bombs on Dresden. From now on, the bombing of Dresden was increasingly portrayed as a 'senseless crime' committed by the Western Allies against a nation that had already been defeated.[6]

The Allied strategic bombing campaign was presented as a terror-attack against German 'women and children' for which the *Anglo-Amerikaner* were solely responsible. The responsibility of fascist Germany for the outbreak of the Second World War and the German attacks on Coventry and Rotterdam that had preceded the Allied bombings were increasingly ignored. This way the Western Allies could be pointed out as the only 'guilty party'. The language used to describe the attacks was charged with metaphors and images of doom and terror. In 1951 a comment in the *Tägliche Rundschau* described the glow of the burning city as the 'räuberische Fratze des amerikanischen Imperialismus, der argste Feind der Menschheit'.[7]

In this clear portrayal of Dresden as an Allied war crime the SED propaganda made use of language and arguments that were remarkably similar to the way this bombardment was exploited by the NSDAP during the last months of the war.[8] Phrases such as *Terror-angriffe* and *anglo-amerikanische Luftgangster* had been invented by Goebbels' propaganda apparatus and now found their way back into the public discourse. But also the special and mythical position of Dresden as the ultimate symbol of Anglo-American criminality was adopted. By portraying Dresden as an innocent victim of ruthless American terror, the SED kept the 'Dresden myth' alive, an image created by Goebbels' propaganda that allowed the adoption of all kinds of legends and falsifications into public consciousness.[9]

This enabled SED propaganda to detach the bombing of Dresden from the Second World War and to explain the events of 13 February 1945 within the new political context of the Cold War. Supported by the frequently repeated notion that the Soviet Army had never engaged in terror attacks, SED propaganda could emphasise that the

Red Army had been the only true liberator of Germany and was morally superior to the half-hearted imperialists from the West. Dresden was used to demonstrate the continuity of American aggression against the German population. Dresden was presented as the historical 'example' of what the imperialist Americans were capable of. Throughout the 1950s and 1960s the commemoration of Dresden was used in the first place as a vehicle to criticise the development of the NATO and the American atomic policies.[10]

This unhistorical and politicised discourse allowed the bombing of Dresden to be explained as a first step in the Cold War. Since Dresden had not been a target of military significance in the Second World War and the war actually already had been won, it was argued, the Allies must have had other reasons for bombing the city. From the mid-1950s, therefore, the idea was spread in the GDR that the actual reason for bombing Dresden had been that the British and Americans wanted to unsettle the future Soviet sphere of influence and at the same time intimidate the Red Army by demonstrating the destructive power of their air forces. By bombing Dresden they were not attacking Hitler but Stalin.[11]

In 1950, Walter Lehwess-Litzmann came to the conclusion that the Allied purposes for bombing Dresden had been twofold. They wanted to conclude their work of 'destruction' by bombing the one last large city that had remained relatively unharmed. More importantly, they had wanted to complicate the later reconstruction of what they knew would become the Soviet zone of influence.[12] A similar perspective was present in the two historical publications on the Dresden bombing attempting to offer a more detailed description of the events that had taken place on 13 February 1945 and giving a more elaborate explanation for the bombing. Former Prime Minister of Saxony Max Seydewitz published *Zerstörung und Wiederaufbau von Dresden* in 1955. It was a highly propagandistic work mainly focusing on a dubious conspiracy theory claiming that the Dresden raid had been the sole responsibility of Charles Noble, a German-American businessman, who embodied the secret conspiracy between Nazism and capitalism.

A decade later Dresden's former *Oberbügermeister* Walter Weidauer produced a slightly more elaborate account, *Inferno Dresden*, based on modest historical research. Weidauer's book became the key text for the dominant SED perspective. Weidauer, like Seydewitz and Lehwess-Litzmann, presented the bombing of Dresden as the beginning of the Cold War. 'Alle Tatsachen beweisen, daß die englische und amerikanische Regierung mit der Zerstörung Dresdens nicht die Hitlerfaschisten, sondern in erster Linie ihre sowjetischen Bundesgenossen treffen wollten', Weidauer concluded.[13] Weidauer took this theory, generally accepted in the GDR, to another level by creating a direct connection between Dresden and the present threat of atomic warfare. Weidauer argued: 'So unwahrscheinlich es auch klingen mag, so sicher ist es: Die erste Atombombe sollte auf eine deutsche Stadt fallen.'[14] This city was going to be Dresden. Dresden lay in the future Soviet zone of influence and had intentionally been spared for the purpose of experimenting with the new bomb. Only because the development of the atomic bomb had taken more time than expected and the Red Army had proceeded very quickly, could the atomic bombing of Dresden not be realised. Churchill had been forced to turn to his only imaginable alternative. To make sure the Soviets wouldn't reach Dresden as an undamaged city, Churchill had quickly decided to bomb the city with 'conventional means'. In this line of argument, the Allied aggression was contrasted to the 'heroic' nature of the Soviets. By proceeding so quickly, the Red Army had 'saved' Dresden from the atomic bomb.[15]

In spite of its obvious propagandistic character, Weidauer's 'atomic bomb' theory was not chosen arbitrarily. It shows to what extent the Cold War determined Weidauer's reference point in his historical interpretations. Weidauer's point is that however dreadful it had been, 'Dresden' was only a preliminary phase of the 'real' threat of the coming atomic war. This was the only real reason for still writing about Dresden, as Weidauer makes clear in the preface to the reedited volume of his book. A second edition was necessary,

weil die großen imperialistischen Staaten in der NATO unter der Führung der reaktionären Monopolgruppen in den Vereinigten Staaten von Amerika gewissenlos einen atomaren Krieg vorbereiten, um andere Völker und damit natürlich auch unser Volk, unsere Städte und Dörfer mit neuen Massenvernichtungswaffen auszurotten.[16]

'So dicht wie möglich an der Wahrheit heranschreiben'. The academic work of Olaf Groehler

In general, East German academic accounts and the general histories that included an interpretation of the Allied bombing war were in line with the dominant political perspective. Here the wild guesses and conspiracy theories of Seydewitz's and Weidauer's books were missing. But, although most of these academic accounts described the Allied bombings in a slightly more distant and neutral way, East German historians generally perceived the Allied bombings as militarily insignificant and morally reprehensible. Most historians emphasised that the Soviet air force had not taken part in the bombing of German city centres. The strategic bombings and especially the destruction of Dresden were interpreted as a clear expression of anti-Soviet politics. The Allied bombings therefore were not seen as an effort to end the war against Germany but more as an act of sabotage against the Soviet Union.[17]

From the late 1960s the Allied bombings became the subject of more serious and academic research. The historian who was almost exclusively responsible for the development of an East German academic perspective on the air war was Olaf Groehler (1935-95). His major works *Geschichte des Luftkriegs* (1975) and *Bombenkrieg gegen Deutschland* (1990) together with various essays, smaller works and contributions to historical overviews form the output of the research Groehler committed himself to for almost three decades. In the academic historical field in the GDR, Groehler was considered to be the leading expert on the Allied air war and strategic bombings. According to his West German friend and colleague Lutz Niethammer Groehler was even nicknamed 'Bomben-Groehler'.[18]

After writing his dissertation on the 'The English and American political and military prearrangement of the Second Front' in 1964, by 1968 Groehler had specialised on the history of the Allied air war.[19] In 1972 he defended his *Promotion B* (Habilitation) on the same topic for the *Zentralinstitut für Geschichte* (ZIG) at the *Akademie der Wissenschaften*. Here he became professor and SED-*Parteisekretär* in 1981 and in 1986 deputy-acting director of the ZIG.[20] Immediately after 1989 Groehler, like many of his colleagues, had to struggle to defend his position as a former GDR historian. He was dismissed from his position and institute in 1990. In spite of his entanglement with the SED state, Groehler was one of the few historians who were given 'a second chance' in one of the newly founded East German academic institutes. He was given the opportunity to work for the new *Forschungsschwerpunkt Zeithistorische Studien* (later *Zentrum für Zeithistorische Forschung*) where he stayed until 1994, when he was exposed as a former *Inoffizieller Mitarbeiter* (IM) for the *Stasi*.[21]

The case of Olaf Groehler is a good example of the difficulty with which the character of modern historical research in the GDR is to be valued in retrospect. Groehler later claimed that in spite of the very clear political limitations GDR historians had to work in, he himself had always made an effort to chose historical topics (like the air war) with which he would be able to write history 'so dicht wie möglich an der Wahrheit heran'.[22] In order to continue writing academic history, Groehler argued, the GDR historians had been forced to operate within the framework of dictatorship.[23] The question of Groehler's academic or political integrity is not the main subject here. But to get a clear view on his work, it should be noted that whatever Groehler's precise role as a Stasi informer might have been, at least it is clear that as a party member and *Parteiseketär* he was clearly a historian who not only conformed to the regime, but also represented the political conformity of the GDR academic climate. Groehler was convinced of the interdependence and inseparability of politics and history. In a speech to his colleagues at the ZIG written by Groehler in 1981, he emphasised the need for conformism to the party's politics, of which especially 'parteilose[n] Mitarbeiter des Instituts' had to be convinced. Further connecting the political and the historical, Groehler summarised the duties of the institute as follows:

> Grundaufgabe des Zentralinstitutes bleibt es, durch geschichtswissenschaftliche Grundlagenforschung auf hohem theoretischen Niveau, mit marxistisch-lenin-istischer Streitbarkeit und intensiver Quellenauswertung sowie der Sicherung der Publikation dieser Ergebnisse den notwendigen politischen und theoretischen Vorlauf zu garantieren, um auf diese Weise politische Entscheidungshilfen realis-ieren und besser, flexibler, anschaulicher und wirkungsvoller als bislang an einem noch breiteren Spektrum von Publikationen zur Stärkung des sozialistischen Geschichtsbewusstseins beitragen zu können.[24]

Groehler had an academic and political career, published a vast number of books and articles and, being a *Reisekader*, was allowed to travel abroad and visit archives and conferences in Western Europe.[25] His work was generally accepted as being the academic answer to West German historiography and was reviewed mostly positively by Groehler's GDR colleagues.[26]

However, does the political position of Olaf Groehler mean his work automatically can be reduced to and dismissed as the mere product of political propaganda? The question to be asked here is how Groehler's work on the Allied bombings is to be interpreted. To what extent he was able to develop a serious academic perspective on the bomber war and in what ways did Groehler's accounts support or contradict the official SED memory politics?

Who sows the wind, shall reap the whirlwind

What is interesting in Groehler's work is that he explicitly connected the importance of determining historical and causal relations and at the same time addressing problems of guilt and responsibility. Both had to be regarded in a differentiated manner, and in relationship to each other. In the introduction to *Bombenkrieg gegen Deutschland* Groehler stated:

> Wenn wir den Blick zurücklenken auf das, was vor über 45 Jahren viele deutsche Städte erlitten, so sollen wir zugleich Augenmaß und historische Perspektive bewahren, die da und dort in hitzigen Auseinandersetzungen mitunter vermisst wurden. Es geht dabei vornehmlich um die Frage von Ursache und Wirkungen und um die Problematik von Schuld und Verantwortung.[27]

This connection between the question of guilt and historical causality was central to Groehler's approach, not only in his 1990 monograph, but is continuously present in his work on the air war since the 1960s. It resulted in a much more differentiated and elaborate depiction of the historical context of the Allied bombings than other GDR accounts on the bombing war had provided.

Where Seydewitz, Lehwess-Litzmann and Weidauer only marginally address the development of air war theory and practice, Groehler described them extensively. By *historically* explaining the backgrounds that led to the Western Allied attacks on German cities, Groehler described the international development of aerial weapons and bombers on a technical as well as on a more theoretical level. Groehler saw an important origin of the bombings in the new concept of total war and the military theories of Guilio Douhet and Hugh Trenchard.[28] In his major article 'Der "strategische Luftkrieg" Großbritanniens gegen Hitlerdeutschland' (1968) Groehler argued that in Britain these theories led to the increasing belief that heavy bombers would be essential in a future war.[29] Though Groehler recognised that ideas of total warfare and strategic bombing on enemy hinterland had spread in Britain and the United States immediately after World War I, he did not believe that Western Allies had started the use of mass bombings in practice. Groehler continuously stressed that fascist

Germany had started the practice of deliberate attacks on civilians.[30]

Groehler contested the idea, first suggested by Nazi propaganda and later often repeated by West German historians, that the German bombings had only been directed at military targets. He emphasised that the death of civilians had not been regarded as collateral damage by the Luftwaffe's command, but had actually been the main target of the German bombers. 'Terror bombing' had been an important strategic concept for the Luftwaffe and consequently the fascist regime had 'caused' the Western Allies to equally shift the moral boundaries of their bombing methods. This causality was closely connected to the question of guilt and responsibility. According to Groehler, it was the Nazi regime which, by 'causing' the Allied bombings, was responsible and guilty of the massive deaths that followed them. To illustrate this causal connection between the fascist bombings and the Allied response Groehler often used the metaphor 'who sows the wind, shall reap the whirlwind'. The metaphor plays a central role in Groehler's argument. Groehler's use of this often used metaphor functions as a constant reminder that German fascism was guilty for starting the war and 'unleashing' the Allied bombs.[31]

Criticising official memory politics?

Contrary to official GDR memory politics, Groehler never lost sight of the historical context and military significance of the Allied air war. He did not only stress that the Allied bombings had to be seen as a 'reaction' to German terror-bombings, he also denied the dominant idea that the Allied strategic air war against Germany had been militarily insignificant and a result of senseless rage and destructiveness. He stated that while the Allies had overestimated the outcome and effectiveness of their air forces throughout the war, it could not be denied that it had significantly damaged German military and economic resources and that therefore had played an important role in the defeat of Germany.[32]

This is a point Groehler made in a remarkably critical book review on Walter Weidauer's book *Inferno Dresden*. In this review written for *Zeitschrift für Geschichtswissenschaft*, Groehler dissociated himself as a serious historian from some of Weidauer's more radical propagandist statements and unfounded theories. Though he praised its many informative assets and especially Weidauer's 'balanced' estimate of the death rate, Groehler also criticised Weidauer's propagandist pamphlet. Groehler concluded that, while Weidauer had filled some information gaps and had introduced some interesting points of discussion, his account had been too unbalanced. Groehler stated: 'Allerdings wäre es vorteilhafter gewesen, wenn der Autor einige seiner Ausführungen, trotz propagandistischer Zielsetzungen, sorg-fältiger und abgewogener formuliert hätte'.[33]

When discussing Weidauer's main thesis, Groehler still remained cautious. He called Weidauer's argument for the theory that the first atomic bomb was meant for Dresden 'worthy of discussion'. Considering the vagueness of this statement and the fact that Groehler later emphasised that 'Operation Thunderclap' had never been planned to be an atomic attack, suggests that Groehler was probably holding back his real thoughts here.[34] At another point, though, Groehler was more explicit. It was the absence of historical context and the brusque simplification of Weidauer's portrayal of the Allied strategic bombing war that troubled him. By reducing the British and American bombings to 'a principle of criminal imperialist military strategy', Weidauer had 'underestimated' the important role the bombings had played as 'a component of the efforts of the anti-Hitler coalition against the Fascist Axis-Powers'.[35]

Groehler called for recognition of the importance of differentiation and chronology. He emphasised that city bombing had mainly been a British strategy and not – as was often suggested in the anti-American climate of the GDR – in the first place an American strategy. The Americans had engaged in 'terror-bombing' but only relatively late.[36] While a strategy that focused on military targets had initially also dominated in the British air force, from 1942 on Bomber Command turned towards a strategy of city bombing. The objective of these bombings was to put pressure on the enemy industrial resources and on its civilian population. An important reason for this new strategy, according to Groehler, was the unwillingness and incapability of the British army to open a 'Second Front' in Western Europe, for which the British had sought to compensate by the bombing offensive. This way they could make clear not only to Hitler but also to their ally Stalin that they had a strong weapon of attack at their disposal.[37] When the Western Front and the Allied achievements came to a halt, the British and later also the Americans again turned to the method of massive 'terror-bombings' in the fall of 1944, that came to a climax in the bombing offensive of 1945. These bombings were in their very essence 'inhumane, terrorist and aimed at the people'.[38]

Integrating the dominant narrative
By eventually classifying the Allied bombings as inhumane and terrorist, Groehler expressed a clear condemnation of the bombings. Especially in his descriptions of the final phase of the bombing war from the fall of 1944 onwards, Groehler also used language and terminology that wholly corresponded with the propaganda language of the official SED discourse. When writing about the city bombings of the Western Allies, Groehler continuously used adjectives like 'murderous', 'barbaric' and 'terrorist'. The bombing of Dresden was described as a 'Massaker aus der Luft'.[39]

Furthermore, Groehler's portrayal of the German civilians underlined the dominant image of a German collective of innocent victims. Though Groehler continuously stressed the fascist 'guilt' for starting the bombing war, this 'guilt' and 'responsibility' hardly seemed to apply to the 'German people' in general. In Groehler's work the political concept of fascism became a coercive force that was implemented by the 'fascist and imperialist' elites on the German people. The 'normal Germans' subsequently were excepted from responsibility for the fascist rule. Instead they were 'double victims': First of immoral Allied strategy and the idle expectations of the impact the bombings would have on their morale,[40] and secondly of the cynical policy of Nazi administration. Groehler stressed that Nazis had provided the German civilians with a totally insufficient air protection. This way the Nazi authorities had knowingly contributed to the enormous scale of destruction and killing.[41] Finally, by the time that the Allied leaders had lost their belief in a victory caused by 'moral bombing' the Germans civilians had become the victim of anti-communist actions. Groehler concluded:

> Unter dem Gesichtspunkt einer auf die Nachkriegszeit abgestimmten Strategie geriet das deutsche Hinterland in die Rolle eines Experimentierfeldes, in der der deutschen Bevölkerung gleichsam die Funktion eines Versuchtieres zugedacht war.[42]

The people that were bombed, were not responsible for their fate: they were innocent. This valuation was constantly present in Groehler's work on an implicit level and sometimes was expressed more directly. When rhetorically discussing the question of whether the German people were 'punished' for the Nazi crimes, Groehler dismissed the responsibility of the Germans altogether by asking rhetorically:

> Doch wenn das uneingeschränkte Flächenbombardement eine Vergeltung für diese ungeheueren Verbrechen sein sollte, wer wurde dann damit bestraft? Etwa die SS-Henker von Maidanek, Treblinka oder Auschwitz oder die profit-machenden Direktoren der IG Farben, die im wahrsten Sinne des Wortes aus dem Schweiß, dem Blut und dem Tod der KZ-Häftlinge Kapital geschlagen hatten?[43]

An Imperialist Air War Doctrine

This does not mean, however, that Groehler lost his sense of historical differentiation. While denouncing this specific element in first German, then British and later American strategy, Groehler did not think that the British and American air war and their bombings in general were to be dismissed. His accusing language was used specifically to emphasize the increasing importance of the focus on civilian morale and city centres in British air war strategy. Groehler pointed at vital documents for Bomber Command air staff that showed that from 1942 on, Bomber Command had focused on city centre bombing in order to cause maximum damage to the German civilian population in order to break their morale.[44]

This combination of historical nuance and moral judgment resulted in the somewhat contradictory fact that in spite of his strong language Groehler remained relatively reluctant in expressing general moral accusations towards 'the Americans' or 'the British' war leaders. Though he called the bombings 'barbaric', Groehler also pointed out that these had to be seen within a 'broader political framework'. He pointed at the situation in which the Allies were confronted with an opponent that had unleashed a 'total war' and had consciously provoked the bombing of its own cities. 'This does not really justify the principle (of city bombing, BvBB); but it delineates the unique historically irrefutable framework.'[45]

What is interesting is that this responsible 'group' remains almost entirely anonymous. Instead of pointing the finger at individuals he rather refers to certain 'Kreise', 'reaktionäre Gruppen' or 'Elemente imperialistischer Kriegsführung'.[46] Although between the lines it becomes clear that at least people like Harris, Churchill and Portal were part of these 'circles', the vagueness of this terminology seems to be chosen with care. What Groehler wanted to illuminate was that these individuals operated within a certain 'political framework'. Especially when discussing Churchill and Harris, Groehler did not so much want to deny their individual responsibility for the planning and execution of the bombing war. Groehler's point was that their strategy was not a result of personal hatred or ruthlessness but of a more far-reaching political agenda.[47]

This political agenda was determined by the structures and politics of 'imperialism'. Groehler consequently used the concept of 'imperialism' to explain the theory and practice of western allied as well as fascist warfare during World War II. The concept of 'imperialism' categorised different non-socialist systems under the same denominator and capitalism and fascism therefore were seen as two fundamentally related political entities. While Western European and American states were seen as examples of 'bourgeois imperialism', fascism was seen as a more aggressive form. This did not mean that Groehler wholly equated 'Western bourgeois imperialism' and 'German fascist imperialism' or that he saw them as natural allies, a view that was defended by political hard-liners like Seydewitz. But by their oppressive nature, their anti-socialism and by the fact that their inner dynamics were created and dominated by big industry, they were essentially similar.

Groehler argued that the German as well as the British and American bombing strategies were grounded in an 'imperialist air war doctrine'. This imperialist doctrine differed 'fundamentally' from 'socialist' strategy, because it accepted the use of terror against civilians as a legitimate method of warfare.[48] While it was significant that German fascism had started the practice of this doctrine the Western Allies came to use same concept in the course of the war. By stressing the 'humanity' and 'tactic premise' of the Soviet Air Force Groehler not only evoked a propagandist and affirmative perspective on the Soviet army and ignored the often savage and brutal practices that the Soviet forces had demonstrated on a massive scale during their advance on German territory. This dichotomy between Soviet and 'imperialist' methods also resulted in the situation that the Western Allies and Nazi Germany eventually were portrayed as two sides of the same 'imperialist' coin. Along the way the Western Allies had descended to the moral depths of fascism. The 'reactionary' circles in the Allied army, politics and industry but above all, 'imperialism' as an abstract political entity, had determined British and American war strategy.[49]

The beginning of the Cold War

Especially Groehler's interpretation of the last phase of the war shows that his notion of the 'imperialist doctrine' was central to his historical narrative and connected his work with the dominant Marxist-Leninist concept of history. According to Groehler the 'imperialism' in British and American air strategy was expressed in the fact that the Western Allies were increasingly concerned with post-war power structures. When it became clear that the Allies were going to win the war against Germany, motifs that looked beyond this war increasingly influenced Allied strategy. The main force that drove this policy was anti-communism and the desire to impose political dominance in post-war Germany.

Groehler motivated this interpretation by analysing the development of 'Operation Thunderclap', the plan that was originally meant as a massive attack on Berlin and is generally seen as the 'blueprint' for the bombing of Dresden. He argued that 'Thunderclap' was supposed to have different functions. On the one hand it was supposed to knock out Berlin as Germany's economic, military and administrative centre. By doing so, a quick victory should be enforced. By turning Berlin into a complete wasteland the Western Allies could claim to have cast the final blow on Germany, in spite of the fact that the real collapse of the German forces had been brought about on the Eastern Front. More importantly, Berlin would be an example of what the air force of the Western Allies would be capable of in the future.[50]

Interestingly (and contrary to the GDR historians and politicians who had made a similar argument), Groehler came up with convincing documents that supported his theory. Not only had an internal directive that preceded the Dresden raid mentioned that an important reason for the attack was to 'show the Russians what Bomber Command is capable of', Groehler showed that this motive had been repeatedly mentioned during the planning of Thunderclap. In a draft of the 'Thunderclap plan' that was recorded by the Joined Planning Staff on 15 August 1945, it was clearly stated that the destroyed Berlin could function as a 'monument' to remind the Russian Allies of the effectiveness of the Anglo-American bomber force. When visiting Berlin the Russians would see with their own eyes what the strategic bombing had caused and 'what could be repeated at any time'.[51]

As such Groehler also saw the final phase of the bombing war as a preliminary stage of an atomic war. Though he rejected Weidauer's theory that Dresden had been the first target for an atomic bomb, he put the impact of the Allied strategic bombing offensive almost on the same level. Moreover, the strategy that the Western Allies had chosen by bombing Dresden as a warning sign, applied more to post-war atomic strategy than to the war against Hitler. Here Groehler saw the main political significance of the Allied bombings, the 'many connections to the present' and the current threat of an 'atomic world inferno'.[52]

Discussions with the West

Recognising this, it must be emphasised that Groehler was not trying to contest the central elements in the East German memory politics. Censorship and a strong 'force of consensus' characterised the academic historiography in the GDR. Publications were censored and differences of opinion were often settled and muted by editorial committees. There was hardly any space for real academic debates and open discussions. In line with the Marxist philosophy of history, Groehler saw the writing of history as a complementary component of the political struggle of Marxism. In Marxist historical philosophy historical insight and political interpretations were seen to be two sides of the same coin. History therefore always had a political meaning and could never be seen as something neutral.[53]

The fact that Groehler explicitly operated within the parameters of Marxist-Leninist history explains why he was able to publish his criticism on Weidauer, without getting into trouble with ideological censorship. He was not arguing from a more neutral and less politically convinced position. But why then was Groehler relatively critical and why was he troubled by the conclusion that Weidauer's approach was insufficiently 'balanced'? The answer might be found in the 'academic self-awareness' of the GDR historians. Apparently Groehler did not feel that political slogans and propagandistic discourse were able to shed a satisfactory light on the matter. A reason for Groehler's emphasis on differentiation, historical context and documentation can be found in another constant element in GDR Marxist-Leninist historiography. East German historical discipline perceived its own identity strongly in a constant competition with Western historiography. This competition with the 'bourgeois historians' was a strong element in the self-perception of East German historians.

Moreover, Groehler's work was strongly characterised by his discussions with what he called 'imperialistische Luftkriegs-historiker'.[54] As his work and his numerous essays and reviews on Western historiography illustrate, Groehler energetically devoted himself to the critical discussion of 'Western' accounts on the Allied bombings by historians and publicists like Eberhard Spetzler, Hans Rumpf, David Irving and Horst Boog. Groehler accused them of ignoring and denying Germany's 'Hauptschuld' for the introduction of terror bombing in the war. He sometimes very sharply and intelligently uncovered certain tendencies to contrast the *Luftwaffe* bombings to the Allied air arracks. Groehler convincingly pointed out that in the interpretations of West German historians the bombing of cities like Rotterdam, Warsaw or Coventry, were often described as 'military relevant' attacks and therefore regarded to be fundamentally different from the allied strategic and 'terrorist' bombings of German cities. Groehler considered this historical interpretation to be a part of a 'neo-fascist' development in the Federal Republic, in which the actions of the *Wehrmacht* and especially the *Luftwaffe* were glamorised and exculpated.[55] On the other hand, he detected in a large amount of English and American accounts, and such West German exceptions as Götz Berganders *Dresden im Luftkrieg*, a tendency to do exactly the opposite, making excuses for the Anglo-American bombings and denying their 'terrorist' nature.[56]

By differentiating both these Anglo-American and West German dominant views Groehler claimed an intermediate position for himself that was supposed to emphasize his distanced and academic point of view. Groehler was convinced that the need to defend and apologise for either Anglo-American imperialism or fascist imperialism was a strong force that distorted the academic interpretations of bourgeois historians. He wanted to counter these distortions; not by simplistic propaganda but by historical and academic arguments based on a Marxist-Leninist historical perspective. It is therefore probable that Groehler's critical distance to Weidauer's book and to the more propagandistic aspects of the dominant SED memory politics can be primarily explained by his focus on an academic debate with the West.[57]

Conclusion

With the work of Olaf Groehler East German historiography produced serious academic research on the Allied bombings. Groehler's works count as the earliest attempts to write comprehensive accounts on the Allied bombings that included the social as well as military aspects of the air war and its consequences. In its differentiated character, the work of Groehler represents a relative distance to the dominant SED perspective as represented in books like Weidauer's *Inferno Dresden*. In this, Groehler's work is different from other East German accounts on the Allied bombings. At times, as is illustrated by Groehler's critical review on *Inferno Dresden*, he even openly criticised certain aspects of the politicised discourse of SED propaganda. He stressed the fascist initiative and 'provocation' of the terror-bombings and did not denounce the efforts of the Western Allies in general.

Still, Groehler worked within the parameters of Marxist-Leninist history. He was interested in an elaborate, academic and historically founded perspective and on a limited level was prepared and able to challenge opinions of SED politicians that he perceived as short-sighted or insufficiently explanatory. On the other hand, he did not challenge the basic historical interpretations of SED memory politics, nor its emphasis on the current moral and political meaning of the air war. Along the lines of Marxist-Leninist historical philosophy, he interpreted the history of World War II from the perspective of a political struggle of socialism against imperialism. Imperialism, and fascism as its most aggressive form, was the responsible and 'guilty' force behind the Allied bombings. The 'innocent' German people had endured its consequences, just like they would if the Western imperialism would unleash a nuclear war. This acknowledgment and the subsequent message of 'peace' gave his work the political significance that was required by his Marxist historical starting point.[58] In spite of the effort to be differentiated, Groehler by no means claimed to pursue a perspective of 'neutral objectivity'.

A closer analysis puts the nature of his criticism into perspective. Groehler's approach did not challenge the main historical and political aspects of the GDR perspective. By using the theoretical concept of an 'imperialist air war doctrine' he underlined the official interpretation that saw 'imperialism' as the main driving force behind war atrocities. Just like the official propaganda view Groehler interpreted 'operation Thunderclap' and the bombing of Dresden as a first step in the Cold

War, but he did so in a more differentiated way and supported this with far more elaborate arguments. He explained the last phase of the Allied bombings as a change of strategy from a generally legitimate attempt to win the war to a criminal phase in which senseless terror and anti-communist motives became increasingly important. A clear distinction between the 'legitimate' side of the Anglo-American bombings and the final phase of terror bombing enabled Groehler to create a differentiated perspective, and at the same time integrate important elements of the official propaganda-discourse.

By morally denouncing the Allied bombings as a criminal outcome of 'imperialism' Groehler's work subscribed to the essence of Marxist-Leninist historical philosophy. He saw his work as an elaboration and illustration of the character of imperialism as a political problem. Also, he seemed to be convinced that it was necessary to support this perspective with differentiated arguments and documentation. As a researcher, he was primarily focused on an academic debate and specifically on an academic debate with the West. For discussions and debates with colleagues political slogans were insufficient. They had to be convinced by historical arguments and by a critical exposure of their 'imperialist' bias and ideological distortions.

Notes

[1] Most notably Groehler, 'Der "strategische" Luftkrieg gegen Hitlerdeutschland (Februar 1942-März 1944)', *Zeitschrift für Militärgeschichte*, 7:4 (1968), 439-53; *Geschichte des Luftkriegs 1910 bis 1970*, Berlin: Militärverlag der DDR, 1975; *Berlin im Bombervisier von London aus gesehen, 1940 bis 1945*, Berlin: Interessengemeinschaft für Denkmalpflege, Kultur und Geschichte der Hauptstadt Berlin im Kulturbund der DDR, 1982; *Kampf um die Luftherrschaft. Beiträge zur Luftkriegsgeschichte des Zweiten Weltkriegs*, Berlin: Militärverlag der DDR, 1989; *Bombenkrieg gegen Deutschland*, Berlin: Akademie Verlag, 1990. Wolfgang Schumann and Olaf Groehler, eds., *Die Zerschlagung des Hitlerfaschismus und die Befreiung des deutschen Volkes (Juni 1944 bis zum 8. Mai 1945)*, Deutschland im Zweiten Weltkrieg 66, Berlin: Akademie Verlag, 1985.

[2] Martin Sabrow, *Das Diktat des Konsenses. Geschichtswissenschaft in der DDR 1949-1969*, Ordnungssysteme. Studien zur Ideengeschichte der Neuzeit. Band 8, Munich: Oldenbourg, 2001.

[3] See for example Gilad Margalit who cites Groehler to demonstrate how much the academic historians contributed to the political propaganda of the SED: Gilad

Margalit, 'Der Luftangriff auf Dresden. Seine Bedeutung für die Erinnerungspolitik der DDR und für die Herauskristallisierung einer historischen Kriegserinnerung im Westen', in: Susanne Düwell and Matthias Schmidt, eds., *Narrative der Shoah. Repräsentationen der Vergangenheit in Historiographie, Kunst und Politik*, Paderborn: Schöning, 2002, pp. 189-208 (here: p. 201). See also David Crew, 'Auftakt zum Kalten Krieg? Wie sich die DDR an die Bombardierung Dresdens im Februar 1945 erinnerte', in: Daniela Münkel and Jutta Schwartzkopf, eds., *Geschichte als Experiment. Studien zu Politik, Kultur und Alltag im 19. und 20. Jahrhundert. Festschrift für Adelheid von Saldern*, Frankfurt/M.: Campus, 2004, pp. 287-95 (here: p. 291). Examples of critical reviews as direct reactions to Groehler's work are: Horst Boog, 'Rezensionen: Olaf Groehler: Geschichte des Luftkriegs 1910 bis 1970', *Militärgeschichtliche Mitteilungen*, 25 (1979), 234-7; Martin Moll, 'Rezensionen. Olaf Groehler: Kampf um die Luftherrschaft. Beiträge zur Luftkriegsgeschichte des zweiten Weltkrieges', *Militärgeschichtliche Mitteilungen*, 48:2 (1990), 199-200; Peter Voegeli, 'Rezension. Olaf Groehler, Bombenkrieg gegen Deutschland', *Schweizerische Zeitschrift für Geschichte*, 42:1 (1992), 160-1.

[4] Jörg Friedrich and others who point to the limited number of serious historical accounts on the Allied bombings have praised Groehler's work as an exception to this rule. See Jörg Friedrich, *Der Brand. Deutschland im Bombenkrieg, 1940-1945*, Berlin: Propyläen, 2002, p. 543. See also Volker Ullrich, 'Weltuntergang kann nicht schlimmer sein' and Nicholas Stargardt, 'Opfer der Bomben und der Vergeltung', in: Lothar Kettenacker, ed., *Ein Volk von Opfern. Die neue Debatte um den Bombenkrieg 1940-1945*, Berlin: Rowohlt, 2003, pp. 55-71 and pp. 110-16.

[5] In a recent article, British historian Richard Overy positively discusses Groehler's perspective on the bombing of Dresden and stresses that Groehler was 'no crude "cold warrior"'. Richard Overy, 'The Post-War Debate', in: Paul Addison and Jeremy A. Crang, eds., *Firestorm. The Bombing of Dresden 1945*, London: Pimlico, 2006, pp. 123-42 (here: p. 543, pp. 135-6). For similar interpretations see e.g. Dietmar Süß, 'Erinnerungen an den Luftkrieg in Deutschland und Großbritannien', *Aus Politik und Zeitgeschichte*, 55:18-19 (2005), 19-26 (here: p. 21); Idem, '"Massaker und Mongolensturm". Anmerkungen zu Jörg Friedrichs umstrittenem Buch *Der Brand. Deutschland im Bombenkrieg 1940-1945*', *Historisches Jahrbuch*, 124 (2004), 521-42 (here: p. 541); Angelika Ebbinghaus, 'Deutschland im Bombenkrieg – Ein missglücktes Buch über ein wichtiges Thema', *Sozal.Geschichte*, 18: 2 (2003), 101-22 (here: pp. 105-6).

[6] Kurt Lieberman, cited in Matthias Neutzner, 'Vom Anklagen zum Erinnern. Die Erzählung vom 13. Februar', in: Oliver Reinhard, Matthias Neutzner and Wolfgang Hesse, eds., *Das Rote Leuchten. Dresden und der Bombenkrieg*, Dresden: Edition Sächsische Zeitung, 2005, pp. 128-64 (here: pp. 137-8).

[7] Cited in Götz Bergander, *Dresden im Luftkrieg*, Cologne, Weimar, Vienna: Böhlau, 1977, p. 220.

[8] This point has been made as early as 1977 by Götz Bergander and e.g. has recently been illuminated in the work of Gilad Margalit and Mathias Neutzner.

[9] Olaf Groehler, 'Dresden: Kleine Geschichte der Aufrechnung', *Blätter für deutsche und internationale Politik*, 40:2 (1995), 137-41 (here: p. 140); Olaf B. Rader, 'Dresden', in: Etienne François and Hagen Schulze, eds., *Erinnerungsorte III*, Munich: Beck, 2001, pp. 451-72 (here: p. 456); Bergander, *Dresden im Luftkrieg*, p. 220.

[10] See the image in: Dresden Deutsches Hygiene-Museum, ed., *Mythos Dresden. Eine kulturhistorische Revue*, Cologne, Weimar, Vienna: Böhlau, 2006, p. 89.

[11] This interpretation had circulated in the Soviet zone since the end of the war and for example was expressed by Victor Klemperer in his diary in 1947. See Neutzner, 'Vom Anklagen zum Erinnern', p. 137.

[12] Walter Lehwess-Litzmann, 'Operation Dresden', *Aufbau: Kulturpolitische Monatschrift*, 6 (1950), 111-24 (here: pp. 113-120).

[13] Walter Weidauer, *Inferno Dresden: über Lügen und Legenden um die Aktion "Donnerschlag"*, Berlin: Dietz, 1965, fourth edition, 1983, p. 20.

[14] Ibid., p. 20.

[15] Ibid., pp. 57-71.

[16] Ibid., pp. 5-6. First mentioned in the second edition published 1966.

[17] Military historians Gerhard Förster, Heinz Helmert and Helmut Schnitter summarised this dryly: 'Während die sowjetischen Fliegerkräfte fast ausschließlich die Kampfhandlungen der Landstreitkräfte direkt unterstützten und nur Objekte von militärischer Bedeutung angriffen, setzten die anglo-amerikanischen Bomberkräfte ihre militärisch sinnlosen Angriffe gegen Städte fort. Die alliierte Luftkriegführung, deren barbarische und terroristische Züge immer deutlicher wurden, richtete sich in zunehmendem Maße vor allem gegen Ziele im künftigen sowjetischen Besatzungsgebiet. Offensichtlich lag diesen Angriffen die Absicht zugrunde, hier ein Chaos und unüberwindbare Schwierigkeiten für den Neuaufbau zu schaffen, die zur Quelle einer antisowjetischen Haltung unter der Bevölkerung werden sollten.' Gerhard Förster, Heinz Helmert and Helmut Schnitter, *Der zweite Weltkrieg. Militärhistorischer Abriss*, Berlin: Militärverlag der DDR, p. 396. See also Gerhard Wissmann, *Geschichte der Luftfahrt von Ikarus bis zur Gegenwart. Eine Darstellung der Entwicklung des Fluggedankens und der Luftfahrttechnik*, Berlin: Verlag Technik, 1960, pp. 378-86 and Rudi Hartwig and Manfred Wille, *Magdeburg im Feuersturm. Ein Dokumentarbericht. Zur Geschichte der Zerstörung der Stadt durch anglo-amerikanische Bombenangriffe im zweiten Weltkrieg*, Magdeburg: Magdeburger Schriftenreihe, Rat der Stadt Magdeburg Abteilung Kultur, 1985.

[18] Lutz Niethammer, *Ego-Histoire? und andere Erinnerungs-Versuche*, Cologne, Weimar, Vienna: Böhlau, 2002, p. 274.

[19] Olaf Groehler, *Die Haltung der herrschenden Kreise der USA, Großbritanniens und Deutschlands zur politischen und militärischen Vorbereitung der zweiten Front 1943-1944*, Dissertation Humboldt-University Berlin, 14 October 1964, later published as: Olaf Groehler, *Der Krieg im Westen*, Berlin: Deutscher Militärverlag, 1968; Groehler, 'Der "strategische" Luftkrieg'.

[20] Lothar Mertens, *Lexikon der DDR-Historiker. Biographien und Bibliographien zu den Geschichtswissenschaftlern aus der Deutschen Demokratischen Republik*, Munich: Bibliographische Information der Deutschen Nationalbibliothek, 2006. See also Klaus Scheel, 'Verteidigte Dissertationen. O. Groehler: Zur Dialektik von Politik und Luftkrieg. Der Platz des strategischen Luftkrieges in der Theorie und Praxis der Sowjetunion und der imperialistischen Grossmächte vor und während des zweiten Weltkrieges, Phill. Diss. B am Zentralinstitut für Geschichte an der Akademie der Wissenschaften der DDR: Berlin 12 September 1972', *Militärgeschichte,* 13:4 (1974), 474-7.

[21] The exact nature of Groehler's Stasi compliance is difficult to judge and was ambivalent. Contacted by the Stasi in 1957, a few years later he had been considered to be of little use to the secret service for 'lacking willingness to cooperate'. It was not until the 1980's when Groehler had become an important historian at the ZIG, that the contacts were revived. Again appointed as an IM in 1984, Groehler now primarily reported his foreign visits and his meetings with Western colleagues. However, while the MfS files show that Groehler was rather reluctant to do so, and almost exclusively concentrated on giving his opinion on discussions with Western historians, reporting on internal problems in his institute was also part of his tasks for the MfS, which he only in few cases, and very carefully, did. See: Bericht über die Kontaktaufnahme, 3-4-1957, MfS AIM 367/61, Bd. P, folder, 13-15; Abschlussbeurteilung, 20-12-1960, Ibid., folder 35; Treffbericht, 18-10-1960 in Ibid., Bd. A, folder 59; Vorschlag zur Werbung eines IM, 15-12-1983, MfS AIM/17697/91, 'Ernst', Bd. 3, folder 163-218 and Werbungsbericht, 29-4-1984, Ibid., folder 156-7. For examples of Groehler's reports on internal issues see his comments on a conflict between two associates and the 'political-ideological stability of his institute'. But again, here Groehler tended to emphasize the political reliability of his colleagues. MfS AIM/17697/91, Bd. 2, folder 121-3. See also: Sabrow, *Das Diktat des Konsenses*, p. 173 (Footnote 230); Niethammer, *Ego-Histoire?*, pp. 274-7 and Mertens, *Lexikon der DDR-Historiker*, p. 248.

[22] Ralf Possekel, 'Tagung der Evangelischen Akademie Berlin-Brandenburg "Wer schreibt die DDR-Geschichte?" Ein Historikerstreit um Stellen, Strukturen, Finanzen und Deutungskompetenz im März 1994', *Zeitschrift für Geschichtswissenschaft*, 42:8 (1994), 535-41 (here: pp. 537-8); Rainer Eckert, Ilko-Sascha Kowalczuk and Ulrike Poppe, eds., *Wer schreibt die DDR-Geschichte? Ein Historikerstreit um Stellen, Strukturen, Finanzen und Deutungskompetenz. Tagung vom 18.-20.3.94 in Zusam-*

menarbeit mit dem unabhängigen Historikerverband im Adam-von-Trott-Haus in Berlin-Wannsee, Berlin: Evangelische Akademie Berlin-Brandenburg, 1995, p. 106.

[23] His West-German friend and colleague Lutz Niethammer backed up Groehler's personal explanation of his position. Niethammer calls Groehler a *'realpolilitischer Diplomat des Geistes'* who engaged in 'continual tightrope act' of keeping the authorities satisfied, while at the same time trying to create an open academic discussion within the boundaries of what was possible. Other historians were much more critical about Groehlers position. For examples of discussions about GDR historiography and Groehler's own position see first some critical remarks on Groehler by the *Unabhängige Historiker-Verband*: Armin Mitter and Stefan Wolle, 'Der Bielefelder Weg. Die Vergangenheitsbewältigung der Historiker und die Vereinigung der Funktionäre', in: Rainer Eckert, Ilko-Sascha Kowalczuk and Isolde Stark, eds., *Hure oder Muse? Klio in der DDR. Dokumente und Materialien des Unabhängigen Historiker-Verbandes*, Berliner Debatte, Berlin: GSFP-Gesellschaft für sozialwissenschaftliche Forschung und Publizistik, 1994, pp. 260-5 (here: pp. 264-5). For Groehler's criticisms and apologies reflecting on the GDR-historiography see Ulrich Herbert and Olaf Groehler, eds., *Zweierlei Bewältigung. Vier Beiträge über den Umgang mit der NS-Vergangenheit in den beiden deutschen Staaten*, Hamburg: Ergebnisse, 1992. For criticisms of Groehlers position by historians of the FU see Klaus Schroeder and Jochen Staadt, 'Die Kunst des Aussitzens', in: Klaus Schroeder, ed., *Geschichte und Transformation des SED-Staates: Beiträge und Analysen*, Studien des Forschungsverbundes SED-Staat an der Freien Universität Berlin, Berlin: Akademie Verlag, 1994, pp. 347-54 (here: pp. 351-3). Groehler's IM activities are mentioned here as well and Groehler is characterised as an active member of the SED oppression. In 1994, Groehler defended his position in discussion platforms: Eckert, Kowalczuk and Poppe, eds., *Wer schreibt die DDR-Geschichte?*, pp. 94-6 and pp. 105-6. Ralf Possekel, 'Tagung der Evangelischen Akademie Berlin-Brandenburg', pp. 537-8.

[24] Archiv der Berlin-Brandenburgischen Akademie der Wissenschaften, Bestand ZIG, 572/1c. pp. 189-92.

[25] Not only was Groehler *Reisekader*, one of his main responsibilities as deputy-acting director was the coordination of the institute's associates' foreign travel. He authorised permissions to travel, organised funds and by this also had influence on the travelling possibilities of his colleagues.

[26] See e.g. Helmut Schnitter, 'Rezensionen. Olaf Groehler, Geschichte des Luftkrieges 1910 bis 1970', *Zeitschrift für Geschichtswissenschaft*, 24:4 (1976), 471-3; Richard Lakowski, 'Rezension. O. Groehler: Geschichte des Luftkrieges 1910 bis 1970 (1975)', *Militärgeschichte* 15:5 (1976), 615-6; Werner Stang, 'Annotationen. Berlin im Bombenvisier. Von London aus Gesehen. 1940 bis 1945. Miniaturen zur Geschichte, Kultur und Denkmalpflege Berlins, Nr.7 (1982)', *Zeitschrift für Geschichtswissenschaft*, 32:2 (1984), p. 173.

[27] Groehler, *Bombenkrieg gegen Deutschland*, p. 8.

[28] Groehler, *Geschichte des Luftkriegs*, p. 36, pp. 114-5, and Groehler, 'Der "strategische" Luftkrieg', pp. 440-2.

[29] Ibid., p. 440.

[30] Groehler especially emphasised the fact that the German *Luftwaffe* had started bombing cities in Spain, Britain, Poland and the Netherlands, before describing the British and American attacks on Germany. With these deliberate 'terror attacks' on Guernica, Warsaw, Rotterdam and Coventry the German fascists had consciously crossed new boundaries of warfare and had provoked the Allies to use the same means in return. The main responsibility for the 'bombing war' therefore was explicitly ascribed to fascist Germany. In *Geschichte des Luftkriegs* Groehler left no doubt regarding this point. 'Denn während dem englischen Commander noch vor dem Gedanken schauderte Deutschland zu bombardieren, brachte die Luftwaffe bereits Tod und Verderben über Hunderte von polnischen Dörfern, Ortschaften und Städten.' Groehler, *Geschichte des Luftkriegs*, p. 217.

[31] Ibid., p. 284 and Groehler, *Kampf um die Luftherrschaft*, p. 23, p. 51. Also as a chapter title in *Bombenkrieg gegen Deutschland*, p. 15. This metaphor is not specific to Groehler and is used by others as well, sometimes with different connotations. See e.g. the chapter titles in David Irving, *The Destruction of Dresden*, London: Kimber, 1963, p. 19, p. 200.

[32] Groehler's conclusion in the 1985 military historical overview *Deutschland im zweiten Weltkrieg* was therefore: 'Obwohl einzelne Zweige der deutschen Kriegs-industrie schwer getroffen wurden – vor allem die chemische Industrie – konnte durch den Luftkrieg zwar keine Kriegsentscheidung herbeigeführt, jedoch die Niederlage des faschistischen Regimes beschleunigt werden.' Schumann and Groehler, eds., *Die Zerschlagung des Hitlerfaschismus*, p. 589. See also Groehler, *Geschichte des Luftkriegs*, pp. 252-53; 'Der "strategische" Luftkrieg', p. 446; 'Militärische Ursachen für die Niederlage des faschistischen Deutschland im zweiten Weltkrieg', *Militär-geschichte*, 16:1 (1977), 443-55 (here: p. 452).

[33] Olaf Groehler, 'Rezensionen. Walter Weidauer: Inferno Dresden. Über Lügen und Legenden um die Aktion "Donnerschlag"', *Zeitschrift für Geschichtswissenschaft*, 13:8 (1965), 1446-7 (here: p. 1447).

[34] E.g. Olaf Groehler, 'Annotationen. Walter Weidauer: Inferno Dresden. Über Lügen und Legenden um die Aktion "Donnerschlag"', *Zeitschrift für Geschichtswissen-schaft*, 33:2 (1985), 187-8 (here: p. 188) and Groehler, *Berlin im Bombenvisier*, p. 41.

[35] Groehler, 'Inferno Dresden (1965)', p. 1447.

[36] Groehler clearly had a problem with a simplistic anti-Americanism that blamed the Americans for everything and completely negated their military contribution to the war against Hitler. This is also reflected in his relatively mild and almost friendly descriptions of American politicians like Roosevelt. In his review, Groehler criticises

Weidauer for insufficiently differentiating between 'militant anti-communist' Churchill and 'personalities like Roosevelt and Morgenthau'. Ibid., p. 1447.

[37] Groehler, 'Der "strategische" Luftkrieg', pp. 444-5.

[38] Ibid., pp. 444-6.

[39] The terminology in *Bombenkrieg gegen Deutschland*, published in 1990, was similarly vivid. The memorandum from November 1942 in which Bomber Command declared that the bombing of German civilians would become the central aim of British bombing raids, was according to Groehler a 'Vision des Schreckens'. Britain had tried to win the war with 'massenhaften Terror', a strategy that had proven to be of very limited effect. Groehler, *Bombenkrieg gegen Deutschland*, p. 74, pp. 294-300. See also Groehler, *Geschichte des Luftkriegs*, p. 458.

[40] Groehler, *Kampf um die Luftherrschaft*, pp. 218-19; Groehler, *Bombenkrieg gegen Deutschland*, pp. 294-5.

[41] E.g. see ibid., p. 140, p. 205.

[42] Ibid., p. 391.

[43] Ibid., p. 378.

[44] For example see the documents Groehler printed in the appendix of *Berlin im Bombenvisier*, pp. 55-97.

[45] Olaf Groehler, 'The Strategic Air War and its Impact on the German Civilian Population' in: Horst Boog, ed., *The conduct of the air war in the Second World War an international comparison: proceedings of the International Conference of Historians in Freiburg im Breisgau, from 29 August to 2 September 1988*, New York/Oxford: Berg, 1992, pp. 279-97 (here: pp. 292-3) See also Groehler, 'Der "strategische" Luftkrieg', p. 446.

[46] Groehler, 'Der "strategische" Luftkrieg', p. 446; Groehler, *Bombenkrieg gegen Deutschland*, p. 338, p. 391.

[47] See e.g. Groehler, 'Der "strategische" Luftkrieg', p. 443. Groehler refers to the work of notorious British historian David Irving, who sees Churchill's personal motivations as an important driving force behind the British air strategy.

[48] Groehler, *Geschichte des Luftkriegs*, p. 507. Groehler's Promotion B (Habilitation) discussed exactly this difference between imperialist and socialist strategy. See Scheel, 'Zur Dialektik von Politik und Luftkrieg', pp. 474-7.

[49] Groehler, 'Inferno Dresden (1965)', p. 1447; Groehler, *Bombenkrieg gegen Deutschland*, p. 180, p. 227, pp. 336-8, p. 391. Even after 1989, Groehler did not,

apart from some minor corrections, essentially change his interpretation. In a some-what schizophrenic manner Groehler criticised the way in which the 'political misuse' of this topic in East Germany had undifferentiatedly interpreted the bombing war as an 'Ausdruck übergreifender imperialistischen Barbarei' and had put 'ein Gleichheits-zeichen zwischen Hakenkreuz und Dollarsymbol'. Groehler corrected some of his previous interpretations, such as the accusation that the British and Americans had deliberately bombed East Germany more extensively than the West to damage and sabotage the future Soviet zone of influence. His theoretical starting point and central approach however underlined exactly this interpretation of the Allied bombing war as an example of 'imperialist warfare'. Ibid., p. 393, p. 450.

[50] Though mainly because the right 'timing' did not occur, the joined and concentrated strike on Berlin was not brought into practice, the desire for a clear demonstrative act remained intact. During the 'reanimated Thunderclap' first Dresden and later other cities like Magdeburg and Pforzheim became the victims of this ruthless first step in the Cold War. Still in 1990 Groehler concluded that 'Die gewaltigen Flächenbombenangriffe des Frühjahrs 1945 […] galten in derartigen Über-legungen nicht mehr ausschließlich der endgültigen Niederringung des sich in Agonie befindlichen faschistischen Regimes, sondern waren zugleich als Demonstration der Stärke, sowie als Warnung und Drohung gedacht. In erster Linie gingen sie an die Adresse der Sowjetunion, aber auch an die der Völker Europas, vor allem diejenigen die mit dem antiimperialistischen Vermächtnis des Krieges Ernst machen und ihr Schicksal in die eigene Hände nehmen wollten'. Groehler, *Bombenkrieg gegen Deutschland*, p. 391; Groehler, *Berlin im Bombenvisier*, pp. 33-42.

[51] Document printed (translated into German, with archival annotation to the original in the Public Records Office) in: Groehler, *Berlin im Bombenvisier*, pp. 83-4. The role of the Soviet Union and the question, whether 'Dresden' was either meant as 'support' for Russian troops or as a 'threat' towards Stalin was a central part of a polemic debate between FRG and GDR historians.

[52] The fact that in 1990 Groehler quite anachronistically claimed that the atomic war had been threatening the world more than ever during 'the last years' shows how much this perceived significance the allied bombings as a 'warning sign' determined his world view. See e.g. Groehler, *Bombenkrieg gegen Deutschland*, p. 8, p. 391, pp. 450-51 and Groehler, *Kampf um die Luftherrschaft*, p. 262 and p. 273.

[53] Sabrow, *Das Diktat des Konsenses* pp. 394-441 and Krijn Thijs, *Elastische Geschichte. Berlin und drei Erzählungen seiner Vergangenheit*. Dissertation Vrije Universiteit Amsterdam 2006, pp. 338-41. Published as: Krijn Thijs, *Drei Geschichten, eine Stadt. Die Berliner Stadtjubiläen 1937 und 1987*, Cologne, Weimar, Vienna: Böhlau, 2008.

[54] E.g. Groehler, 'Der "strategische" Luftkrieg', p. 439; Groehler, *Geschichte des Luftkriegs*, p. 265.

[55] Olaf Groehler, 'Der "strategische" Luftkrieg', p. 443 and Olaf Groehler, 'Neuere bürgerliche Publikationen zur Luftkriegsgeschichte', *Militärgeschichte* 17:2 (1978), 491-7 (here: p. 491).

[56] Groehler, 'Der "strategische" Luftkrieg', p. 443; Groehler, 'Annotationen. Götz Bergander: Dresden im Lufttkrieg', *Zeitschrift für Geschichtswissenschaft*, 25:12 (1977) 1494-5; Groehler, *Bombenkrieg gegen Deutschland*, p. 402. For a more detailed analysis of the discussions Groehler had with Bergander and Boog see Bas von Benda-Beckmann, 'De "imperialistische Luftkrieg" en de Koude Oorlog. DDR-historici over de Geallieerde bombardementen op Duitse steden', in: Patrick Dassen, Ton Nijhuis and Krijn Thijs, ed., *Duitsers als slachtoffers. Het einde van een taboe?*, Amsterdam: Mets en Schil, 2006, pp. 389-430 (here: pp. 411-18).

[57] In private notes Groehler made in 1964 he concluded that in these discussions the GDR side had rightly been criticised for its cut and dried opinions and lacking differentiation. See the citation and interpretation of Groehler's private notes, dated 11 October 1964 in Sabrow, *Das Diktat des Konsenses*, pp. 322-23. Here Groehler even doubted the strong connection between capitalism and fascism. This seemingly very dissident thought never found its way into Groehler's published work and as his 1981 speech to his ZIG colleagues shows (see note 24), did not encourage Groehler to any form of objection to the merging of politics and historical research. Though he repeated his complaint towards GDR historiography in *Bombenkrieg gegen Deutschland*, the use of 'imperialism' as a comprehensive and inclusive concept that connected reactionary capitalism and fascism remained a central theoretical premise to his work. This demonstrates the intellectual balancing act of Groehler's obviously not very successful attempt to integrate the concept Marxist-Leninist historiography into a Western academic discourse.

[58] Even after 1989 his work was characterised by strong elements of a seemingly deliberate partiality. Groehler claimed that the goal of his 'historical documentation' was 'to objectify' his own 'subjectivity', without renouncing his 'personal concern'. Groehler, *Bombenkrieg gegen Deutschland*, p. 6.

Nicholas JSteneck

Hitler's Legacy in Concrete and Steel: Memory and Civil Defence Bunkers in West Germany, 1950-65

The Nazi civil defence programme left a huge visible legacy in German cities in the form of air raid shelters and bunkers. This chapter analyses the role of bunkers in post-war public memory and their impact on the public's relation to the Federal Republic's civil defence programme, arguing that the German public's reluctance to embrace the post-war building of bunkers originated in their memories of victimisation during the war.

During the opening decades of the Cold War, millions of West Germans believed they were victims of Third Reich terror, or rather the terror that resulted from the Nazi regime's aggressive, racially motivated policies. The West Germans who internalised this role of victim were, for the most part, the ordinary men and women who had lived, worked, and supported the Nazi regime to a greater or lesser degree. They came from a broad cross-segment of post-war society, representing all the political, socio-economic, educational, religious, and geographical groups that made up West Germany. They were unified by experience, having lived through or knew people who had lived through the Allies' use of strategic bombing to reduce civilian morale and war-fighting capability. From this common experience came three central beliefs that formed this particular type of West German victimhood. First, the strategic bombing campaign waged against German civilians had caused widespread physical destruction and human misery. Second, this misery and devastation was made worse by the Nazi regime's inadequate civil defence policies. Finally, it was unacceptable that the West German government planned a civil defence programme nearly identical to its Nazi predecessor. This final, common belief shared by millions of West German 'victims' had severe consequences for their country's early Cold War civil defence programme.

It is the connection between these consequences and post-war national memory that constitutes this chapter's central focus. Specifically, the question is how wartime memories about civil defence shaped post-war policy. Because of the pivotal role they played both during the war and after, this chapter focuses on bunkers. It does so in two parts. In the first, the evolution of West Germany's civil defence programme from its inception in the late 1940s through its final demise in the late 1960s will be summarised.[1] During this period, West German civil defence planners drew upon their wartime experience to embrace and support a massive bunker construction programme. However, most West Germans were reluctant to follow their lead and throughout the 1950s and early 1960s maintained an ambivalent relationship, at best, with the idea. Although the reasons for this rejection were manifold, an important factor was wartime experience, which will be explored in part two. Here it is suggested that wartime experience caused millions of West Germans to think of bunkers as powerful symbols of their wartime victimisation. As a result, when it looked as if their government was resurrecting the Nazi programme, West Germans decided to not repeat the past's mistakes.

Civil Defence and the Federal Republic's Post-war Bunker Policy
For those Germans in the Western occupation zones after the end of the war, survival rather than thoughts about the possibility of future conflict dominated daily existence. However, as the literature on the immediate post-war period reminds us, most Germans, especially those living in cities, could not escape the war's legacy, especially its visible legacy.[2] One aspect of this legacy was the omnipresence of bunkers, tens of thousands of which remained after the war.[3] Admittedly, Allied occupation authorities demolished many, but they focused mostly on military installations, such as the massive complexes in Hamburg and Bremen which had protected Germany's submarine force, or the structures that formed the core of the country's wartime air-defence system. Thousands more were converted to other roles. For example, in the immediate aftermath of the war bunkers became homes for people whose pre-war houses and apartments were destroyed during the bombing raids. City governments also converted bunkers into offices, hospitals, warehouses, and even schools. In Berlin, the rudimentary first-aid station in the city's massive Zoo Air Defence Tower became the well-equipped Robert Koch Hospital. Later, as conditions in the cities improved, enterprising entrepreneurs converted bunkers into more comfortable accommodation, sometimes as apartment buildings but more frequently as hotels. As the bunker historian Michael Foedrowitz notes, until the mid-1960s travellers

could find cheap accommodation in the Hotel Aude, a former air-raid shelter located in front of the Bremerhaven train station.[4]

Even unused bunkers intruded physically into the lives of urban Germans long after hostilities ended. This was especially true in the north, where ground water had forced the Nazis to build upwards rather than tunnel into the earth. Massive, intact structures such as Berlin's flak towers, Hamburg's *Heiligengeistfeldbunker*, and the 18,000-person shelter in Emden were so stoutly constructed that Allied and local city officials could find no easy way to purge West Germany of their existence. (The Zoo Tower remained intact in the early 1950s; the *Heiligengeistfeldbunker* remains a dominant feature of the city's skyline; and more than 150 bunkers remain in Emden.) Only slightly less intrusive were the ruined bunkers that dotted West Germany's urban landscape. One example from the industrial city of Wilhelmshaven is illustrative. The large, round civil defence bunker built during 1943-1944 in the *Freiligrathstraße* (known before 1945 as *Fortifikationsstraße*) was partially demolished by Allied occupation forces in August 1949. Sizeable ruins remained long after, however, as evidenced by photographs from the 1950s which show large piles of relatively intact masonry covered with pro-Communist graffiti.[5]

The presence of such graffiti highlights the international tension of the time, and the fact that it rekindled West Germans' interest in bunkers. By the early 1950s, West Germany's political leadership believed escalating international tension between the US and Soviet Union required the country to prepare for a future war. These preparations focused on two separate strategies: re-establishing a robust, active military defence and recreating an extensive national civil defence system. Planning for the latter began in 1949. Very soon thereafter, federal planners settled on a tripartite civil defence strategy of evacuation, post-attack rescue and recovery services, and physical protection, or bunkers, which ultimately proved the most controversial of the three.

From the archival record we see that West Germany's civil defence community very quickly embraced bunkers as a viable and important element of their overall strategy. Within the West German Interior Ministry – the government agency with overall responsibility for the country's civil defence programme – influential experts made the case for physical protection. Typical were the arguments of Heinz Dählmann who concluded that bunkers were absolutely imperative, both physically and psychologically, and wrote that 'in order to provide the public with a sense of security [...] easily accessible protective shelters of suitable construction' were absolutely necessary.[6] Other government agencies supported the Interior Ministry. The influential Housing Ministry, which oversaw much of West Germany's reconstruction efforts, called for 'as much protection as possible' and urged learning the lessons of the last war by implementing a comprehensive bunker construction programme.[7]

Given these opinions, it is not surprising that bunker construction was at the centre of the civil defence legislation the Adenauer government sent to the West German *Bundestag* in June 1955.[8] According to the proposed legislation, new housing in large cities (those with more than ten thousand inhabitants) was to include 'adequate' protection against aerial bombardment. Moreover, the law obligated state and local authorities to preserve, and where necessary renovate, civil defence facilities dating back to the Second World War, unless it was impossible to do so or the renovation was clearly not in the best interest of the common good. Ultimately, the Interior Ministry's belief that West Germany's civil defence future was best served by bunkers proved problematic. In October 1957, *Bundestag* representatives approved the government's programme, but because of its projected cost imposed a five-year moratorium on the shelter requirement for new residential building, effectively killing off the programme.[9]

West Germany's civil defence community was undeterred by the failure of this first effort to reintroduce bunkers. Indeed, their commitment grew stronger. For example, a year after the 1957 Civil Defence Law's passage the retired police major turned consultant Hans Schmidle authored a three-part article entitled 'Bunker Construction Must Be the "Prime" Consideration of All Civil Defence Planning.' In his final analysis Schmidle argued,

> after reviewing all the positive and negative factors that influence [the government's] bunker policy one must conclude (whether one wants to or not) that constructing the necessary shelters within a generation (the next fifteen to twenty years) is possible.[10]

Nor did technological innovation in the form of more powerful bombs and faster delivery systems end bunker enthusiasm among experts even as public scepticism grew. As a result, when the Interior Ministry unveiled its new civil defence vision in January 1963 – the Emergency Laws [*Notstandsgesetze*] – bunkers still featured prominently. The 'Shelter Construction Law' [*Schutzbaugesetz*] once again required all new buildings to contain protective bunkers, some of which could withstand the full effects of a nuclear explosion. Moreover, clearly influenced by Germany's wartime experience, the law's authors included in its provisions a requirement that municipal authorities construct 'open shelters' for people caught away from home or work at the start of an attack.[11]

As was the case during the public debate leading up to the 1957 Civil Defence Law's passage, the government's emphasis on bunkers during this second attempt to create a comprehensive civil defence system proved controversial. Pointing to the fact that the Nazi bunker programme had failed to save the lives of hundreds of thousands, critics asked – not unreasonably – why civil defence proponents believed a similar programme would work any better should the Soviet Union (once again) attack the country? Among the voices condemning the government's programme was that of Professor Friedrich Tamms, a well-respected architect who had spent most of the war in Berlin overseeing construction of the massive anti-aircraft towers and heading the office that oversaw reconstruction efforts in Aachen and Lübeck.[12] In contrast to his colleagues in the Federal Interior Ministry, Tamms offered frequent and sharply worded criticisms of the government's bunker strategy, which he called 'largely illusionary' [*weitgehend illusorisch*].[13] Tamms's criticism was not unique. Many of the programme's opponents decried it as nothing short of useless in the face of the Soviet Union's ability to attack with weapons capable of instantly annihilating whole cities, and accused Adenauer's government of embracing disastrous militarism.

Pro-bunker forces rejected these charges and mounted a spirited defence of their work. Expressing no doubt about the future role of protective shelters, proponents constantly referred to scientific and technical evidence that backed their use. For example, in a January 24, 1963 *Bundestag* speech in which he introduced the new law, Interior Minister Hermann Hörcherl informed his colleagues that extensive studies by leading scientists and technical experts and the results of NATO military exercises left no doubt about the usefulness of physical protection.[14] Twenty-four months later, as they conducted the law's second reading, representatives from West Germany's major right of centre political parties, the Christian Democratic Union (CDU) and Free Democratic Party (FDP), remained committed to this position. 'Bunkers', one CDU representative stated, 'are the centre-piece and foundation of all civil defence [...] without which all other action is senseless.'[15] Support from the majority CDU/CSU is not surprising. What is interesting, however, is that fact that the political opposition, the Social Democratic Party (SPD), also embraced bunkers. After noting that his party had long pressed the government to provide protective shelters for the public, the SPD's Hermann Hansing informed the house of his party's intention to approve the law despite misgivings about its possible ramifications on state and local finances.[16]

As a result, in May 1965 a slightly modified form of the Shelter Construction Law was passed almost unanimously in the *Bundestag*. For civil defence proponents it was a short-lived victory. Just over six months later, in an attempt to stave off budgetary crisis, the same legislators voted to delay implementation of the Shelter Construction Law for three years. This delay proved fatal. In 1968, the dramatic changes in West Germany's domestic political landscape signalled by Willy Brandt's ascension to power led to new directions in security policy, and a bunker-based civil defence strategy was replaced by the beginning of *Ostpolitik* and engagement with the Communist bloc.

The preceding summary of West Germany's early experience with bunkers reveals tepid support on the part of politicians and many civil defence experts. This ambivalence was even more visible in the West German public. Through the 1950s and early 1960s, various segments of West German society – including clergy, scientists, students, and leading cultural icons – banded together to resist the government's civil defence programme. Admittedly, not all critics of West German civil defence were as biting as the Committee Against Nuclear Armament [*Komitee gegen Atomrüstung, e.V.*], but the archival and press records of the period support the conclusion that a healthy majority of people were at least sceptical about the government's support of bunkers. Why? Although several factors account for this tepid support, wartime experience was clearly important. Bunkers, which in the late 1940s and 1950s were an omnipresent part of daily existence, served as constant reminders of the Nazi regime's inability to protect its people during the war. Let us turn now to that experience.

Germany's Second World War Bunker Experience and Its Effect on Post-war Policy

As recent studies have revealed, bunkers became a defining element of German civilians' Second World War experience.[17] Nazi leaders failed to anticipate this before 1939. The fact that civilians became the target of aerial bombardment during the First World and that interwar thinkers saw such action as a war-winning strategy was lost upon the Nazis, who for the most part abhorred the very idea of bunkers. This disdain for bunkers stemmed from a number of different factors, the most important of which were their financial and psychological cost. In other words, Nazi leaders worried that a large-scale bunker construction programme might impede rearmament plans and impede the public's 'war-fighting' capability. As a result, the Nazis embraced civil defence planning that focused on programmes stressing active public participation and strengthening civilian morale.[18] Erich Hampe, whose civil defence experience spanned the Weimar, Nazi, and early Federal Republic eras, exemplified this approach. Although not a committed Nazi, Hampe argued that the sound of air-raid sirens should instil in Germans the physical and psychological strength necessary to achieve final victory rather than the desire to retreat underground.[19] Notably, the Nazis' emphasis on physical and psychological strength was in direct contrast with the Weimar government's preference for technologically-based civil defence strategies, in which bunkers played an important role. For Weimar's leaders, bunkers were nothing more than an effective means of protection. In the minds of Nazi leaders, however, the passive protection provided by bunkers represented nothing less than an admission of collective and individual weakness.

Not surprisingly, pre-war Nazi directives and propaganda made it clear that bunkers, especially public bunkers, were useful only for the very young, the elderly, and the sick. In times of war, 'real' Germans would remain above ground and actively participate in their nation's defence. Admittedly, in the late 1930s official attitudes towards physical protection began to change when Nazi officials ordered 'block wardens' [Blockwarte] to help people seek protection in basements and cellars in the event of aerial attacks.[20] However, this slight policy shift was motivated primarily by concern about maintaining strict control over the German population rather than a new-found acceptance of the value of physical protection. The end result of the Nazis' attitudes was mixed. Although the country entered the Second World War with the most robust civil defence programme of all the combatant nations, it was one that paid little attention to physical protection.

Nazi attitudes towards physical protection barely survived the war's opening month. In September 1939, Hitler ordered three massive 'anti-aircraft fortresses' constructed in Berlin, Hamburg, and Vienna. In addition to housing heavy artillery, communications equipment, and emergency medical facilities, each fortress contained shelter space for several thousand civilians. The first British attacks against Berlin in August and September 1940 intensified Nazi concern about civilian vulnerability, and in October Hitler authorised an emergency bunker-construction programme, the *Führer-Sofort-programm*.[21] Like most of his architectural visions, Hitler's bunker construction programme was monumental in scope. He planned to achieve his goal of 'complete protection for the entire civilian population' by constructing thousands of bunkers each capable of sheltering hundreds of people from direct hits of two thousand-pound bombs. However, as was also the case with many of his visions, Hitler's bunker plans proved impossible to achieve. Initial bunker construction was limited to sixty-one cities that contained critical war industries, with railroad and utilities personnel and armaments workers receiving priority. By the end of the war, an expanded national programme and efforts by local governments increased the number of bunkers available, although overall quality differed dramatically, ranging from massive, above-ground structures in Hamburg, Bremen, Düsseldorf, and Berlin, to smaller cellar shelters. Tragically, not all bunkers offered the same level of protection. Rushed or shoddy construction sometimes allowed bombs to penetrate the roofs of 'bomb-proof' bunkers before exploding in the crowded chambers below while indiscriminate area bombing entombed shelter occupants or caused their death through asphyxiation or carbon-monoxide poisoning.[22]

How did the German public respond to the Nazi bunker programme? In general, wartime public attitudes towards the bunkers were mixed. On the one hand, Germans clearly supported the idea of government-financed bunkers. Despite the best efforts of Nazi officials to instil in Germans the idea that bunkers were only for those who could make no useful contribution to the country's war effort, even the small-scale Royal Air Force attacks in the spring and summer of 1940 resulted in a public outcry for more shelter. Some top Nazi officials preferred to ignore this outcry. Those tasked with overseeing and reinforcing public will, such as Josef Goebbels, did not. As the air war intensified from mid-1944 onwards, public support grew until, as reports from Wehrmacht authorities written during the war's final winter demonstrate, many people reordered their lives around the daily trek to the public shelters, and in some cases actually lived there.[23] Extensive public demand for bunkers is also evidenced by the fact that regime officials constantly reported general and specific complaints about the inadequate number available. As one official noted in a March 1945 report, the lack of public bunkers was a frequent topic of conversation. Public consensus, according to the report's author, was that the regime had had sufficient time and resources to build enough shelters, especially if it had used prisoners-of-war labour. The government's failure to do so represented nothing less than indifference to Germans' fates.[24]

On the other hand, contemporary police reports, post-war oral histories, and published memoirs also reveal widespread public discontent. Admittedly, most that came to officials' attentions likely resulted from growing frustration with and concern about the war's impact on daily life. Goebbel's succinct diary entries about the massive Anglo-American attacks against Germany's cities – such as his observation on 23 November 1943 that Berlin had experienced an 'extensive catastrophe' and his comment in the wake of Royal Air Force's attack on 16 February 1944, that the city's situation was 'not very pleasant' – portray only poorly the consequences of the attacks.[25] Regular, frequent attacks by Anglo-American bomber forces destroyed housing, disrupted transportation, ground vital city services to a halt, killed hundreds of thousands of civilians, and wounded many, many more.[26] Moreover, as historians of the aerial war against Germany make clear, the Anglo-American bomber offensive also inflicted a heavy psychological and physical toll. Rates of alcoholism and smoking increased as did cardiac deaths, nervous disorders, accidents caused by sleep deprivation, anxiety and depression.[27]

Thus, it is not surprising that as the number of Germans affected by strategic bombing increased, so, too, did anger about the government's bunker policies. According to many Germans, the Nazi regime's inability (some argued unwillingness) to provide adequate protection was the root cause of much of this anger. As noted above, by the winter of 1944-45 public sentiment in the country's cities had condemned the Nazi leadership as callously dismissive of Germans' fate. The inevitable failure of bunkers to withstand all attacks only exasperated this sentiment. Public sentiment in Berlin was shaken, for example, when a huge, above-ground concrete bunker sheltering 20,000 people received a direct hit from a five-ton 'earthquake' bomb. After the explosion, rescue workers found only cement powder, small pieces of clothing, and body parts, soaked through with blood.[28] Nazi leaders worked hard, but ultimately unsuccessfully, to suppress knowledge about such disasters.

Nazi officials also found it difficult to counter widespread concern about the official rules and regulations governing bunkers' use. Criticism about the government's bunker policies ranged from annoyance that local officials routinely ignored rules intended to ensure mothers with young children were given priority to limited space to complaints that too many scarce spots were reserved for functionaries. For example, in his report on public sentiment in Berlin from 9 December 1944, Lieutenant-Colonel Wasserfall noted widespread complaints that the public shelters were 'so filled with men that women and children often found no space and were even frequently denied access' to the bunkers. In the same report, Wasserfall also noted the public's annoyance that 'foreigners' sought shelter during air-raids but then refused to help with post-attack rescue and recovery efforts. Previously, Wasserfall had informed his superiors about public anger over the fact that the Lehrter Bahnhof contained two, unequal types of protection. 'Normal' people were forced to shelter in a difficult-to-reach, dank, dark cellar less than sixty feet away from an easily-accessible, well-ventilated and lighted 'comfort bunker' the door to which contained the strict injunction 'Railroad Personnel Only!' Wasserfall's colleague in Hamburg, Major Schubert, wrote that local officials were routinely 'impudent' and 'arrogant' to those seeking shelter, threatened to report people to the police for the most trivial offences, and in general increased rather than mitigated tension in the bunkers.[29]

Failure to provide actual protection was the single most important reason for this mistrust – a fact the Nazis tacitly acknowledged by attempting to suppress catastrophic bunker failure – but was by no means the only cause for concern. For many people, spending extended periods of time amongst a crushing press of strangers in the dank, often dark and airless confines of a bunker was an experience best avoided. In her account of growing up in wartime Kaiserslautern, for example, Siegrid Mayer tells of a neighbour who rejected the local public bunker in favour of the safety offered by her basement. Mayer's mother's warning that the basement shelter was 'no good' proved accurate. When an incendiary bomb hit the house the burning phosphorous flowed down to the basement, covering the occupants and causing deadly injuries. Mayer's mother's mistrust of the local public bunker also proved accurate, however, when several months later an attack resulted in liquid phosphorous flowing down its steps. The subsequent mass panic and whole-scale flight to the escape tunnels crushed many people to death.[30] Hans Herzmann, who was a teenager when the war ended, avoided air raid shelters after helping in the rescue of two cousins who were entombed in the ruins of a partially destroyed bunker.[31] In writing about his own experiences in Würzburg during the war, Hermann Knell describes his efforts to cope with an embarrassing physical reaction to the bombing – a severe form of diarrhoea – feelings of fatalism, and tremendous anxiety about being buried alive in an air-raid shelter.[32] The work of Knell and other scholars show widespread 'bunker anxiety' existed in the German population by the end of the war.

Conclusion

The benefit of hindsight reveals that memory of wartime experience with bunkers posed an insurmountable obstacle for West Germans who embraced them as part of Cold War civil defence. For millions of people bunkers served as powerful symbols of the country's recent inglorious past. Long after the war's end in May 1945 they existed as monumental testimony to the efficiency and dedication of a ruthless authoritarian government that led the country into a ruinous war. At the same time, by conjuring up memories of long, unpleasant nights spent sheltering from Allied bombing raids bunkers also represented the Nazi regime's absolute failure to fulfil its pre-war promise to protect the country's civilian population. Whereas the subject was rarely spoken of publicly in the decades following the war, recent writing on the German wartime home-front leaves little doubt that the emotional scars that resulted from this trauma persisted long after the country's physical recovery. For supporters of an atomic-era civil defence system predicated on protective shelters, this emotional trauma was devastating. To muster support for their programme, civil defence officials needed to convince people to forget, or at least ignore their wartime memories and embrace bunkers as a necessary part of Cold War West German existence. Sparse bunker-related resources made this extremely difficult, however. Because they lacked the money to build or renovate existing protective shelters, state and local governments were forced to make difficult decisions about resource allocation. Understandably, they focused on measures designed to maximise chances for recovery, which in practical terms meant building bunkers to shelter key governmental personnel and rescue and recovery units. While eminently logical, such policies did little to alleviate widespread apprehension about bunkers. Rather than functioning as a potent symbol of a commitment to protecting as much of the country's population as possible, the government's bunker strategy served only to reawaken wartime memories and reinforce wide-spread public scepticism about civil defence.

Notes

[1] A detailed history of the programme is found in Nicholas J. Steneck, *Everybody Has a Chance: Civil Defense and the Creation of Cold War West German Identity, 1950-1968*, Ph.D. diss., The Ohio State University, 2005, and Nicholas J. Steneck, 'Eine verschüttete Nation? Zivilschutzbunker in der Bundesrepublik Deutschland 1950-1965', in: Inge Marszolek and Marc Buggeln, eds., *Bunker: Kriegsort, Zuflucht, Erinnerungsraum*, Frankfurt/M.: Campus Verlag, 2008, pp. 75-88.

[2] See, for example, Frank Biess, *Homecomings: Returning POWs and the Legacies of Defeat in Post-war Germany*, Princeton: Princeton University Press, 2006, and Giles MacDonogh, *After the Reich: The Brutal History of the Allied Occupation*, New York: Basic Books, 2007.

[3] Michael Foedrowitz estimates that more than 25,000 bunkers remained in northern Germany at the turn of the century. See Foedrowitz, *Bunkerwelten: Luftschutzanlagen in Norddeutschland*, Berlin: Ch. Links Verlag, 1998.

[4] Additional examples are found in Foedrowitz, *Bunkerwelten*, and Helga Schmall and Tobias Selke, *Bunker: Luftschutz and Luftschutzbau in Hamburg*, Hamburg: Christians Verlag: 2001.

[5] See http://www.luftschutzbunker-wilhelmshaven.de/bu_sites/lenau.html (accessed 24 June 2007).

[6] Heinz Dählmann, 'Gedanken über den Schutzraumbau', *Ziviler Luftschutz*, 17:7/8 (1953), p. 1969.

[7] Bundesarchiv Koblenz [hereafter BA] B106.17569, Letter (Copy), Beutler and Meendsen-Bohlken to Kristen, 4 November 1952; Subject: 'Schutzraumbau im Industrie-Luftschutz.'

[8] Bundestag Drucksache [hereafter BD] II/1978, 'Entwurf eines Gesetzes über Maßnahmen auf dem Gebiete des zivilen Luftschutzes', in *Anlagen zu der Verhandlungen des deutschen Bundestags*, Second Electoral Period, Vol. 39, Bonn: Bundesdruckerei, 1955, pp. 1931-53 (hereafter cited as *Bundestag Anlagen*).

[9] *Bundestag Anlagen*, BD II/1978, 'Begründung', Section III, §§11-12.

[10] Hans Schmidle, 'Schutzraumbau für die Bevölkerung muß "das Primäre" aller Luftschutzmaßnahmen sein (3. Teil)', in *Zivil Luftschutz*, 23:11 (November 1959), p. 323.

[11] *Bundestag Anlagen*, BF IV/896, 'Entwurf eines Gesetzes über bauliche Maßnahmen zum Schutz der Zivilbevölkerung (Schutzbaugesetz)'.

[12] On Tamms' work during the war see Ernst Klee, *Das Kulturlexikon zum Dritten Reich. Wer war was vor and nach 1945*, Frankfurt/M.: Fischer, 2007, p. 607.

[13] See 'Überleben in Schutzraumbauten', *Die Welt*, 17 January 1963, 'Kritik an Bonner Schutzbauplänen', *Deutsche Zeitung*, 4 March 1963, Staatsarchiv Hamburg (hereafter cited as SHH) 614-2/12, Packet 39.

[14] *Verhandlungen des Deutschen Bundestages. Stenographische Berichte*, Fourth Election Period, Vol. 52, 56th Meeting [January 24, 1953], Bonn: Bundesdruckerei, 1958, pp. 2481-2. Hereafter cited as *Bundestag Verhandlungen*. The proceedings show that Hörcherl ignored the Opposition's repeated cries that the information he cited was classified and therefore unavailable to most West Germans.

[15] *Bundestag Verhandlungen*, Fourth Election Period, Vol. 49, 192nd Meeting [24 June 1965], p. 9746.

[16] *Ibid.*, p. 9749.

[17] See, for example, Dietmar Arnold, et. al., *Sirenen und gepackte Koffer: Bunkeralltag in Berlin*, Berlin: Ch. Links Verlag, 2003; Ralf Blank, 'Kriegsalltag und Luftkrieg an der Heimatfront', in: Jörg Echternkamp, ed., *Das Deutsche Reich und der Zweite Weltkrieg*, Vol. 9/1: *Die Deutsche Kriegsgesellschaft, 1949 bis 1945: Politisierung, Vernichtung, Überleben*, Munich: Deutsche Verlags-Anstalt, 2004, pp. 357-461; Thomas Childers, *'Facilis descensus averni est'*: The Allied Bombing of Germany and the Issue of German Suffering', *Central European History* 38:1 (2005), 75-105; Peter Fritzsche, 'Machine Dreams: Airmindedness and the Reinvention of Germany', *American Historical Review* 98:3 (June 1993), 685-709; Angela Martin and Claudia Schoppmann, eds., *'Ich fürchte die Menschen mehr als die Bomben.' Aus den Tagebüchern von drei Berliner Frauen, 1938-1946*, Berlin: Metropol Verlag, 1996; and Mary Nolan, 'Germans as Victims in the Second World War: Air Wars, Memory Wars', *Central European History*, 38:1 (2005), 7-40. A more well known addition to the literature is Jörg Friedrich's *Der Brand: Deutschland im Bombenkrieg, 1940-1945*, Berlin: Propyläen, 2002, which includes a lengthy (pp. 371-464), if not

completely documented, section on Nazi civil defence measures.

[18] Fritzsche, p. 690.

[19] Erich Hampe, 'Luftschutz als Schicksalsfrage des deutschen Volkes', in: Kurt Knipfer and Rich Erich Hampe, eds., *Der zivile Luftschutz: Eind Sammelbuch über alle Fragen des Luftschutzes*, Berlin: Stollberg, 1934, pp. 135-43.

[20] The lowest-ranking Nazi officials, the block wardens, formed the link between the Party and the general population. Administrative guidelines issued in August 1939 gave block wardens the responsibility of ensuring apartment blocks had strengthened cellars sufficient to provide adequate protection during air raids. See Friedrich, *Der Brand*, 375. On the Nazi block wardens see Detlef Schmiechen-Ackermann, '"Der Blockwart." Die unteren Parteifunktionäre im nationalsozialistischen Terror- und Überwachungsapparat', *Vierteljahrshefte für Zeitgeschichte*, 48:4 (2000), 575-602.

[21] Foedrowitz, p. 12.

[22] A near-contemporary discussion of the technical failures of German bunkers can be found in the U.S. government study *Impact of Air Attack in World War II: Selected Data for Civil Defense Planning, Division I: Physical Damage to Structures, Facilities, and Persons*, Vol. I: 'Summary of the Civil Defense Experience', Washington, D.C.: U.S. Government Printing Office, 1953, pp. 22-26.

[23] 'Bericht des Wehrmacht-Propaganda-Offiziers des Wehrkreiskommandos III, Berlin, Oberstleutnant Wasserfall, über den "Sondereinsatz Berlin" für die Zeit vom 21.2 bis 27.2.1945', in: Wolfram Wette, et. al., *Das Letzte halbe Jahr: Stimmungsberichte der Wehrmachtpropaganda 1944/45*, Bd. 13. Schriften der Bibliothek für Zeitgeschichte – Neue Folge. Essen: Klartext Verlag, 2001, pp. 284-6.

[24] Wette, p. 311.

[25] *Die Tagebücher von Joseph Goebbels*, ed. Elke Fröhlich, Teil II: *Diktate, 1941-1945*, vol. 10: *Oktober-Dezember 1943*, Munich: K.G. Saur, 1994, p. 399; and ibid., vol. 11: *Januar-März 1944*, p. 299. On 23 November, a 764-bomber raid caused extensive damage to the city's western residential districts, key government buildings such as the Ministry of Weapons and Munitions, and war industries. The 900-bomber raid of 15 February, the RAF's largest, destroyed large sections of Berlin's city centre and south-western districts, damaging critical war industries, including the large *Siemensstadt* area.

[26] The total number of German civilian casualties remains unknown. Blank notes (pp. 459-61) that initial estimates were as high as 422,000. In 1956, the West German government revised the number downward to 410,000. More recent work places civilian casualties at between 360,000 and 465,000. This number includes forced labourers, prisoners of war, and active duty military personnel on leave. See Olaf Groehler, *Bombenkrieg gegen Deutschland*, Berlin: Akademie-Verlag, 1990, pp. 316-20.

[27] Hermann Knell, *To Destroy a City: Strategic Bombing and Its Human Consequences in World War II*, Cambridge, MA: Da Capo Press, 2003, p. 308, and

Martin K. Sorge, *The Other Price of Hitler's War*, Santa Barbara/CA: Greenwood Press, 1986, pp. 111-12.

[28] Sorge, p. 97.

[29] Wette, pp. 168, 203, 299, and 393.

[30] Wolfgang W. E. Samuel, *The War of Our Childhood: Memories of World War II*, Jackson: University of Mississippi Press, 2002, pp. 84-5.

[31] Ibid., p. 116.

[32] Knell, p. 309.

Christian Groh

Expressions of Memory in Pforzheim, a City hit by Air War

Far from ever having been a taboo, the air war has always been part of the public memory in Pforzheim and elsewhere. There is a lively and locally well-known and debated memorial culture that is living proof against the idea of a taboo of the air war in the post-war period. This chapter traces the history of this local memorial culture and the way that the depiction of the air war in literature, exhibitions, newspapers and speeches made it possible for many Germans to see themselves as victims.

'Dürfen Täter sich als Opfer fühlen, wenn die militärischen Macht-verhältnisse sich umkehren und die Angegriffenen mit furchtbarer Vergeltung zurückschlagen?' This is the question Romain Leick asks in his epilogue to the re-edition of one of the most successful books on German history in the past years: Jörg Friedrich's *Der Brand*.[1] After the first edition in 2002, in which the author according to the epilogue had lifted the veil of forgetting and for the very first time had written 'eine umfassende, packende, glänzend geschriebene Darstellung der Bombardierung deutscher Städte durch die Alliierten',[2] a host of books, articles and special editions were published which, according to what the publishing houses told us, lifted a taboo of silence on the air war.

Before attempting to give an answer to the moral question whether the perpetrators of the Second World War may be entitled to feel as victims one should ask whether they really did feel as victims. Are there any expressions of grief in the German population? Has there been a discourse on the strategic air war at all? Or has the topic really been hidden behind a veil of forgetting?

Contrary to what the media – eager to sell their products – tell us, there had been publications and a public discourse on the air war since the end of the war. Studies by social scientists as well as literary writings from the 1950s can be quoted as evidence.[3] The *Bundes-ministerium für Vertriebene, Flüchtlinge und Kriegsgeschädigte* published a *Dokumentation deutscher Kriegsschäden* in 1958. Besides this there is a vast body of local history. Memorials and articles in local newspapers may be cited as further evidence.[4] In the respective cities the citizens held commemorations. Monuments were erected to remember the dead, streets and places were renamed.

Pforzheim, one of the most severely hit cities during the bombing campaign, laid in ruins ten days after the bombing of Dresden, has 21 sites and memorials with reference to the years 1933 to 1945. Fifteen of these, that is more than two thirds, recall the bombing of the city. Given this evidence, the supposed taboo can easily be unmasked as a 'modern legend'.[5] One reason why this legend has been so successful may be the fact that the discourse about the air war was restricted to private,[6] small half-public, and local circles. Not before 1995, when Federal President Roman Herzog attended a memorial service in Dresden, was the air war a central element of federal memorial politics. One has to go down to the local level in order to ascertain the ways in which Germans talked, felt, and thought about the air war.[7]

In the early evening hours of 23 February 1945, 368 bombers of the Royal Air Force had dropped their lethal load of almost 1,600 tons of bombs on Pforzheim. The city centre was completely destroyed and more than 17,000 people died. Pforzheim shared its fate with most German industrial cities and bigger towns. In relation to its size, however, it was second in the line of most damaged cities after Dresden. Alfred Döblin, who visited Germany as officer in the French army wrote in a letter: 'Das Tollste ist Pforzheim; vom Erdboden verschwunden, rasiert, komplett kurz und klein geschlagen. Keine Menschenseele mehr vorhanden. Pforzheim kannst Du vom Atlas streichen.'[8]

Indeed, the old city had vanished, but it has not ceased to exist as Döblin had stated. However, the reconstruction radically altered the city's appearance. City planners designed an urban space to suit modern individual traffic with all the commodities for shoppers and all the disadvantages this entails for the residents. The new and modern face of the city led to feelings of alienation among the inhabitants. The local paper wrote about one of the first exhibitions of the 'old Pforzheim before the war': 'Eine modern gewordene Stadt auf der Suche nach ihrer Seele.'[9]

For months, even years after February 1945, life was marked by the consequences of the air raid: removal of the ruins and rubble, burial of human remains, shortage of housing, debates about the reconstruction etc. Nearly every measure taken by the French and then the American military government and by the city officials in the first months, years, and even decades after the war had to and could be put down to the air raid. Consequently, there could hardly have been silence around it. It was rather always present, at least in the back of people's minds. It is even present in our days: Today the old city is idealised, books with pictures of 'Alt-Pforzheim' sell well, reconstructions of historical buildings are celebrated enthusiastically.

There is a widespread body of literature about Pforzheim's history and especially about the bombing. Historical overviews, memorial literature, and newspaper articles published every year on the 23 February provide an insight into the way public memory on the air war has been influenced.

In 1946, only weeks after Pforzheim citizens were able to read the first licensed newspapers a small booklet of 24 pages was published titled: 'Pforzheim – Geschichte und Zerstörung'. The concise historical overview ends with the description of early 20th century Pforzheim and the idyllic town's rapid growth to a big industrial city. The author then continues immediately: 'Nun wurde die gesamte Innenstadt bis auf kleine Reste am Rande und auf die Vororte ein einziges Trümmerfeld, unter dem noch so mancher Tote aus der Katastrophe des 23. Februar 1945 verschüttet liegt.'[10]

The so-called 'Katastrophe' or 'disaster', meaning the air raid, seems to have appeared out of the blue. The years and decades between the early 20th century and 1945 are omitted by the book. There is not a word about the rise of National Socialism, which had received an above-average share of voters in the city;[11] no mention of 'Gleichschaltung' and the formation of a Nazi society. German responsibility for the Second World War and the German war crimes are not worth a single sentence, neither is the Holocaust. The fact that the whole economic, social and ultimately cultural life had been subjected to the goals of warfare, this being one of the reasons for aerial bombing, is not touched upon. It was easier to see the night of the bombing as a disaster than to try to explain the path that had led to the wide areas of ruins and rubble.

Of course, a small pamphlet of only 24 pages could not provide well thought-out explanations. Nevertheless, the depiction of the war as a disaster out of the blue is a typical feature of the local literature of the early post-war years and has even been repeated in some publications up into the 1980s.[12]

The local press in its annually recurring articles wrote about the number of the dead, about the loss of historic buildings and of cultural heritage, about the clearing up work, and about the reconstruction. However, even here there is no reference to the years before. In 1954, an article in the *Pforzheimer Kurier* outlined the development of World War II in the city, listing the growing restrictions during the war, from the introduction of rationing to the summoning of youths and elderly people for war services. At least the article also mentioned that city and party officials had been informed about the risk of an air attack in 1943 – a fact that is frequently omitted in later publications in order to create the impression of an unknowing and innocent city struck without any reason. However, there is no reference whatsoever to the strategic background of aerial bombing and to the fact that this was a response to Nazi Germany's conduct in the war.

The first historical account on the bombing of Pforzheim that reconsidered the strategic background was significantly written by an American historian. Ursula Moessner-Heckner's *Pforzheim. Code Yellowfin*,[13] published in 1991, gives a detailed overview over all air raids against the city. The Pforzheim-born author was the first historian writing about the city's war history to make extensive use of archival resources from the Public Record Office (PRO) and other British and US archives. Her sources reveal that on the one hand the British and American military knew that the factories, many of them based in the centre, had been turned into armament factories in the course of the war. On the other hand it was clear that the operation also was part of the strategic air war intended to hit Germany's morale.

Moessner-Heckner specifically stresses this second aspect. Although she gives an accurate overview of her findings in the archives, her motives and subsequent lack of distance to the topic become too clear, when she writes about the strategic air war as a 'terror developing into futile mania of destruction'.[14] In a letter she explains why she had written the book: 'Ich schrieb […] für meine Mutter. […] [F]ür jene, die den Schrecken des 23. Februar entronnen waren, war der Angriff eine traumatische Zäsur, […], die eine Erklärung benötigte.'[15]

In an interview in 2004 she told a Pforzheim newspaper she had wanted to know 'warum mein Pforzheim zerstört wurde. Trotz der

Kriegsindustrie war das ja nicht der Grund, sondern das schöne Wetter an jenem Tag. [...] Es war ein reiner Terrorangriff.'[16]

The interpretation of the bombardment as 'terror', seemingly confirmed by a supposedly independent scholar from the United States, fitted all too well into many people's frame of mind. And it was much easier to accept than the more complex truth. Moessner-Heckner's study gave the first detailed account of the military background of Pforzheim's bombing night. However, it did not change pre-existing notions of victimhood that had been spread before, as for example in a special edition of the *Pforzheimer Zeitung* published on the occasion of the 25th anniversary of the bombing in 1970. The city's bombardment, so the argument there, had been 'sinnlos wie der ganze Krieg', the inhabitants had been 'durch ein Bomben-Massaker ausgelöscht'. The evaluation of the air attack as futile implies a hidden accusation of a war crime. Moreover, it puts all victims of World War II on one level. Germans are portrayed as victims from two sides: first they had fallen victim to a dictator, and then even had to pay for his atrocious deeds. The attack on the city, so the article, had been

> eine Aktion ohne jeden militärischen Nutzeffekt [...]. Es war ein mörderischer Amoklauf der Sieger. Freilich – 'wir Deutschen' haben mit dem Luftkrieg begonnen. Wer kann Schuld gegen Schuld aufrechnen? Die diktatorischen Maßnahmen eines Wahnsinnigen werden uns noch auf Generationen hinaus als Kollektivschuld angelastet.[17]

A narrowly focused view on the air war made it easier for many Pforzheim citizens to live on. To confront oneself with the past and with German guilt would have been much harder than it was to mourn the dead and to describe one's own suffering. Witnesses' accounts, which are up to today a very popular section of the literature and which are printed almost every year in the newspapers contributed to the general feeling of victimisation because their perspective was emotional and full of suffering.[18] In 1963 eyewitness accounts were published in a book after mayor Johann Peter Brandenburg had called on his fellow citizens to write down their experiences.[19] In the two re-editions of this book the reports are accompanied by a selection of pictures which can likewise be found in many newspaper articles and in exhibitions to this day. The first illustrated book about Pforzheim to appear after 1945 was the 1953 *Pforzheim im Bild*, subtitled: 'Vor der Zerstörung – Nach dem Angriff – Beim Wiederaufbau'.[20] The collection seems to try to reconcile those who criticised the modern reconstruction. The pictures show quiet places in the reconstructed town and clean streets along with schools or buildings of social housing.

Other books, most notably Friedrich's *Brandstätten* which contains Pforzheim pictures,[21] contrast the 'ugly' modern face of post-war Pforzheim with the allegedly beautiful, picturesque and quiet image of the pre-war years. To print pictures of the old city alongside those of the destroyed and/or the rebuilt city is a prominent feature of memorial culture.[22] This can be interpreted as trying to regain a degree of continuity that seemed to have been lost in the bombing nights, especially in a city like Pforzheim where the reconstruction hardly made any references to the historic predecessor. At the same time the contrasting of old and new pictures in publications was and is a popular strategy to highlight the losses German cities had suffered through the Allies' air attacks. Descriptions of the town before the destruction leave out any negative aspects of the industrial city. Indeed, the picture books and texts make us believe that a peaceful and romantic life has been lost forever: 'So endete die einst blühende Stätte von Kunstfleiß und Gewerbe, die Stadt froher und schaffensfreudiger Menschen, der Ort fröhlichen Lebens und emsigen Strebens in Nacht und Grauen.'[23]

Many of the photographs published depict damaged or destroyed cultural monuments, churches, or schools. Public buildings, which had been ornated with Nazi insignia, however, are hardly ever printed.[24] In the 'before' sections of the illustrated books such pictures would not have underlined the main argument of an innocent victim. Likewise, factories which were legitimate targets for the Allied bombers are neither shown in the 'before' nor in the 'after' sections. This way, any debate on the legitimacy of air war in general was omitted; thus, the impression of an innocent German city was much easier to deliver – not regarding its factories producing war goods, the adjacent railway stations and trails transporting military goods and personnel, the Nazi institutions within the city limits.[25]

The fire kindled by the bombs had burnt in an indiscriminate way, it did not and could not make a halt in front of churches, museums, archives, schools, or similar buildings. This is especially true for cities like Pforzheim, where factories of minor size were situated in the city centre and next to workers' housing and other buildings. However, our perception of the destroyed German cities, which is highly influenced by the transmission of pictures, is highly selective as the photographs show mostly destroyed cultural artefacts and monuments, one of the most prominent examples being the angel on top of the Dresden town-hall tower pointing on the fields of ruins below.

Further prominent motifs of pictures are seemingly ageless objects of art or religion, suggesting a moment of eternity, detached from history. This seeming timelessness, along with the perceptible preponderance of depictions of destroyed residential houses, social, cultural, and religious buildings has helped people to forget about the context of the destructions. The myth of the 'Stunde Null', of a totally new beginning without looking back could be and was backed by the very look of the cities in ruins.

In addition, human beings are hardly ever depicted in the ruined cities. They do not reappear in the visual memory before the time of reconstruction, when Germans played a constructive role again and cleared away the mess that Hitler or the Allied bombers had left behind. Public memory has been influenced by these pictures, which did not show Germans as perpetrators but instead their destroyed homes; thus they could more easily be depicted as victims, not as representatives of a Nazi state.

In a city like Pforzheim, in which 17,000 people had died after one bombing raid, it was hard to address the role of Germans as perpetrators. As a consequence, well into the 1970s the city's public memory concentrated on its suffering, not on the complicated entanglements of competing roles as perpetrators, sufferers, and beneficiaries. Every year since 1946 the city of Pforzheim has held a ceremony at its main cemetery, with attendances in the hundreds. There were even campaigns to make 23 February a local public holiday. Since 1952 the flags have been hoisted at half-mast, and every year the mayor gives a speech.

During the 1950s and 1960s the mayors' speeches focused on reconstruction and reflected a kind of pride in the progress made so far. After giving feeble expressions of mourning, the mayor usually stressed the duties of the present time. These were first and foremost to rebuild the city physically, followed by a spiritual rebuilding by working to maintain peace. The annually repeated appeal to peace was justified by reference to the city's own fate. Mayor Brandenburg's speech of 1948 may serve as an example:

> Sehen wir Pforzheim! Städte wie Pforzheim dürfen […] nicht nur als Trümmer-
> stätten Mahnmale sein. Sie sollten darüber hinaus Stätten der Erneuerung unseres
> inneren und äußeren Lebens werden, sie könnten beispielgebend wirken für die
> ganze Welt, wenn sie die Forderungen der Zeit erkennen.[26]

Mayor Brandenburg's call to 'look at Pforzheim' was not just a
warning against cities' fates in a threatening future war turning from
'cold' to 'hot'. It was at the same time intended to raise the discourse
about the air war to a higher level with a wider public. Brandenburg
did not overstress the role of Germans as victims. He never left any
doubt that it was the Nazi state which was responsible for the suffering of its own people during the air raids. In 1957 he admonished

> von dem Geschehenen nichts [zu] vergessen, dass wir die Ursachen, die den Krieg
> auslösten, erkennen und Ursache und Wirkung nicht verwechseln. Das Vergessen
> jener Zusammenhänge mag vielen willkommener und bequemer sein, aber gerade
> an einer solchen Stätte muss daran erinnert werden, welcher Weg die Deutschen
> und auch unsere Stadt in jenes Unglück der Jahre 1939 bis 1945 geführt hat.[27]

The interpretation of Nazi Germany as an 'Unglück', as it was
expressed in Brandenburg's speech, lead to the interpretation of the
dead of 23 February as victims of the war, but also as victims of the
Nazi regime. In many Germans' views the dead of the bombing nights
were all innocent, whether they had been workers, soldiers, party
officials, policemen, housewives, forced labourers or whatever:

> Unsere gegen Kriegsende in einer schrecklichen phosphor-erhellten Abendstunde
> gestorbenen Vorfahren und Mitmenschen waren großenteils die schuldlosen Opfer
> schwerer Verfehlungen, welche andere Menschen veranlasst haben.[28]

The air raid and its totality of destruction also influenced the
process of coming to terms with questions of guilt and responsibility.
The distinction between those who had become guilty, those who had
to suffer and those who tried to get through – often hard to make
anyway – has been even harder to make in Pforzheim because – in a
literal and a metaphorical sense – all were covered by the ruins.

In the speeches of the mayors the Pforzheim dead were not only
signified as victims, they were also interpreted as human sacrifices,
the German word 'Opfer' having both connotations. The local paper
wrote in 1955 about the 'Opfertod der teuersten Bürger'.[29] In the
effort of trying to give a meaning to the bombing night and its
aftermath mayors up to this day have stressed the importance of peace.

The meaning of the thousandfold deaths on 23 February 1945 was 'to plant the love of peace in the hearts of future generations'.[30]

However seriously the city's mayors may have articulated the call for peace, they ran the risk of equating and homogenising different victims. Their commemoration speeches frequently contained references to contemporary theatres of war, civil wars or other crises. In 1967 Vietnam had to stand in as a comparison, the Middle East and Biafra were mentioned in 1969, and three years later Cambodia and Northern Ireland. In the suggested unity with the casualties of wars wholly different from World War II the victims of the air war were turned into sufferers of developments they had not influenced; more so: they had never been able to influence. In this perception, the context, the pre-history of the air raid vanished into vagueness. War thus was turned into a personified evil. It was no longer the result of human actions. As a result even the survivors, not only the many dead of the bombing nights could look at themselves as victims.

In this way of thinking not only German politics between 1933 and 1945 was relieved of responsibility but so, too, were the bombers of the Royal and the US Air Force, who had since become partners in the Cold War. There seemed to be no more need to inquire into the actions and the decisions which had led to the air war. The multi-faceted questions about the air war, which would have included a reflection both of German guilt and of a moral evaluation of modern warfare in general, were avoided well into the later years of the 20th century.

The ways of remembering the Second World War have changed in recent years, both on the national stage as well as in the city.[31] German suffering is now remembered in public, especially the consequences of the air war and of expulsion. At the same time difficult subjects like the role of the 'Wehrmacht' in the Holocaust have been discussed and have found their way into a wider audience beyond the limits of the academy.

When Federal President Roman Herzog attended the commemoration of the bombing of Dresden in 1995 there were still debates about whether the presence of the highest-ranking politician of the Federal Republic would not bestow too much honour on the event. Ten years later even politicians from the former Allied countries were present in Dresden.

On 23 February 2005 Sir Peter Torry, the then British Ambassador to Germany, gave a speech at the commemoration in Pforzheim and spoke of the 'extraordinary capability to reconcile and reconstruct'.[32] The sixtieth anniversary of the Pforzheim bombing night was remembered in many diverse ways. In addition to the ritual-like commemoration on the cemetery and similar hours of remembrance and wreath-laying ceremony there were peace rallies, exhibitions, events at schools and round-table discussions with historians. The manifold ways of remembering, especially the growth of debates and of educational efforts alongside the older more ritualised forms of remembrance will hopefully lead to a rationalisation. A less personal view could then contribute to differentiated ways of looking at the past. Then, answers to the introductory question, whether former perpetrators may be entitled to feel as victims, could not be answered as easily as Roman Leick's answer suggests. A wider public would take notice of the debates and findings of historical enquiry and consequently pied pipers would find it harder to sustain claims about taboos that never existed.[33]

Notes

[1] Jörg Friedrich, *Der Brand. Deutschland im Bombenkrieg 1940-1945,* Hamburg: Spiegel-Verlag, 2007 (= Spiegel-Edition 35), originally Munich: Propyläen, 2002.

[2] Ibid., p. 580.

[3] In 1950 Hannah Arendt discovered symptoms of post-traumatic distress among Germans. See Hannah Arendt, 'Besuch in Deutschland 1950. Die Nachwirkungen des Naziregimes', in: Hannah Arendt, *Zur Zeit. Politische Essays*, Munich: dtv, 1989, pp. 43-70 (here: p. 44). Hans Rumpf interpreted his observation of remarkable indifference among Germans in 1961 as a long-term consequence of the air raids fifteen to twenty years earlier. See Hans Rumpf, *Das war der Bombenkrieg. Deutsche Städte im Feuersturm*, Oldenburg, Hamburg: Stalling, 1961, p. 9.

[4] Thomas W. Neumann, 'Der Bombenkrieg. Zur ungeschriebenen Geschichte einer kollektiven Verletzung', in: Klaus Naumann, ed., *Nachkrieg in Deutschland,* Hamburg: Hamburger ed., 2001, pp. 319-42 (here: p. 335).

[5] See Ralf Blank, 'Einleitung – Bombenkrieg', in: *historicum.net*, http://www.historicum.net/no_cache/persistent/artikel/1859/ (accessed 27 November 2009) and Robert G. Moeller, 'The Politics of the Past in the 1950s: Rhetorics of Victimisation in East and West Germany', in: Bill Niven, ed., *Germans as Victims.*

Remembering the Past in Contemporary Germany, Basingstoke: Palgrave Macmillan, 2006, pp. 26-43 (here: p. 38).

[6] Jürgen Habermas, 'On how Post-war Germany has Faced its Recent Past', *Common Knowledge,* 5:2 (1996), p. 6.

[7] For Dresden see Gilad Margalit, 'Der Luftangriff auf Dresden. Seine Bedeutung für die Erinnerungspolitik der DDR und für die Herauskristallisierung einer historischen Kriegserinnerung im Westen', in: Susanne Düwell and Matthias Schmidt, eds., *Narrative der Shoah. Repräsentationen der Vergangenheit in Historiographie, Kunst und Politik,* Paderborn: Ferdinand Schöningh Verlag, 2002, pp. 189-207. See also Bill Niven, 'The GDR and Memory of the Bombing of Dresden', in: Bill Niven, ed., *Germans as Victims,* pp. 109-29. For Hamburg see Malte Thiessen, *Eingebrannt ins Gedächtnis. Hamburgs Gedenken an Luftkrieg und Kriegsende 1943-2005,* Weilerswist: Dölling und Galitz, 2007; for Kassel see Jörg Arnold, '"Krieg kann nur der Wahnsinn der Menschheit sein!" Zur Deutungsgeschichte des Luftangriffs vom 22. Oktober 1943 in Kassel', in: Dietmar Süß, ed., *Deutschland im Luftkrieg. Geschichte und Erinnerung,* Munich: Oldenbourg Verlag, 2007, pp. 135-49.

[8] Alfred Döblin, *Briefe II,* Düsseldorf, Zurich: Walter Verlag, 2001, p. 217.

[9] *Pforzheimer Zeitung,* 23 February 1965.

[10] M. Heinrich, *Pforzheim. Geschichte und Zerstörung,* Klosterreichenbach, no publisher, 1946, p. 24.

[11] Stefanie Wolfinger, 'Aufstieg der NSDAP und Wahlverhalten in Pforzheim am Ende der Weimarer Republik', in: Hans-Peter Becht, ed., *Neue Beiträge zur Stadtgeschichte I,* Sigmaringen: Thorbecke, 1999, pp. 185-234.

[12] For example: 'Ich war jetzt ganz allein, und auf dieser einsamen Wanderung sollte mir erst ganz zum Bewußtsein kommen, wie groß das Ausmaß des Unglücks war. Von oben blickte ich auf das Stadtgebiet herunter, das ein einziges ungeheures Flammenmeer war, und ich erkannte zu meinem Entsetzen, daß diese Stadt aufgehört hatte, eine Wohnstätte von Menschen zu sein. Der Moloch Krieg hatte sie verschlungen.' In: Alfons Schler, *Pforzheim's Schicksalsnacht. Ein Erlebnisbericht zur Erinnerung an den 23. Februar 1945,* Baden-Baden: Koelblin, 1949, p. 12.

[13] Ursula Moessner-Heckner, *Pforzheim. Code Yellowfin. Eine Analyse der Luftangriffe 1944-1945,* Sigmaringen: Thorbecke, 1991.

[14] Ibid., p. 155.

[15] *Pforzheimer Kurier,* 30 August 1991.

[16] *Pforzheimer Zeitung,* 23 October 2004.

[17] *Pforzheimer Zeitung*, 23 February 1970.

[18] Ralf Blank, 'Einleitung – Bombenkrieg'.

[19] Esther Schmalacker-Wyrich, *23. Februar 1945. Augenzeugenberichte vom großen Fliegerangriff auf Pforzheim*, Pforzheim: Verlag Esslinger, 1963.

[20] Karl Hillenbrand, *Pforzheim im Bild. Vor der Zerstörung – Nach dem Angriff – Beim Wiederaufbau*, Waiblingen-Stuttgart: Verlag Späth, 1953.

[21] Jörg Friedrich, *Brandstätten*, Munich: Propyläen, 2003, pp. 232f.

[22] See for example Bärbel Rudin, *Pforzheim – Die neue Stadt. Zerstörung – Aufbau – Umbau. Eine Fotoreportage aus fünf Jahrzehnten*, Kieselbronn: Windrose, 1993.

[23] Alfons Schler, *Pforzheim's Schicksalsnacht*, p. 14.

[24] Klaus Naumann, *Der Krieg als Text. Das Jahr 1945 im kulturellen Gedächtnis der Presse,* Hamburg: Hamburger ed., 1998, p. 36.

[25] For my argument it makes no difference whether the lack of such pictures is the result of limited means to take pictures in the destroyed cities or whether it is due to a willing selection. The impression left by this deliberate or unintentional selection remains the same. For photographers' possibilities to take pictures in the destroyed cities see Ludger Derenthal, 'Trümmerbilder. Fotografien der Kriegszerstörungen von Walter Frentz (1939-1947)', in: Hans Georg Hiller von Gaertringen, ed., *Das Auge des Dritten Reiches. Hitlers Kameramann und Fotograf Walter Frentz*, Munich, Berlin: Deutscher Kunstverlag, 2006, pp. 226-33 (here: p. 230).

[26] *Süddeutsche Allgemeine Zeitung*, 23 February 1948 (Gedenkbeilage).

[27] *Pforzheimer Kurier*, 25 February 1957.

[28] Walter Heidegger, *Pforzheim. Leben zwischen Ruinen,* Pforzheim: Verlag Weber, 1955.

[29] *Pforzheimer Kurier*, 23 February 1955.

[30] According to Mayor König's speech in 1950, see *Süddeutsche Allgemeine Zeitung*, 24 February 1950.

[31] Klaus Naumann, *Der Krieg als Text*, p. 35.

[32] *Pforzheimer Kurier*, 24 February 2005.

[33] See the argument developed by Stefan Berger in 'On Taboos, Traumas and Other Myths: Why the Debate about German Victims of the Second World War is not a Historians' Controversy', in: Niven, ed., *Germans as Victims*, pp. 210-24.

Jeffrey Luppes

'*Den Toten der ostdeutschen Heimat*': Local Expellee Monuments and the Construction of Post-war Narratives

This chapter focuses on the narrative constructed by more than 1,400 local expellee monuments located throughout Germany. Ignored in the debate over the proposed national memorial/documentation 'Zentrum gegen Vertreibungen' in Berlin, these local monuments – erected throughout the entire post-war period – have made permanent contributions to discourses on 'German wartime suffering' by generating and reflecting a one-sided narrative of German victimhood. Emphasising the loss of 'Heimat' and asserting the collective innocence of the expellees, the narrative comes at the expense of an inclusive, contextualised account of the Second World War and its aftermath, thus contesting the centrality of the Holocaust in German post-war memory.

Monuments to the Expulsion – A 'Blank Spot' in Germany's Memory Culture?

Since its inception in September 2000, the private foundation 'Zentrum gegen Vertreibungen' has spearheaded an effort to construct a large-scale memorial/documentation and research center in Berlin dedicated to twentieth-century victims of forced migration in Europe. Proclaiming, 'Alle Opfer von Genozid und Vertreibung brauchen einen Platz in unseren Herzen und im historischen Gedächtnis',[1] the foundation, under the aegis of the *Bund der Vertriebenen* (BdV – League of Expellees),[2] sought the German government's official sanction and financial support of its project. Although in a 2002 vote, the Social Democrat-led *Bundestag* approved merely the initiation of a Europe-wide discussion on the emplacement of an international memorial in a location to be determined, the Grand Coalition headed by Chancellor Angela Merkel passed legislation in late 2008 which opens the door for a state-sponsored centre in the German capital and grants the BdV an advisory role as well as a legitimate say in the ultimate form the memorial will take.[3]

From the start, the idea of a national memorial to the expulsion was contentious. Not only did the opponents of the idea fear the possibility of a self-absorbed, revisionist presentation of the German experience in WWII which might overshadow the innumerable crimes of the Nazis, they also could not forget the long-standing revanchist policies espoused by some members of the League, which included their boisterous opposition to the recognition of the Oder-Neisse border.[4] Seeking to assuage the concerns of their opponents, the League and the foundation 'Zentrum gegen Vertreibungen' stated repeatedly their combined desire to include representations and documentation of all expulsions of the twentieth century, not just that of the Germans. Nevertheless, even a cursory look at the foundation's objectives listed on its website indicates the preponderance of the German experience.[5]

As could be expected, the League's reaction to this recent development was positive. Nevertheless, in a statement by Erika Steinbach released to the press the day after the German parliament's decision, the BdV president declared that the government's resolution of this issue 'comes late, but not too late'. For the '*Erlebnisgeneration*', the release continued, the building of the centre would provide comfort, 'dass ihr Schicksal nicht vergessen ist, sondern einen festen Ort im kollektiven Gedächtnis unseres Vaterlandes hat'.[6]

The last point is particularly striking. The BdV's argument had always been that commemoration of flight and expulsion had been a '*weißer Fleck*', a blank spot, in German and European history and that there had been no place for the expellees in German memory culture. The 'Zentrum gegen Vertreibungen' would thus fill a significant lacuna in the Federal Republic's understanding of World War II and its aftermath.

Overlooked in this argumentation, however, are the ubiquitous monuments on the local level already commemorating flight and expulsion. Erected in every decade following the war, the 1,400+ monuments dot the landscapes of reunited Germany, are located in small numbers throughout the former 'German East', and can even be found as far away as the United States and Africa. Taken as a whole, these concrete examples of cultural production – up to now, never systematically and comprehensively analysed by scholars[7] – comprise an important component of Germany's memory culture and make an unequivocal but overlooked statement about the expellees' understanding of their war experience. These monuments and their contribution to discourses on German suffering in the Second World War are the focus of this chapter.

Monuments and Memory

It is a commonly held notion that monuments say a lot more about the time in which they are established than about the person(s) or event(s) they commemorate. Local expellee monuments are no different and reflect the political climate and societal mood at the time of their erection. Particularly interesting in this case, however, is the general uniformity in the contributions to public discourse made by expellee monuments throughout the decades since WWII despite paradigmatic shifts in memory culture at the national level. Indeed, the memorials, taken as a whole, make a profound statement about their initiators' understandings of the past –understandings, in many cases, which deviate substantially from standard post-war historical interpretations that have focused since the 1970s on Nazi crimes.

Of what importance are these commemorative spaces and the memorials they contain? After all, as Robert Musil so perceptively pointed out, '[…] Monuments are conspicuously inconspicuous. There is nothing in this world as invisible as a monument'.[8] However, this chapter regards these memorials to the expulsion as James E. Young sees memory-sites dedicated to the Holocaust, namely, as the multi-dimensional, meaning-creating public art which contributes to the shaping of public discussions of the past and comprises a significant portion of what he calls the 'texture of memory'.[9] Local expellee monuments offer an alternative 'texture of memory'.

Comparing or even connecting Holocaust memorials with local expellee monuments is, to say the least, problematic. In addition to the stark thematic differences, expellee monuments do not match the scale and public awareness of former concentration camps and other public monuments dedicated to the Shoah. Nor do they share the enhanced commemorative effect and the historic verisimilitude of Holocaust memorials located at the *authentischer Ort*. Local expellee monuments thus lack what Peter Reichel calls the 'authority of unreconstructed realities'.[10] Nevertheless, they do share one commonality in that they are dedicated to civilians and contrast sharply with German monuments of the past. About all post-WWII monuments, Heinz Ladendorf writes:

> Instead of the war memorials of the First World War, one encounters everywhere – not just in Germany – memorials to the fallen which are devoted to commemoration, not only glory and which are testimonies of mourning, not triumph.[11]

Furthermore, like virtually all monuments, those dedicated to the expulsion of Germans after WWII are used to memorialise, prompt, mobilise, communicate, and decry. Again, like all other intentional monuments, they have an agenda. Indeed, by their very nature, they privilege a selective interpretation of the past – in this case, one that reifies memories of Germans as victims of WWII. Moreover, they reflect, shape, and undergird the memories which help make up the historical narratives at the grassroots level. While not the only representations of this historical chain of events, expellee monuments constitute a significant public and (semi)permanent component of historical consciousness.

General Observations

In general, one can make three interrelated, larger observations about local expellee monuments and the role they play in post-war memory discourses in Germany. First of all, contrary to suggestions of silence about German suffering, the monuments serve as incontrovertible evidence that the topos 'Germans as victims' was never 'taboo' in the sense the word is used in current German memory discourse, i.e., that assertions and discussions of 'Germans as victims' were not permitted or nonexistent, and have been, instead, an ever-present topic on the minds and in the memories of significant numbers of Germans.[12] While this study is not the first that has set out to demystify this notion, it is the first which uses expellee monuments to do so.[13]

Secondly, local expellee monuments have been part and parcel of a deliberate and sustained effort to shape discussions of victimisation as a result of the Second World War. That significant numbers of the memorials were erected within the first decade after WWII demonstrates the immediate but also persistent attempts to assert the pre-eminence of German suffering in the face of Nazi atrocities and official measures of reconciliation and reparation that have been taken by the federal government. As Robert G. Moeller points out:

> Focusing on German suffering also made it possible to talk about the end of the Third Reich without assessing responsibility for its origins, to tell an abbreviated story of National Socialism in which all Germans were ultimately victims of a war that Hitler started but everyone lost.[14]

The exculpatory implications of this stance are self-evident. The hundreds more dedicated in subsequent decades, including many erected post-1990 in the former GDR show, in fact, how this endeavour continues, at least on the local level. Indeed, the local memorials are a public expression of popular, as opposed to official, memory, and a clear and concrete (figuratively and literally) example of how a German-centred post-war narrative has been constructed despite the emergence of the Holocaust-centred narrative.[15]

The third observation addresses the query, what narrative(s) or historical interpretation(s) do local expellee monuments – ranging from simple and austere 'Eastern crosses', to gravestones, commemorative plaques, bas-reliefs, signposts, stelae, sculptures and statues – make manifest? Instead of constructing – as their defenders would contend, and as the proponents of the 'Zentrum gegen Vertreibungen' in Berlin maintain – an innocuous, more inclusive parallel narrative that merely augments Holocaust-centred narratives, close readings of the local monuments reveal the building blocks of a counter-narrative that contests the centrality of the Holocaust in German memory. Indeed, the initiators of the local monuments have had an agenda that has gone beyond commemorating the dead to obfuscating causal links between the Nazi war of aggression and the forced migration of Germans from their homes in the East, thus challenging official memories of the war. More specifically, local expellee monuments facilitate the construction of a singular, de-contextualised German-centred narrative based on two thematic clusters: the loss of 'Heimat' and the concomitant territorial claims this forfeiture engendered and assertions of collective innocence.[16]

What follows is a breakdown of the two thematic clusters into categories which allow a broader analysis of all these memorials. Obviously, space limitations prohibit a full examination of all local expellee monuments. It must also be noted that this interpretive scheme cannot capture all local expellee monuments. As will be apparent, some monuments fit into more than one category. Others defy simple categorisation. Thus, some of the most striking and salient examples have been chosen, based ultimately on the questions: *What* story does the monument depict? And, *whose* story does the monument tell? Posed another way, is this a memorial that commemorates solely the undeniably tragic plight of Germans forced to leave their homes in Eastern and Central Europe *or* are the fates of other victims of WWII included?

Loss of 'Heimat' and Territorial Claims
'Großdeutschland' motif (Figures 1 and 2)
Most arresting and germane about the first category is that the monuments go beyond merely lamenting the loss of homeland and instead boldly decry the forfeiture of German territory as a result of WWII. The territories beyond the Oder-Neisse ceded by the Reich at the Potsdam Conference – the monuments seem to say – were and always will be German. Indeed, they exhibit revisionist iconography insofar as they display maps of Germany in its pre-1937 borders. Not only limited to monuments with nationalistic motifs (e.g. regional coats of arms), this category also includes the monuments with traditional Germanic forms, for example the 'erratic boulders' used mainly in northern Germany.[17]

Cold War Conflation (Figure 3)
The second category is called 'Cold War Conflation'. In some cases, iconography from the previous category is included linking the loss of Germany's eastern territories to its division between the Federal Republic and the GDR. Interestingly, East German cities like Eisenach, Erfurt, and Magdeburg are treated as 'lost' just like the cities of the truly lost eastern provinces Danzig and Königsberg. This category examines memorials erected after the division of Germany into two states (though many expellees to this day refer to Germany's division as a 'triple partition'), especially after the much-celebrated uprising in East Germany on 17 June 1953.[18] Commemorations of the revolt and the desire for unification it was said to have expressed were appropriated and combined by expellee organisations with their hope for unification of all former German territory.

Why this conflation? Especially in the early days of the Cold War, the expellees could couch their rhetoric about the right to homeland and the desire for a return home in the rhetoric of German reunification usually reserved for the two German states. Moreover, emphasis on the division of Germany and the parallel drawn between the Cold War and the expulsion reflects efforts to disconnect the expulsion from the Nazi war of aggression. The loss of their homes was less a consequence of WWII, and more a result of what they saw as the arbitrary and spiteful 'Siegerjustiz' of the Allies, especially the pernicious and vengeful Soviets. No memorials were erected in the territory of the GDR until after 1990.[19] However, the similarities of the memorials erected there in the years since to those in West Germany suggest that the will to commemorate the expulsion in the form of enduring monuments was not an ephemeral phenomenon reflecting anti-Soviet, anti-GDR rhetoric in the early years of the Federal Republic.

Germans as 'Kulturträger' – Accomplishments of German Settlement
The third category is comprised of a smaller number of monuments which highlight the longevity of German settlement in Eastern and Central Europe and laud the cultural contributions and accomplishments there. Indicating an organic, permanent connection to 'Heimat', these memorials once again express territorial claims and putative cultural superiority in that they celebrate the specific role of Germans, for example, in bringing culture to the area and making the land inhabitable and agriculturally bounteous. While the majority of these memorials were erected in West Germany by expellee organisations representing Germans from territory never incorporated into the German Reich (for example, by the 'Landsmannschaften' of Germans from Hungary or the Siebenbürger Saxons from Romania), the notion of Germans as bearers of culture has been a component of all discussions of the German 'Drang nach Osten'.[20]

'Den Toten der Heimat' – Territorial Claims through Cemeteries
This group of monuments is quite complex. First, it is unclear specifically to whom the monuments in this category are dedicated. Are the 'dead of the homeland' – easily the most common inscription of all expellee monuments – those who died during flight and expulsion? Are they the deceased expellees buried not in the German East but in the West? Are these monuments – as argued by Stephan Scholz – merely ersatz graves for the now inaccessible cemeteries containing the earthly remains of ancestors and loved ones behind the Iron Curtain?[21] Are they dedicated to the fallen soldiers from the eastern provinces? Does this terse inscription apply to the non-'Aryan' population of the East as well? How did these people die? In combat? In an air raid? In a gas chamber? Of natural causes?

Presumably, Scholz is correct and the monuments of this group are memorials for otherwise inaccessible gravestones and cemeteries in the former 'German East', but it could be argued that more is at play here, that in addition to memorialising, they were erected to serve another purpose. These monuments connect to the dead left behind in the East in a way that disputes the permanence of the newly established borders. Here, the monuments correspond to the view of Katherine Verdery, who, in her study of the 'political lives of dead bodies', writes about the 'symbolic capital' possessed by human remains.[22] Much like the gravesites in the Balkans about which Verdery writes, the memorials dedicated to 'Den Toten der Heimat' behind the Iron Curtain are used to make territorial claims. Where German graves lie was, is, and always will be German territory.

Exculpation through Collective Innocence
'Mutterliebe' – Allegory of the Female Form (Figures 4 and 5)[23]
The first category of the second cluster deals with how the female form – above all as mother – has become iconic in representations of the expulsion and is used to convey a brand of collective innocence. Elizabeth Heinemann writes how the 'stereotypically female experience' of WWII was universalised in West German collective memory to provide 'vital alternatives to representations of militaristic and genocidal Germans'.[24] As depicted in this category, the experiences of putatively innocent women, especially mothers with young children – apparently untainted by any connection to the Nazi war machine – were chosen to represent flight and expulsion. Thus, in order to make the notion of German victimhood more palatable, local expellee monuments display non-specific female figures to posit the presumed innocence of all the expellees, further distancing them from the Nazi regime. Gender is instrumentalised to exculpate all expellees, and by extension, all Germans.

Christian Symbolism (Figure 6)
The second category of this cluster features monuments that display religious motifs. Memorials in the form of crosses and crucifixes, crowns of thorns, or which quote Bible passages have always constituted a significant subset of all war memorials but those erected by the expellees are qualitatively different. The cross is by the far the most frequently implemented form in expellee monuments. Meinhold Lurz argues that religious symbolism was employed in public commemorations in the immediate post-war era to console in lieu of the more familiar and traditional (but since disavowed) nationalism.[25] According to Lurz, Christian motifs were used to 'level off'

('nivellieren') the difference between death caused by war and normal civilian death. As in the next category as well, the use of Christian symbolism blurs the distinction between different ways of dying and between perpetrator and victim because, as Lurz points out, 'everyone is equal before God'.[26] What is more, as Scholz observes, 'Das Kreuz mit seinem zentralen Bedeutungselement des Opfers diente dazu, die Vertriebenen als christusgleiche Opfer zu stilisieren und die Vertreibungserfahrung im Rahmen der göttlichen Heilsgeschichte zu sakralisieren.'[27] The sacrifice of the expellees – as depicted in the monuments employing Christian symbolism – was perhaps greatest of all.

Subsumptive assertions of victimhood (Figure 7)
The final category is closely related to the previous one. In a war in which everyone was a 'victim', so the thinking goes, no-one (or only a few, i.e. Hitler and the upper echelon of the National Socialist regime) was a 'perpetrator'. Germans suffered just as everyone else did. This is the thinking behind the final category of memorials. Here, all casualties of WWII are grouped together in a universalised victim-hood collective. Rather than a war in which some were active agents and some passive recipients, these memorials ostensibly collapse categories like 'German' and 'Jew' or 'Pole', or 'civilian' and 'soldier', or 'perpetrator' and 'victim' without addressing how or why the people fell victim. As Sabine Behrenbeck observes, this type of memorial treats all the nameless, faceless war dead as the victims of 'an accident, like a tragic fate, or a natural disaster'.[28] Once again, causality is ignored, and, much like in the previous category, attribu-tions of guilt or responsibility are muted. This type of monument is especially prevalent in the eastern states, where a substantial number bear the vague inscription 'DEN OPFERN DES KRIEGES DER FLUCHT UND VERTREIBUNG'.

Conclusion
In conclusion, in no way is this critique intended to diminish human suffering. After all, how does one differentiate between revanchism and legitimate mourning over real loss? Does any amount of complicity in a criminal regime preclude genuine bereavement? However, it appears that acknowledgement of German suffering in the form of local expellee monuments leads, at minimum, to equalisation,

and in many cases borders on eclipsing and effacing. The monuments
discussed here and the scores of others dedicated exclusively to
'*UNSEREN* TOTEN' (my emphasis) or which swear eternal loyalty to
the long-lost German East are at the heart of discourses on German
wartime suffering because they facilitate the construction of an
exculpatory narrative in which the causal links between the Nazi war
of aggression and the expulsion are dissolved. Indeed, the
monuments' one-sided inscriptions suggest that their sponsors have
not viewed what befell the expellees as connected to WWII at all. The
processes and the actors that unleashed the events which precipitated
the expulsion are almost never mentioned. The local monuments thus
reflect an immediate and sustained effort to shape post-war debates
over victimhood and culpability in a concerted endeavour to muddle a
strict victim/perpetrator binary.

Of course, these issues mirror those in the debate over the
'Zentrum gegen Vertreibungen'. Many opponents of the proposal fear
official recognition of the expulsion in the form of a monument would
be tantamount to an exculpation of German perpetrators.
Acknowledgement in the form of a state-sanctioned memorial, they
believe, would lead to equalisation which would continue down the
slippery slope toward effacing and forgetting. For, as Robert G.
Moeller noted, accounts of German suffering often contain an
'implicit "too," [...] and from "too" it has sometimes been a short step
to "like" and the equation of German and Jewish suffering'.[29]

Remarkably, the group which might be most affected if such a plan
came to fruition has not been opposed, at least not in principle, to the
'Zentrum gegen Vertreibungen'. In December 2005, the Central
Council of Jews in Germany issued a press release which after
expressing some misgivings stated,

> Es ist völlig legitim und längst überfällig, auch der deutschen Opfer von
> Vertreibung und Krieg zu gedenken. Ein solches Gedenken darf jedoch
> keinesfalls der Versuchung erliegen, die nationalsozialistischen Mensch-
> heitsverbrechen zu relativieren oder auch nur den Hauch eines Eindrucks
> aufkommen zu lassen, dass hier Opfer- und Täterrollen beliebig ausge-
> tauscht werden.[30]

Such a nuanced approach seems to be the best way to balance the
expellees' obvious desire for recognition and remembrance with
potential relativisation through memorials. This balance is precisely
what is lacking in so many of the local monuments.

Illustrations

Figure 1: 'Großdeutschland' Motif – This monument in Lengerich, North Rhine-Westphalia, was erected in 1956 before hopes for a border adjustment had been permanently dashed. Not only does it look retrospectively at the past, it also makes an optimistic claim on the future.

Figure 2: 'Großdeutschland' Motif – The territorial claims raised by the expellees persisted even after Willy Brandt's 'Ostpolitik' recognised *de facto* the Oder-Neisse border. This monument in Plüderhausen, Baden-Württemberg, was erected in 1980.

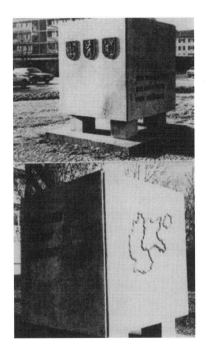

Figure 3: Cold War Conflation – This monument in Böblingen, Baden-Württemberg, with the inscription 'Wir wollen sein ein einig Volk von Brüdern' bears the coats of arms of both Berlin and Breslau as well as a map of pre-1937 Germany with emphasis on the inner-German border.

Figure 4: 'Mutterliebe' – Allegory of the Female Form – This bronze statue was erected in Oberursel, Hessen in 1981. Privately donated and located in a cemetery, the figures are of a visibly downtrodden, hunched-over mother trudging arduously with her three young children during winter with all their possessions in small bundles. *Where* they are headed can only be speculated. The location of the husband and father can also only be presumed. *Why* they were forced to flee, however, is inscribed at their feet: '1945/1946 Flucht und Vertreibung aus der Heimat im Osten'. They were the blameless German victims of either the advancing Red Army or local partisans at the end of WWII.

Figure 5: 'Mutterliebe' – Allegory of the Female Form – Another example is the sculpture titled MUTTERLIEBE found in Pforzheim, Baden-Württemberg. Erected in 1994, this memorial features a loving mother protectively cradling her babies and is dedicated specifically to mothers and children.

Figure 6: Christian Symbolism – The plinth of this commemorative cross in Steinhagen, North Rhine-Westphalia bears the inscription: '90. Psalm. Den Opfern des großen Trecks aus dem Osten 1945'.

Figure 7: Subsumptive Assertions of Victimhood – In this monument in Radeberg, Saxony, erected in 1994, all victims are to be commemorated without any specificity as to who the actual 'victims' are and without reference to the causes of this calamity.

Notes

My thanks to the *Bund der Vertriebenen* for permission to use its photographs in this contribution.

[1] As cited on the foundation's website www.z-g-v.de (accessed 30 January 2010).

[2] In the interest of simplicity and brevity, I follow this nomenclature and henceforth use the terms 'expulsion' and 'expellees' to refer respectively to the events and those Germans who left their homelands in the 'German East' either in anticipation of the Red Army's advance starting in the fall of 1944, those forcibly driven out of their homes and driven west during the 'wilde Vertreibungen' immediately after the end of the war, and those formally expelled during the last quarter of 1945 and beyond as a result of the Allied agreements reached at the Potsdam Conference, fully aware that the terms are not semantically neutral and that not all the Germans were 'expelled' per se. This three-part periodisation is based on Philipp Ther's article 'The Integration of Expellees in Germany and Poland after World War II: A Historical Reassessment', *Slavic Review*, 55:4 (Winter 1996), 779-805.

[3] In addition to Berlin, less 'offensive' cities like Wrocław (Breslau) and Priština were proposed.

[4] For an investigation of the expellee lobby's influence on West German foreign policy, see Pertti Ahonen, *After the Expulsion: West Germany and Eastern Europe, 1945-1990*, Oxford and New York: Oxford UP, 2003. Other critics remember the involvement in National Socialism of many of the BdV's founding members, including its first chairman Hans Krüger, who resigned in 1964 from his cabinet post as expellee minister because of his Nazi past. For more on the organisation's nefarious connections to National Socialism, see Hans Michael Kloth & Klaus Wiegrefe, 'Unbequeme Wahrheiten', *Der Spiegel*, 33 (2006), p. 46, as well as Erich Später's chilling examination of the Sudetendeutsche Landsmannschaft. *Kein Frieden mit Tschechien: Die Sudetendeutschen und ihre Landsmannschaft*, Hamburg: KVV Konkret, 2005.

[5] According to its website (www.z-g-v.de), the 'Zentrum gegen Vertreibungen' foundation has four tasks: the first calls for the creation of a museum dedicated to the experience of the German expellees. Deeming this act a 'task for the whole of Germany', the first task foresees a museum/research centre with 'additional space for sadness, sympathy and forgiveness [...] to be accommodated in a requiem rotunda'. The second task is to 'illuminate the changes in Germany as a result of the integration of millions of uprooted compatriots' which 'has had its effects on all areas of life'. Task three aims at providing a space 'in our hearts and in historical memory' for all the victims of genocide and displacement'. Interestingly, in undoubtedly another concession to potential opponents of the centre, the foundation does include a (very brief) mention of European Jews in their lists of representative groups. However, this trite reference ostensibly equates the systematic extermination of the Jews with the

forced migration of the Greek Cypriots and other oppressed minorities on the list. The fourth task calls for the bestowal of a prize to individuals or groups who work against human rights violations.

[6] Erika Steinbach, *Bund der Vertriebenen*. Press Release: 'Wir haben viel erreicht', 5 December 2008. Available online: http://www.bund-der-vertriebenen.de/presse /index.php3?id=802.

[7] While scholarly work on the monuments is limited, there have been two major efforts to document this public art. The first is a catalogue listing a large but incomplete number of the monuments compiled privately and independently by the amateur historian Kurt Schmidt. The other is the BdV's useful documentation project (actually based in large part on Schmidt's work) posted on the organisation's website http://www.bund-der-vertriebenen.de/infopool/inmemoriam.php3.   Otherwise, examples of scholarship exclusively on this topic are rare and are generally limited in scope, for example, Kathrin Panne's localised sketch of expellee monuments in *Land-kreis* Celle, 'Erinnerungspolitik – Erinnerungsspuren: Zur Funktion symbolischer Erinnerung an Flucht und Vertreibung im öffentlichen Raum. Eine Skizze', in: Rainer Schulze, Reinhard Rohde and Rainer Voss, eds., *Zwischen Heimat und Zuhause: Deutsche Flüchtlinge und Vertriebene in (West-)Deutschland 1945-2000*, Osnabrück: Senoco, 2001, pp. 201-15. Hans-Werner Retterath published two articles on expellee monuments in Baden-Württemberg: 'Geschichtsbilderkampf und zwiespältige Beheimatungsversuche – Vertriebenendenkmale in Südbaden', *Jahrbuch für deutsche und osteuropäische Volkskunde*, 47 (2005), 83-121 as well as 'Gedenkstein und Wegweiser. Zur Symbolik von zwei Vertriebenendenkmalen in Lörrach/Südbaden', *Jahrbuch für deutsche und osteuropäische Volkskunde*, 48 (2006), 1-33. Most recently, Stephan Scholz investigated the use of religious symbols in the monuments in '"Opferdunst vernebelt die Verhältnisse" – Religiöse Motive in der bundes-deutschen Gedenkorten der Flucht und Vertreibung', *Schweizerische Zeitschrift für Religions- und Kulturgeschichte*, 102 (2008), 287-313.

[8] '[D]as auffallendste an Denkmälern ist nämlich, daß man sie nicht bemerkt. Es gibt nichts auf der Welt, was so unsichtbar wäre wie Denkmäler'. Robert Musil, *Nachlass zu Lebzeiten*, Hamburg: Rowohlt, 1962, p. 59

[9] James E. Young. *The Texture of Memory: Holocaust Memorials and Meaning in Europe, Israel, and America*, New Haven: Yale UP, 1993.

[10] Peter Reichel. *Politik mit der Erinnerung: Gedächtnisorte im Streit um die nationalsozialistische Vergangenheit*, Munich: Hanser, 1995, p. 29.

[11] Heinz Ladendorf, 'Denkmäler und Mahnmale seit 1945', in: Konrad Schilling, ed., *Monumenta Judaica: 2000 Jahre Geschichte und Kultur der Juden am Rhein eine Ausstellung im Kölnischen Stadtmuseum*, Cologne: Kölnisches Stadtmuseum, 1963, pp. 656-67 (here: p. 658).

[12] The suggestion that German suffering in WWII was unmentionable and unacceptable except in the most radical circles is widely shared. Setting off the 're-emergence' of the topic on the national stage in part were the works of some leading literary and cultural figures which purportedly 'broke' the taboo once and for all. One of the most celebrated examples was Günter Grass, winner of the 1999 Nobel Prize for Literature, who in *Im Krebsgang* (Göttingen: Steidl, 2002) lamented the fact that moderate Germans of a certain generation faced a self-imposed restriction when discussing German experiences of war because of the shame over what their parents had done or overlooked during the Third Reich. Writing about the Allied aerial bombardments, W.G. Sebald (*Luftkrieg und Literatur*, Munich: Hanser, 1999) and Jörg Friedrich (Der *Brand: Deutschland im Bombenkrieg 1940-1945*, Munich: Propyläen, 2002) were said to have finally spoken out about the destruction of German cities. Even earlier, director and author Helke Sander purported the existence of a taboo regarding the rape of German women by Allied soldiers. She wrote, 'The film and the book *BeFreier und Befreite* are about the mass rapes in Germany in the last weeks of World War II and the immediate post-war period. I am often asked how I came up with this topic. I, on the other hand, ask myself why it wasn't a topic for nearly fifty years'. Helke Sander, 'Erinnern/Vergessen', in: Sander & Johr, eds., *BeFreier und Befreite: Krieg, Vergewaltigungen und Kinder* Munich: Kunstmann, 1992, pp. 9-20 (here: p. 9).

[13] Indeed, the number of attempts to refute this position involving various modes of cultural representation including literature and film continues to grow. For notable recent counters see Robert G. Moeller's *War Stories: The Search for a Usable Past in the Federal Republic of Germany*, Berkeley: Univ. of California Press, 2001 and 'Sinking Ships, the Lost *Heimat* and Broken Taboos: Günter Grass and the Politics of Memory in Contemporary Germany', *Contemporary European History* 12:2 (2003), 147-81, as well as '"Germans as Victims?" Thoughts on a Post-Cold War History of World War II's Legacies', *History and Memory* 17:1/2 (Fall 2005), 147-94. See also Eric Langenbacher, 'Changing Memory Regimes in Contemporary Germany?', *German Politics and Society*, 67 (Summer 2003), 46-68, and 'The Return of Memory – New Discussions about German Suffering in World War II', *German Politics and Society*, 21:2 (2003), 46-68. In addition, Atina Grossmann convincingly disproves Helke Sander's claim about taboos surrounding rape. See Grossmann, 'A Question of Silence: The Rape of German Women by Occupation Soldiers', *October* 72, Special Issue: Berlin 1945: War and Rape "Liberators Take Liberties" (Spring 1995), 42-63. In response to W.G. Sebald, Susanne Vees-Gulani, in *Trauma and Guilt: Literature of Wartime Bombing in Germany* (Berlin/New York: de Gruyter, 2003) contests both the lack of literary depictions of the air war and provides psychological reasons for why aerial bombardment was such a difficult topic to tackle. Lastly, nearly all the contributors to Bill Niven's valuable edited volume *Germans as Victims: Remembering the Past in Contemporary Germany* (Basingstoke and New York: Palgrave Macmillan, 2006) 'test the relative validity', as Niven puts it, of the taboo thesis (p. 21). Most succeed in disproving it.

[14] Robert G. Moeller, 'War Stories: The Search for a Usable Past in the Federal Republic of Germany', *The American Historical Review*, 101:4 (October 1996), 1008-48 (here: p. 1013).

[15] No less important, this point further illustrates the multi-leveled nature of a nation's memory culture, an argument which echoes the work of John E. Bodnar, who persuasively uncovers this inherent tension in the American context through examination of the Vietnam Veterans Memorial. John E. Bodnar, *Remaking America: Public Memory, Commemoration, and Patriotism in the Twentieth Century*, Princeton: Princeton UP, 1992.

[16] Lars Rensmann persuasively describes how Germany's right wing propagated the notion of 'collective innocence' and 'collective victimhood' as a defensive strategy to counter its own self-imposed claims of collective guilt supposedly thrust upon them by Jews, the Allies, and foreign academics. Most arresting about this notion, Rensmann argues, is '[...] the image of a collective innocence reproduced a glorifying narrative about German history and identity in political culture: a public whitewashing of the past and a presentation of ordinary Germans [...] as victims and heroes'. Rensmann, 'Collective Guilt, National Identity, and Political Processes in Contemporary Germany', in: Nyla Branscombe and Bertjan Doosje, eds., *Collective Guilt: International Perspectives*, Cambridge: Cambridge UP, 2004, pp. 169-90 (here: p. 180).

[17] For more on 'erratic boulders', see Christian Fuhrmeister, 'Findlinge als Denkmäler: Zur politischen Bedeutung erratischer Steine', *Museumsdorf Hösseringen Landwirtschaftsmuseum Lüneburger Heide Materialien zum Museumbesuch.* 32 (2000) and Fuhrmeister, 'The Advantages of Abstract Art: Monoliths and Erratic Boulders as Monuments and (Public) Sculptures', in: Charlotte Benton, ed., *Figuration/Abstraction: Strategies for Public Sculpture in Europe 1945-1968*, Aldershot and Burlington, VT: Ashgate, 2004, pp. 107-26.

[18] For an outstanding rendering of the instrumentalisation of the uprising of 17 July 1953 as the source of West German national pride and identity, see Edgar Wolfrum's *Geschichtspolitik in der Bundesrepublik Deutschland: Der Weg zur bundesrepublikanischen Erinnerung 1948-1990*, Darmstadt: Wissenschaftliche Buchgesellschaft, 1999.

[19] Since 1990, expellee memorials have been erected in a number of East and Central Europeans states. According to the registry of the 'Bund der Vertriebenen', however, only a single memorial was erected in the Eastern Bloc during the time of the Cold War, in Hungary in 1979.

[20] Wolfgang Wippermann has written extensively about the Germans and 'the East' as a construct. See Wippermann, *Der "deutsche Drang nach Osten": Ideologie und Wirklichkeit eines politischen Schlagwortes*, Darmstadt: Wissenschaftliche Buchgesellschaft, 1981 and *Die Deutschen und der Osten: Feindbild und Traumland*, Darmstadt: Primus, 2007.

[21] Scholz, 'Opferdunst vernebelt die Verhältnisse'.

[22] Katherine Verdery, *The Political Lives of Dead Bodies: Reburial and Postsocialist Change*, New York: Columbia UP, 1999, p. 33.

[23] The second part of the title I borrow from the subtitle of Marina Warner's *Monuments & Maidens: The Allegory of the Female Form*. Berkeley: Univ. of California Press, 1985, in which she demonstrates how generic female figures are often employed allegorically in public art to embody high-minded ideals such as liberty, justice, or virtue.

[24] Elizabeth Heinemann, 'The Hour of the Women: Memories of Germany's "Crisis Year" and German National Identity', *American Historical Review*, 101:2 (April 1996), 354-95 (here: p. 388).

[25] Meinhold Lurz, 'Die Verdrängung der Gewalt in den Denkmälern und Friedhöfen des 2. Weltkriegs', in: Jörg Calliess, ed., *Gewalt in der Geschichte: Beiträge zur Gewaltaufklärung im Dienste des Friedens*, Düsseldorf: Schwan, 1983, pp. 119-29 (here: p. 122). Lurz is also the author of a colossal, six-volume study of German war memorials entitled *Kriegerdenkmäler in Deutschland*. Volumes I-VI, Heidelberg: Esprint, 1984-1987. In the last volume of his investigation into how death was dealt with in the form of monuments in Germany, Lurz briefly looks at expellee monuments but his analysis remains largely superficial.

[27] Scholz, 'Opferdunst vernebelt die Verhältnisse', p. 304.

[28] Sabine Behrenbeck, 'Heldenkult oder Friedensmahnung? Kriegerdenkmäler nach beiden Weltkriegen', in: Eds. Gottfried Niedhart and Dieter Riesenberger, eds., *Lernen aus dem Krieg? Deutsche Nachkriegszeiten 1918/1945*. Munich: C.H. Beck, 1992, pp. 344-64 (here: p. 361).

[29] Robert G. Moeller, 'Germans as Victims?', p. 151.

[30] Zentral der Juden in Deutschland. Press Release: 'Zur geplanten Schaffung eines Vertriebenenzentrums in Berlin', 2 December 2005. Available online: http://www.zentralratdjuden.de/de/article/812.html?sstr=vertreibung (accessed 30 Jan 2010).

Michael Heinlein

Das Trauma der deutschen Kriegskinder zwischen nationaler und europäischer Erinnerung: Kritische Anmerkungen zum gegenwärtigen Wandel der Erinnerungskultur

At present, a new generation of eye witnesses of World War II is forming in Germany: The memories of war children, i.e. of persons who were born between 1930 and 1945 and who experienced the war in their everyday life as children, are emerging as a prominent subject of public discourse. This article shows that this phenomenon is not merely documenting a new group of memory carriers, but argues that the ongoing attention to memories of 'Kriegskinder' needs to be situated within a broader trend about tendencies of self-victimisation in Germany's political culture of the last decade.

Die Entdeckung der Kriegskinder

Je weiter sich die Vergangenheit des Zweiten Weltkriegs entfernt, so lässt sich in Anlehnung an Aleida Assmann[1] formulieren, desto näher scheint sie uns zu rücken.[2] Spätestens seit dem Gedenkjahr 2005 ist klar, dass in Deutschland von der vielfach beklagten Last der Erinnerung keine Spur mehr zu sehen ist. Erinnern wird vielmehr zu einer öffentlich ausgelebten *Lust*, die, wie Harald Welzer in der *Frankfurter Rundschau* vom 7. Mai 2005 bemerkt, bisweilen auch in eine 'Lust an der Schauseite des Nationalsozialismus' umschlägt. Die Ursache für dieses Phänomen lässt sich auf einen zunächst schleichenden, in den letzten Jahren jedoch zunehmend an Brisanz gewinnenden Umbruch innerhalb der Erinnerungslandschaft zurückführen: Die Menschen, die die Zeit des Nationalsozialismus und den Zweiten Weltkrieg selbst miterlebt haben, beginnen uns zu verlassen – und damit droht auch das auf 'Primärerfahrungen' beruhende Gedächtnis dieser Generationen verloren zu gehen.[3] Der öffentliche Erinnerungsdiskurs reagiert auf diesen bevorstehenden Gedächtnisverlust mit einem *Mehr* an Erinnerung: Kaum eine Zeitung kommt ohne individuelle Erlebnisberichte zum Kriegsende aus, und auch andere populäre Medien wie Bücher, Dokumentationen und Spielfilme bemühen sich um authentische Einblicke in das zivile Gedächtnis des Krieges.

Der Historiker Norbert Frei bringt dieses verschärfte Interesse an der deutschen Kriegsvergangenheit mit der einprägsamen Formel 'Soviel Hitler war nie' auf den Punkt.[4] Blickt man auf den gegenwärtigen Erinnerungsdiskurs, dann macht jedoch auch eine Änderung der Formel Sinn: Soviel *Kriegskindheit* war nie. Mehr als sechzig Jahre nach dem Ende des Zweiten Weltkriegs wird die sogenannte Generation der Kriegskinder von der öffentlichen Erinnerung als die letzte lebende Kriegsgeneration entdeckt, der man, so der allgemeine Tenor, zuhören müsse, 'bevor es zu spät ist'.[5] Im deutschen Kontext sind damit die Menschen gemeint, die kurz vor, während und nach dem Zweiten Weltkrieg geboren wurden – in der Regel also die Geburtsjahrgänge zwischen 1930 und 1945 – und seine Schrecken bzw. Nachwirkungen in ihrer Kindheit unmittelbar miterlebt haben. Die Erinnerungen deutscher Kriegskinder werden dabei nicht nur in Form von unzähligen Autobiografien – Schätzungen gehen davon aus, dass 'im deutschsprachigen Raum jährlich bis zu 1000 Autobiografien und autobiografische Romane in Buchform neu auf den Markt kommen'[6] – sowie populärwissenschaftlichen Büchern[7] publiziert und publikumswirksam vermarktet, sondern auch gesammelt und archiviert, in das Zentrum wissenschaftlicher Veranstaltungen gerückt und zum Gegenstand therapeutischer Diskurse gemacht.

Auch wenn sich mit dieser Konzentration auf das deutsche Leiden im und am Krieg in jüngster Zeit (noch) nicht der von manchen Autoren befürchtete 'triumph of the private over the public, of emotion over enlightenment, and of uncritical empathy over pedagogy'[8] eingestellt hat, erlangen im öffentlichen Erinnerungsdiskurs dennoch Narrative eine nicht zu unterschätzende Deutungsmacht, die im Vergleich zur institutionalisierten Erinnerungskultur in Deutschland eine andere Geschichte erzählen. Mit den neu entdeckten Kriegskindern beginnt sich in diesem Zusammenhang ein Narrativ zu etablieren, das dem Leiden der Zivilbevölkerung einen Namen gibt: Der aus dem medizinisch-psychologischen Bereich entlehnte Begriff des (kollektiven) *Traumas* wird nicht nur zur Metapher für leidvolle Kriegserfahrungen, sondern immer mehr auch zu einem zentralen Bezugspunkt des öffentlichen Erinnerns. Das Ziel dieses Beitrags besteht darin, danach zu fragen, auf welche Weise das deutsche Kriegsleid im Zusammenhang mit den Kriegskindern entlang des Traumabegriffs konstruiert und erinnert wird und welche Folgen

damit für die öffentliche Erinnerung verbunden sind. Besonderes
Gewicht wird dabei auf die Verortung der deutschen Erinnerungskultur in einem sich langsam entwickelnden europäischen Gedächtnisraum gelegt. Die Argumentation stützt sich auf unterschiedliche
Quellen und Materialien: Zum einen werden wissenschaftliche und
populärwissenschaftliche Texte und Bücher herangezogen, die sich
mit dem Trauma von Kriegskindern beschäftigen. Zum anderen speist
sich das empirische Material aus Interviews mit Experten,
insbesondere Ärzte, Psychologen und Psychotherapeuten, die sich mit
dem Thema deutsche Kriegskindheiten auseinander setzen und in dem
Verein *kriegskind.de e.V.* bzw. in der interdisziplinären Studiengruppe
weltkrieg2kindheiten organisiert sind.[9]

Das deutsche Kriegstrauma
Der Begriff des Traumas ist Ende des 20. Jahrhunderts zu 'one of the
key interpretive categories of contemporary politics and culture'[10]
geworden, mit der ganz unterschiedliche Phänomene exzessiver
Gewalt und daraus resultierende Folgen bezeichnet und gedeutet
werden. Trauma verweist damit nicht mehr ausschließlich auf
individuelle Zusammenhänge (wie es beispielsweise bei der Post-
traumatischen Belastungsstörung der Fall ist), sondern wird zu einer
Metapher für *kollektive* Erfahrungen von politischer, kultureller oder
religiöser Unterdrückung und Verfolgung, Genozid, Terrorismus und
Krieg. Auch in der gesellschaftlichen Praxis des Erinnerns nutzen
verschiedene Erinnerungsgemeinschaften zunehmend den Begriff des
Traumas, um leidvolle Erfahrungen öffentlich zu artikulieren und
Anerkennung als Opfer zu erhalten.[11] Auf welche Weise und in
welchen Zusammenhängen der Traumabegriff auf die deutschen
Kriegskinder bezogen wird und zur Erinnerung des deutschen
Kriegsleids beiträgt, lässt sich paradigmatisch an dem im Jahr 2006
erschienenen Buch *Die deutsche Krankheit – German Angst* der
Journalistin Sabine Bode ablesen. Bode vertritt dort die These, dass
die deutsche Gegenwartskultur von einer Krankheit befallen sei, die
sich in kollektivem Pessimismus, Mutlosigkeit und Zukunftsangst
äußere. Als Beispiele für diese 'German Angst' werden unter anderem
das Unvermögen der deutschen Gesellschaft, den Sozialstaat zu
reformieren, die kaum vorhandene Identifikation der deutschen
Bevölkerung mit der eigenen Nation, der mangelnde Weitblick
politisch Verantwortlicher in Zeiten des Umbruchs, die andauernde

Inszenierung neuer Bedrohungen durch die Medien und die daraus resultierende Darstellung der Zukunft 'als eine einzige Kette von katastrophenähnlichen Zuständen' angeführt.[12] Auch wenn diese Beobachtungen auf den ersten Blick nur wenig miteinander zu tun haben, verbindet sie laut Bode jedoch ihr gemeinsamer Ursprung – sie alle lassen sich als Folge der traumatischen, gesellschaftlich jedoch nicht verarbeiteten Kollektivvergangenheit des Zweiten Weltkriegs begreifen. Die kollektive Mutlosigkeit und das zögerliche politische Handeln der Deutschen stellten eine direkte Konsequenz nicht nur der kollektiven Erfahrung des Zweiten Weltkriegs, sondern auch der seit Mitte der 1960er Jahre unterdrückten Erinnerung an das eigene Leid dar: Die deutschen Opfer des Zweiten Weltkriegs wären nicht zuletzt mit dem Aufkommen der sogenannten Generation der 68er beschwiegen und vergessen worden – und die deutsche Nation leide heute mehr denn je darunter. Den Kriegskindern weist Bode dabei eine 'Schlüsselrolle' zu,[13] da es ihr unverstandenes Trauma sei, auf das sich die kollektive Lähmung der Deutschen zurückführen lasse: Die traumatisierte Generation der Kriegskinder habe nicht nur die deutsche Kultur all die Jahre 'auf eine stille, verschwiegene Art' geprägt, sondern ihre unbewussten Ängste auch 'an Nachgeborene weitergegeben'.[14] Daher überrascht es nicht, dass die Spuren dieses Traumas, die ihr Buch aufdecken und bewusst machen will, nicht nur im politischen Handeln zu finden sind, sondern auch in der unentschlossenen Haltung der Deutschen gegenüber ihrer eigenen Nation: 'German Angst und eine diffuse nationale Identität bedingen sich gegenseitig.'[15]

Hinter dieser Argumentation, die der politischen Kultur Deutschlands ein tief verborgenes Trauma zuschreibt, verbirgt sich ein Konzept, das im Rahmen der wissenschaftlichen und therapeutischen Auseinandersetzung mit den Nachkommen jüdischer Holocaust-Überlebender entwickelt wurde: das medizinisch-psychologische Konzept der *transgenerationellen Weitergabe von Trauma*. Wie eine Vielzahl von Studien zeigen, können Kinder von Holocaust-Überlebenden durch vielfältige psychische und soziale Mechanismen zum Opfer von in der Familie weitergegebenen Traumatisierungen werden.[16] Im Zuge der Entdeckung der Kriegskinder wird dieses Konzept jedoch nicht nur von der Opfer- auf die Täterseite übertragen,[17] sondern auch in ein *kulturelles Erinnerungsnarrativ* verwandelt, das das deutsche Kriegsleid auf verschiedenen Ebenen festmacht:

Mit der Annahme einer transgenerationellen Weitergabe von Trauma gelingt es nämlich *erstens*, die Familie als einen zentralen Ort der Erinnerung an das deutsche Kriegsleid einzubeziehen. Die Erinnerungsgemeinschaft der Familie wird in dieser Lesart zur Keimzelle eines Traumas, das von den Eltern, die in den Nationalsozialismus und den Zweiten Weltkrieg verstrickt waren, unbewusst an ihre Nachkommen weitergegeben wird. *Zweitens* erlaubt sie aber auch die Konstruktion einer historischen Generationenfolge, die auf der Idee des kollektiven Traumas aufbaut und über die enge Familiengeschichte hinausgeht. Folgt man der Studiengruppe *weltkrieg2kindheiten*, dann beginnt diese Abfolge nicht bei den Kriegskindern, sondern bei deren Eltern, die zwischen 1905 und 1920 geboren wurden. Diese Jahrgänge sind selbst in einem Krieg – dem Ersten Weltkrieg – aufgewachsen und könnten somit als die 'erste kriegsbetroffene Generation' in Deutschland gelten,[18] die unter dem Verlust des Vaters im Krieg und den Auswirkungen elterlicher Traumata zu leiden gehabt hätte. Die zweite kriegsbetroffene Generation stellen die Kriegskinder des Zweiten Weltkriegs dar, die sich dadurch auszeichnet, dass sie nicht nur durch eigene Erlebnisse im Krieg und in der unmittelbaren Nachkriegszeit traumatisiert wurde, sondern auch durch Elternteile, die selbst sowohl in ihrer Kindheit im Ersten Weltkrieg als auch als Erwachsene im Zweiten Weltkrieg Traumatisierungen erlitten haben. Als dritte kriegsbetroffene Generation werden die Kinder dieser Kriegskinder bezeichnet, von denen sich viele 'zurzeit in psychotherapeutischer Behandlung' befänden.[19] Der Zweite Weltkrieg wurde dabei nicht selbst erlebt, sondern wirkt sich nur noch auf indirektem Wege über die Eltern aus. Sie klagten

insbesondere über den Widerspruch zwischen äußere Sicherheit gebender Verwöhnung und psychischem Desinteresse dieser Eltern an alltäglichen Schwierigkeiten, und über innere Unerreichbarkeit bei gleichzeitig unbekannter Familienvorgeschichte. Ihre Kinder wiederum (d.h. die Enkelkinder der Kriegskinder des Zweiten Weltkriegs) verkörpern die bereits *vierte* (wiederum indirekt) *kriegsbetroffene Generation*.[20]

Diese Konstruktion einer Generationenfolge kann als Versuch gelesen werden, die Generation der Kriegskinder nicht als isolierten Generationszusammenhang, sondern im Verhältnis zu anderen Generationen zu begreifen. Auffällig ist dabei jedoch, dass die für Generationsbeziehungen typischen Spannungen zwischen den Generationen ausgeblendet und einem alle Generationen durchziehenden und letztlich alles bestimmenden Trauma untergeordnet werden. Selbst dort, wo die in dieser Lesart erste und zweite kriegsbetroffene Generation in destruktiven Familienkonflikten aufeinander trifft, sehen die Forscher unbewusste Bindungen am Werk, die auf eine Weitergabe von Trauma verweisen und die Generationen integrieren. Die Annahme eines solch simplen Mechanismus der Weitergabe legt jedoch nicht nur das Bild einer 'unilinearen Bewegung' von einem aktiven Geber zu einem passiven Empfänger nahe, das die komplexen Austauschprozesse, die zwischen den Generationen stattfinden, nicht abzubilden vermag.[21] Vielmehr hat diese 'Reduktion einer komplexen Wirklichkeit'[22] auch zur Folge, dass das Trauma der Kriegskinder als ein Trauma der Generation*en* thematisierbar wird, das seine Relevanz sowohl aus seiner *historischen Tiefe* als auch seiner *Verlängerung in die Zukunft* erhält. Historisch tief ist das kollektive Trauma der Generationen deshalb, da es seine Wurzeln im Ersten Weltkrieg hat; in die Zukunft verlängert wird es aufgrund der linearen – und wie es scheint: nur schwer zu unterbrechenden – Weitergabe. Damit werden, so die Logik, auch immer mehr Menschen von einem kollektiven Trauma infiziert und ergriffen, das sich aus der Familie heraus auf die Generationen und damit auch die deutsche Nation überträgt.[23]

Das deutsche Trauma in Europa
Die hier skizzierte, auf medizinisch-psychologischen Narrativen beruhende Konstruktion des deutschen Kriegstraumas berührt dabei auch ein Thema, das in den vergangenen Jahren sowohl in der Öffentlichkeit als auch in der Wissenschaft intensiv debattiert wurde: die Möglichkeit eines europäischen Gedächtnisses. Das Interesse am Gedächtnis Europas speist sich dabei vor allem aus der Frage, wie sich eine gemeinsame europäische Identität herstellen lässt. Kollektive Erinnerungen werden dabei immer wieder als der Kitt in Betracht gezogen, der die unterschiedlichen nationalen Erzählungen und verschiedenen historischen Erfahrungsräume, die Europa auszeichnen, zusammenhalten und verbinden könnte.[24] Auch die in der Erinnerung an deutsche Kriegskindheiten eingebettete Konstruktion des deutschen Kriegsleids nimmt immer wieder Bezug auf Europa – auch wenn sie sich dabei erst sehr zögerlich aus dem Binnenraum des nationalen Gedächtnisses herauslöst: Die einheimische Diskussion beschränkt sich im Wesentlichen auch auf die deutschen Kriegskinder. Dieser nationale Fokus schließt die Orientierung an transnationalen bzw.

europäischen Erinnerungsnarrativen jedoch nicht aus.[25] Vielmehr ist das Gegenteil der Fall: Gerade *durch* die Europäisierung der Erinnerung wird das kollektive Trauma der deutschen Kriegskinder legitimiert und als Gegenstand der öffentlichen Erinnerung verankert. Im gegenwärtigen Erinnerungsdiskurs lassen sich dabei zwei Strategien unterscheiden: Zum einen wird mit Verweis auf die *gemeinsame Vergangenheit* Europas ein Gedächtnisraum konstruiert, in dem auch die Erinnerung an das deutsche Kriegstrauma ihren legitimen Platz hat; zum anderen wird das kollektive Trauma der deutschen Kriegskinder in den Dienst einer Erinnerung gestellt, die für die *gemeinsame Zukunft* in Europa und auf der ganzen Welt Frieden sichern will.

Das 'psychische Zusammenwachsen' Europas
Zur ersten Strategie: Hier wird Europa als unvollendet angesehen, da der europäischen Identität aus medizinisch-psychologischer Sicht eine wichtige Komponente fehlt: das kollektive Erinnern an das gemeinsame Leid. Dieses Argument findet sich an exponierter Stelle im Rahmen des im April 2005 veranstalteten Frankfurter Kongresses 'Die Generation der Kriegskinder und ihre Botschaft für Europa sechzig Jahre nach Kriegsende' wieder: Ein ausgewiesenes Ziel der Tagung, an deren Planung die Studiengruppe *weltkrieg2kindheiten* beteiligt war, bestand darin, Europa 'psychisch zusammenwachsen' zu lassen, wie der sich selbst als Kriegskind begreifende Psychoanalytiker Hartmut Radebold dies in seinem Eröffnungsvortrag formulierte:

> Die internationale Kooperation würde ermöglichen, die weit reichenden Folgen des Zweiten Weltkrieges, von denen unsere Nachbarländer genauso und teilweise noch viel schlimmer betroffen waren, gemeinsam und im Vergleich zu erkunden. [...] Der zweite Teil unseres Kongresstitels drückt unsere Hoffnung aus, dass unsere Forschungen dazu beitragen, dass Europa nach der politischen, ökonomischen, sozialen Einigung auch psychisch zusammenwächst. Erst das sich selbst zugestandene Leid erlaubt, das Leid der anderen gefühlsmäßig besser zu verstehen, sich dann über das gemeinsame Leid auszutauschen sowie schließlich diese gemeinsame Erfahrung an die nächsten Generationen weiterzugeben.[26]

Folgt man Hartmut Radebold, der als Mitglied der Studiengruppe zu den Organisatoren des Frankfurter Kongresses gehörte, dann darf das kollektive Trauma der deutschen Kriegskinder nicht isoliert von den traumatischen Erfahrungen anderer Länder betrachtet werden, sondern muss in einem europäischen Rahmen verstanden und verortet

werden. Dieser Schritt zur Europäisierung von Erinnerung und
Forschung wird damit begründet, dass erst durch das gemeinsame
Erkunden der traumatischen Vergangenheit Europa vollends, und das
heißt: auch 'psychisch' geeint werden könne. Hinter dieser Forderung
steht die Erkenntnis, dass der Zweite Weltkrieg nicht nur Kinder in
Deutschland traumatisiert hat, sondern es kaum ein europäisches Land
gibt, in dem Kinder nicht vom Zweiten Weltkrieg betroffen waren. Im
Vergleich zu heute hätten sich, wie die ebenfalls der Studiengruppe
angehörige Psychologin Insa Fooken herausgearbeitet, damals jedoch
eine Vielzahl europäischer Organisationen und Forschungsprojekte
um das Schicksal dieser Kinder gesorgt:

> In den ersten fünf Nachkriegsjahren war [...] im europäischen Raum ein Grund-
> stein gelegt worden für unmittelbare Hilfsmaßnahmen aber auch für vergleichen-
> de Forschung über sowohl generalisierbare als auch spezifische kurz-, mittel- und
> langfristige Entwicklungsfolgen von Kindern mit Kriegsschädigungen.[27]

Angesichts des Kalten Krieges und des Wiederaufbaus in West-
europa geriet diese europäische Herangehensweise, in deren Rahmen
auch deutsche Kriegskindheiten thematisiert wurden, jedoch zunehmend in Vergessenheit: Auf eine Phase, in der das Thema Kriegskindheit in europäischer Perspektive erforscht und verhandelt wurde,
schloss sich, so Fooken, bedingt durch politische und gesellschaftliche
Entwicklungen der 1950er Jahre, eine Phase der nationalen Be-
grenzung des Themas an. Die Folge war, dass keine internationale
Forschung und kein internationaler Austausch mehr über die Folgen
des Krieges für die Kinder in Europa – die jüdischen Kinder stellen
eine Ausnahme dar – stattfanden. Ihr Trauma verschwand gleichsam
hinter den Grenzen national spezifischer Verarbeitungsweisen der
Vergangenheit, was laut Fooken in Deutschland dazu führte, dass das
Schicksal der Kriegskinder auch aus dem öffentlichen und wissenschaftlichen Diskurs verschwand. Blickt man vor diesem Hintergrund
auf die Zielsetzung des Frankfurter Kongresses und die von Radebold
erwähnte Forschungsarbeit, dann kann beides als ein Versuch verstanden werden, die Kriegskindheitsthematik erneut zu europäisieren:
Durch die vergleichende Forschung der Studiengruppe, die sich
insbesondere an polnischen Kriegskindheiten orientiert, und der
bewussten Öffnung des Erinnerungsdiskurses für die Erinnerungen
anderer Nationen, soll ein gemeinsamer europäischer Gedächtnisraum
geschaffen werden, in dem nicht nur alle Kinder des Zweiten Welt-

kriegs als eine gleichermaßen europäische Generation repräsentiert sind, sondern auch die Einigung Europas vollendet wird.

Diese Form der Europäisierung hat jedoch auch Folgen dafür, wie das kollektive Trauma deutscher Kriegskinder erinnert wird. So sieht Radebold den Zweiten Weltkrieg zwar als Ursache des Traumas von Kriegskindern in ganz Europa, geht in seinen Ausführungen aber nicht näher darauf ein, dass Deutschland diesen Krieg verursacht hat: Im Zweiten Weltkrieg haben, so die dahinter liegende Botschaft, alle Kinder gelitten. In dieser Logik stellt das deutsche Trauma einen legitimen Bestandteil des nationalen wie europäischen Gedächtnisses dar – auch wenn wohlwollend angemerkt wird, dass die Nachbarländer Deutschlands 'genauso und teilweise noch viel schlimmer betroffen waren' (siehe oben). Gerade *weil* Europa den normativen Hintergrund der nationalen Erinnerung abgibt, gerade *weil* die Erinnerungen anderer europäischer Länder in das eigene, nationale Erinnern einbezogen werden sollen, wird das deutsche Trauma somit zu einem objektiven Tatbestand, der nicht nur wissenschaftlich, sondern auch erinnerungskulturell anerkannt werden muss. Unterstützt wird diese Konstruktion durch die These, dass das Leid der Anderen – sprich: der Opfer der Deutschen – erst dann verstanden und ein gemeinsamer Austausch in Gang gesetzt werden könne, wenn die deutschen Opfer ebenfalls anerkannt und Teil der deutschen Erinnerungskultur werden. Damit ist nicht nur der kognitive, sondern auch der emotionale Zugang zum Trauma der deutschen Kriegskinder von entscheidender Bedeutung dafür, dass die deutsche Nation in der Lage ist, auf das Leid Anderer einzugehen. Will man Europa auch auf der psychischen Ebene zusammenwachsen lassen, dann ist es aus medizinisch-psychologischer Sicht somit nicht nur legitim, sondern auch notwendig, das kollektive Trauma der Generation der Kriegskinder und der deutschen Nation öffentlich anzuerkennen und zu verarbeiten.

Das deutsche Leid und die Zukunft Europas
Im Gegensatz zu einer in der Erinnerungspraxis selbst erst herzustellenden gemeinsamen europäischen Vergangenheit rückt im Rahmen der zweiten Strategie die gemeinsame Zukunft in den Vordergrund. Auf welche Weise dies geschieht, lässt sich an Sabine Bodes Antwort auf ihre Frage ablesen, wie heute mit den immer noch unverarbeiteten Traumatisierungen deutscher Kriegskinder umzugehen sei:

Erstens müssen wir uns darum kümmern, damit nicht länger traumatische Erfahrungen an die nachfolgenden Generationen weitergegeben werden. Zweitens müssen wir es tun, um einen neuen Opferkult zu verhindern. Und drittens sind wir dazu verpflichtet, um den Frieden in Europa zu erhalten.[28]

Die Anerkennung des kollektiven Traumas der deutschen Kriegskinder hat aus der Sicht von Bode nicht nur Folgen für die deutsche Nation selbst, indem die generationsübergreifende Weitergabe von Trauma unterbrochen und einem 'neuen Opferkult' zuvorgekommen werden kann. Vielmehr stellt das öffentliche Erinnern dieses Traumas auch einen friedenspolitischen Akt dar, zu dem Deutschland als Bestandteil Europas verpflichtet ist. Begründet wird diese Forderung folgendermaßen:

Der Ausbruch der Gewalt im Balkan in den neunziger Jahren hat gezeigt, dass das Langzeitgedächtnis für unverarbeitete kollektive Schrecken nachtragend und unberechenbar ist. 50, sogar 100 Jahre können verstrichen sein, und man glaubt, die Zeit habe alle Wunden geheilt – aber dann eskaliert irgendein Konflikt, und eine ungeheure Zerstörungskraft bricht auf. Unverarbeitete kollektive Traumata können sich in Ressentiments niederschlagen wie auch in blutigen Auseinandersetzungen. Ähnlich wie bei Blindgängern und Giftmülldeponien bestünde verantwortliches Handeln darin, die Gefahr zu entschärfen, bevor sie zum Ausbruch kommt.[29]

Folgt man dieser Argumentation, dann lassen sich die Kriege in Slowenien, Kroatien, Bosnien und dem Kosovo als eine direkte Folge gesellschaftlicher und politischer Versäumnisse begreifen: Da in der Vergangenheit erlittene kollektive Traumatisierungen in der Öffentlichkeit nicht aufgearbeitet und thematisiert worden sind, konnten sich diese unbemerkt in das gesellschaftliche 'Langzeitgedächtnis' einschreiben und – mit zum Teil erheblicher zeitlicher Verzögerung – zu der Gewaltexplosion auf dem Balkan führen. Bode prangert damit eine Politik der Verdrängung an, die sie nicht nur im Kontext des deutschen Umgangs mit der insbesondere für Kinder belastenden Vergangenheit des Zweiten Weltkriegs ausmacht, sondern auch in den südosteuropäischen Ländern des Balkans am Werk sieht. Der Zusammenhang, der hier zwischen der fahrlässig versäumten Aufarbeitung kollektiver Traumata und dem Ausbruch von Kriegen konstruiert wird, wird dabei nicht nur als universal gültig angenommen, sondern auch als Aufforderung zu verantwortlichem Handeln verstanden: Ebenso wie im vorherigen Fall wird die Anerkennung des deutschen Traumas als eine gesellschaftlich zu meisternde Aufgabe gesehen, die an dieser Stelle jedoch nicht primär zur Einigung Europas beiträgt, sondern unvermeidlich ist, wenn zukünftige Auseinandersetzungen in einem von Kriegen gezeichneten Europa vermieden werden sollen. Das europäische Gedächtnis, das Bode vor Augen schwebt, orientiert sich dabei nicht nur am Ideal einer gemeinsam gestaltbaren Zukunft, sondern auch an der ebenso populären wie normativen Zielsetzung 'Nie wieder Krieg'. Dass sich diese auf Prävention ausgerichtete Erinnerung nicht allein auf Europa beschränkt, wird mit der Arbeit des in Kiel ansässigen Vereins *kriegskind.de* sichtbar. Für Helga Spranger, Ärztin und 1. Vorsitzende des Vereins, ist auch der globale Raum von Bedeutung:

> Also, für mich persönlich ist die Geographie nicht so wichtig. Ich weiß, wo überall Kriegskinder entstanden sein könnten. Für mich ist eine andere Verbindung, eine vertikale, zeitliche Verbindung das Wichtige, und zwar von der Vergangenheit in die Gegenwart. Wenn Sie bedenken, wir haben, 2003 haben wir 40 virulente Kriege auf der Welt gehabt. [...] Das heißt, wir produzieren all over the world neue Traumatisierte. [...] Und ich, ich, da ist meine Verbindung, dass ich sage: Mensch, wir haben jetzt ja Daten, wir haben Daten von vor 50 Jahren, wir haben Kosovodaten, wir haben Irakdaten, wir haben Afghanistandaten. Das liegt ja alles vor. Und wir brauchen ja nur zu kucken, welche Schädigungen da sind. Da sind ja sehr differenzierte Arbeiten inzwischen entstanden. Dann müssten wir doch eigentlich wissen, dass wir diese Art von Kriege nicht mehr tun dürfen. Zumal jeder weiß inzwischen, dass die Schädigung der Soldaten wesentlich geringer ist, also der Anteil der geschädigten Soldaten wesentlich geringer ist als der Anteil der geschädigten Zivilbevölkerung.[30]

Wie dieses etwas längere Zitat zeigt, verfolgt auch Helga Spranger mit ihrer Arbeit einen friedenspolitischen Anspruch: Die Beschäftigung mit dem Trauma von Kriegskindern erhält ihren Sinn unter anderem auch dadurch, dass auf diesem Wege die Sinnlosigkeit von Kriegen herausgestellt und über das Leiden und die dauerhaften Schädigungen der Zivilbevölkerung aufgeklärt werden kann. Für Spranger ist dabei ein Perspektivenwechsel entscheidend, der bereits bei Sabine Bode anklingt: Sie begreift Kriege nicht in ihrer räumlichen Ordnung, sondern versucht, kriegerische Auseinandersetzungen, die zu unterschiedlichen Zeiten stattgefunden haben, in Beziehung zueinander zu setzen. Entsprechend sinnvoll ist es, die Daten, die über die Auswirkungen des Zweiten Weltkriegs für die deutsche Zivilbevölkerung vorliegen, mit aktuellen Daten über den Irak, Afghanistan und dem Kosovo zu kombinieren und zu vergleichen, um neue Erkenntnisse über Kriegsschädigungen zu gewinnen oder aber

die Wahrscheinlichkeit bestimmter psychischer Kriegschädigungen
für zukünftige Kriege abschätzen zu können (was nicht zuletzt die
medizinisch-psychologische Betreuung in den von Krieg betroffenen
Gebieten erleichtern würde).

Aus einer Perspektive, die daran interessiert ist, wie das Trauma
deutscher Kriegskinder vor dem Hintergrund europäischer bzw. trans-
nationaler Narrative konstruiert und legitimiert wird, lässt sich dies als
ein Versuch interpretieren, das Trauma der deutschen Kriegskinder in
einen universalen Opferdiskurs einzubetten, in dem Kriege unabhängig von ihren politischen, kulturellen und historischen Kontexten
als menschliche Tragödien begriffen werden:

> The universal idea of victimhood begins with the idea that modern warfare made
> everyone victims. It does not matter if you start, win, or lose the war because war
> is a human tragedy affecting all. This is why in the universalized discourse on
> victimhood, war is seen as a tragedy and an aberration in the cosmopolitan path to
> peace.[31]

Indem Kriege als Ereignisse erinnert werden, die in ihrem Kern alle
zu Opfern machen, verschwinden jedoch wichtige Differenzierungen
zwischen Siegern, Besiegten und Auslösern des Krieges. In der
Konstruktion des deutschen Kriegstraumas verstärkt sich dieser Effekt
dadurch, dass der Blick auf die traumatischen Folgen von Kriegen
gerichtet wird, von denen in letzter Konsequenz auch die Verursacher
betroffen sind – einerlei, ob es sich um die Verknüpfung des Zweiten
Weltkriegs mit europäischen (Sabine Bode) oder globalen (Helga
Spranger) Kriegen handelt oder aber um die Konstruktion einer
europäischen Opferidentität, die auf dem Argument beruht, dass in der
Vergangenheit alle vom Zweiten Weltkrieg betroffenen Länder in
ähnlicher Weise gelitten hätten. Der Begriff des Traumas ist somit aus
zwei Gründen der Schlüssel zum Verständnis des gegenwärtigen
Wandels der Erinnerungskultur: Zum einen wird Trauma durch die
Bezüge auf Europa und den globalen Raum als ein deutsches Trauma
konstruiert und legitimiert. Zum anderen ermöglicht der dem Trauma
eingeschriebene 'universal code of suffering'[32] erst eine Form der
Erinnerung, die gleichzeitig national, europäisch und global orientiert
ist. Die Erinnerung an den Holocaust spielt dabei eine wichtige Rolle:
'The Holocaust has become the iconic trauma. It is now a concept that
has been dislocated from space and time resulting in its inscription

into other acts of injustice and traumatic national memories across the globe.'[33]

Indem der Holocaust als Schlüsselereignis des 20. Jahrhunderts im Laufe der Zeit auf seinen traumatischen Kern reduziert und aus seinen raum-zeitlichen Bezügen herausgelöst wurde, gibt er die Folie ab, vor deren Hintergrund Jahrzehnte später partikulare Erinnerungen reformuliert und mit einem universalen Opfernarrativ verknüpft werden. In der Erinnerung an das deutsche Kriegsleid zeigt sich dies darin, dass die traumatischen Folgen des Zweiten Weltkriegs gleichzeitig als universal und partikular ausgewiesen werden. Wenn also Norbert Frei konstatiert, dass – vorangetrieben von den einstigen Achtundsechzigern, die sich plötzlich als Generation der Kriegskinder entdecken' – in 'den Gedächtnisraum einer globalisierten Holocaust-Erinnerung [...] die intensive Verlebendigung von Bombenkrieg, Flucht und Vertreibung'[34] drängt, dann übersieht er einen wesentlichen Punkt: Es ist gerade die Globalisierung und Universalisierung der Holocaust-Erinnerung, die dieses Hineindrängen möglich macht. Die deutsche Erinnerung an das deutsche Kriegsleid ist nicht nur eine rein nationale Angelegenheit, sondern findet auch in einem europäisierten und globalisierten Gedächtnisraum statt, den es nicht als Gegenpart, sondern als *integralen Bestandteil* einer nationalen Erinnerungskultur zu begreifen gilt.

Kritische Schlussbetrachtung

Die vorhergehenden Ausführungen haben gezeigt, dass sich im Zuge der Entdeckung der Kriegskinder als die letzten Kriegszeugen ein Erinnerungsnarrativ etabliert, dass das deutsche Kriegsleid als kollektives Trauma erinnerbar macht. Durch die Verknüpfung unterschiedlicher medizinisch-psychologischer und europäischer Diskurse und Narrative wird versucht, das Trauma der deutschen Nation zu konstruieren und zu legitimieren. Die Unterfütterung und Veränderung der deutschen Erinnerungskultur mit dem Traumabegriff ist dabei jedoch alles andere als unproblematisch. Die Übertragung von Trauma auf die kollektive Ebene birgt die Gefahr, unterschiedlichste Erfahrungen extremer Gewalt auf den gemeinsamen Nenner eines Opfernarrativs zu bringen und die mit diesen Erfahrungen verbundenen historischen, sozialen, politischen und kulturellen Kontexte auszublenden. Installiert man mit Hilfe medizinisch-psychologischer Diskurse einen Traumabegriff, dem es an 'historical and moral precision'[35] mangelt, als einen zentralen Bezugspunkt der deutschen Erinnerung an den Zweiten Weltkrieg, dann macht man damit die Grenzen zwischen Tätern und Opfern unkenntlich – die Rede vom kollektiven Trauma lässt unabhängig von der historischen Wahrheit *alle* zu Opfer werden.[36] Dass solch eine Angleichung auf fragwürdigem Boden erfolgt, liegt auf der Hand. Die Versuche, das deutsche Kriegsleid mit Hilfe des Traumabegriffs in einem europäischen Gedächtnis zu verorten, zeigen jedoch auch, dass sich die gegenwärtige, angesichts des Sterbens der letzten Zeitzeugen in einem Suchstadium befindliche Erinnerungskultur in einem Spannungsfeld bewegt, das sich mit den Begriffen der Eindeutigkeit und der Ambivalenz umreißen lässt. Micha Brumlik schreibt dazu:

> Während es im Gedenken an die ermordeten Juden Europas darum geht, den unschuldig ausgegrenzten, vertriebenen, vernutzten und unter unsäglichen Qualen ihrer Würde beraubten und schließlich ermordeten Juden, Roma, Polen und Russen sowie aller Opfer der eugenischen Politik der Nationalsozialisten zu gedenken, geht es bei der Erinnerung an das durch Krieg, Bombennächte, Flucht und Vertreibung erzeugte Leiden um die ungleich schwierigere Aufgabe, ein Leiden an und von Menschen zu artikulieren, die oft genug nicht nur Opfer von Kriegshandlungen, sondern auch deren Verursacher oder Nutznießer waren. Damit werden höchste Ansprüche an das gestellt, was die Sozialpsychologie als 'Ambivalenztoleranz' bezeichnet. Sich dabei jener liturgischen und museographischen Formen zu bedienen, die bisher im Rahmen der Gedenkkultur des Holocaust entwickelt wurden, liefe nicht nur in der historischen Sache auf eine Geschichtsklitterung hinaus – die deutschen Opfer waren nicht die Opfer eines Genozids –, sondern versagte auch vor der selbst gestellten Aufgabe, der objektiven Ambivalenz dieses Erinnerns gerecht zu werden.[37]

Die Kernfrage lautet somit: Wie kann dem im Zweiten Weltkrieg verursachten Leid der deutschen Bevölkerung gedacht werden, ohne dabei die eigene Rolle als Täter zu verdecken und das Leid der jüdischen Opfer des Holocaust zu relativieren? Auch wenn es bei der Rede vom deutschen Kriegstrauma nicht unmittelbar um das Aufrechnen von Leid oder um Opferkonkurrenzen gehen mag, stellt sich dennoch die Frage, wie viel Ambivalenz das Erinnerungsnarrativ des Traumas erlaubt. Die vorhergehenden Ausführungen legen nahe, dass mehr Eindeutigkeit produziert als Ambivalenz anerkannt wird: Traumatisierte Kriegskinder werden kaum als Täter wahrgenommen, und auch durch die Konzentration auf die traumatischen Folgen des Zweiten Weltkriegs geraten die Täter und Mitläufer des Nationalsozialismus als Täter und Mitläufer – und nicht als Opfer, die durch die Konsequenzen ihres eigenen Tuns oder Unterlassens traumatisiert wurden – leicht aus dem Blick. Aus einer kritisch-soziologischen Perspektive muss sich der medizinisch-psychologisch orientierte Erinnerungsdiskurs demnach fragen lassen, ob Trauma – so sinnvoll und hilfreich diese Diagnose bei der Therapie von Kriegskindern sein mag – ein angemessener Begriff ist, mit dem das deutsche Leid in einer zukünftigen europäischen Gedenkkultur repräsentiert und erinnert werden soll. Zu fragen wäre einerseits nach Alternativen, andererseits aber auch danach, wie das Erinnerungsnarrativ des Traumas so reflektiert, umgebaut und kontextualisiert werden kann, dass es der von Brumlik angesprochenen 'objektiven Ambivalenz' des Erinnerns gerecht wird. Es geht dabei nicht darum, Kriegskindern ihr subjektiv empfundenes Leiden abzusprechen, sondern um eine dringend notwendige öffentliche Reflexion und Diskussion der Erinnerung an das deutsche Leiden im und am Krieg, deren Argumente nicht allein einem medizinisch-psychologisch geprägten Diskurs entstammen.

Notizen

[1] Aleida Assmann, *Erinnerungsräume. Formen und Wandlungen des kulturellen Gedächtnisses*, München: C.H. Beck, 2003, S. 14.

[2] Dieser Aufsatz stellt einen gekürzten Auszug aus meiner Dissertation über die gegenwärtige Konstruktion der Erinnerung an deutsche Kriegskindheiten dar. Für die Gesamtargumentation siehe Michael Heinlein, *Die Erfindung der Erinnerung. Deutsche Kriegskindheiten im Gedächtnis der Gegenwart*, Bielefeld: transcript, 2010.

[3] Hans Günter Hockerts, 'Zugänge zur Zeitgeschichte: Primärerfahrung, Erinnerungskultur, Geschichtswissenschaft', *Aus Politik und Zeitgeschichte*, B28 (2001), 15-30.

[4] Norbert Frei, *1945 und wir. Das Dritte Reich im Bewusstsein der Deutschen*, München: C.H. Beck, 2005, S. 7.

[5] Bruni Adler, *Bevor es zu spät ist: Begegnungen mit der Kriegsgeneration*, Tübingen: Klöpfer und Meyer, 2004.

[6] Jürgen Zinnecker, 'Autobiografisches Schreiben als Erinnern einer Kriegsgeneration', in: Kulturwissenschaftliches Institut, Hg., *Jahrbuch 2005*, Bielefeld: transcript, 2006, S. 89-112 (hier: S. 109).

[7] Für viele: Sabine Bode, *Die vergessene Generation: Die Kriegskinder brechen ihr Schweigen*, Stuttgart: Klett-Cotta, 2004; Margarete Dörr, *'Der Krieg hat uns geprägt': Wie Kinder den Zweiten Weltkrieg erlebten. 2 Bände.* Frankfurt/M. und New York: Campus, 2007; Guido Knopp, *Hitlers Kinder*, München: Bertelsmann, 2000; Hilke Lorenz, *Kriegskinder: Das Schicksal einer Generation*, Berlin: List, 2005.

[8] Bill Niven, 'Introduction: German Victimhood at the Turn of the Millennium', in: Bill Niven, ed., *Germans as Victims. Remembering the Past in Contemporary Germany*, Basingstoke und New York: Palgrave Macmillan, 2006, S. 1-25 (hier: S. 20).

[9] Die Interviews wurden im November und Dezember 2005 geführt. Der Verein *kriegskind.de* wurde im Jahr 2003 in Kiel gegründet und will neben seiner öffentlichen Aufklärungsarbeit als Therapie- und Beratungsstelle für Menschen dienen, die im Alter von den Erinnerungen an ihre beschwerliche Kindheit im Zweiten Weltkrieg heimgesucht werden und unter den Folgen kriegsbedingter Traumatisierungen zu leiden haben. Die im Jahr 2002 ins Leben gerufene Studiengruppe *weltkrieg2-kindheiten* ist interdisziplinär ausgerichtet und bietet Forschern aus den Bereichen der Zeitgeschichte, Literaturwissenschaft, Psychologie, Psychoanalyse und Psychotherapie sowie Medizin die Möglichkeit zum Austausch und gemeinsamen Arbeiten. Für die Gruppe, deren Mitglieder sich zum Teil selbst zur Generation der Kriegskinder hinzudefinieren, steht dabei die wissenschaftliche und politisch-kulturelle Auseinandersetzung mit deutschen Kriegskindheiten im Vordergrund.

[10] Wulf Kansteiner, 'Genealogy of a Category Mistake: A Critical Intellectual History of the Cultural Trauma Metaphor', *Rethinking History*, 8:2 (2004), 193-221 (hier: S. 193).

[11] Vgl. Paul Antze und Michael Lambek, Hg., *Tense past: cultural essays in trauma and memory*, New York und London: Routledge, 1996.

[12] Sabine Bode, *Die deutsche Krankheit – German Angst*, Stuttgart: Klett-Cotta, 2006, S. 22f.

[13] Ebd., S. 32.

[14] Ebd., S. 32f.

[15] Ebd., S. 277.

[16] Siehe z.B. Ilany Kogan, 'Die Durchlässigkeit der Grenzen in Holocaust-Überlebenden und ihren Nachkommen', in: Hartmut Radebold, Werner Bohleber und Jürgen Zinnecker, Hg., *Transgenerationale Weitergabe kriegsbelasteter Kindheiten: Interdisziplinäre Studien zur Nachhaltigkeit historischer Erfahrungen über vier Generationen*, Weinheim und München: Juventa, 2008, S. 119-27; Miriam Rieck, 'Die Nachkommen der Holocaust-Überlebenden. Ein Literaturüberblick', in: Hans Stoffels, Hg., *Schicksale der Verfolgten. Psychische und somatische Auswirkungen*

von Terrorherrschaft, Berlin, Heidelberg, New York, London und Paris: Springer, 1991, S. 129-47.

[17] Aus medizinisch-psychologischer Sicht wurden nicht nur die Holocaustüberlebenden und die Bürger besetzter Länder schwer traumatisiert, sondern 'auch die Angehörigen der Täternation [...], die Soldaten durch den Fronteinsatz ebenso wie die Zivilbevölkerung durch Bombardierungen, Flucht und Vertreibung'. Vgl. Werner Bohleber, 'Wege und Inhalte transgenerationaler Weitergabe. Psychoanalytische Perspektiven', in: Radebold, Bohleber und Zinnecker, Hg., *Transgenerationale Weitergabe kriegsbelasteter Kindheiten*, S. 107-118 (hier: S. 107). Trauma wird somit als ein Überbegriff für die Folgen der sehr heterogenen und damit auch nicht vergleichbaren Ereignisse von extremer Gewalt verwendet, in die Täter, Opfer und auch Mitläufer des Nationalsozialismus eingebunden waren.

[18] Hartmut Radebold, Werner Bohleber und Jürgen Zinnecker, 'Einleitung. Kriegskindheiten – transgenerationale Auswirkungen', in: Radebold, Bohleber und Zinnecker, Hg., *Transgenerationale Weitergabe kriegsbelasteter Kindheiten*, S. 7-12 (hier: S. 8).

[19] Ebd.

[20] Ebd., S. 8f.; Hervorhebung im Original.

[21] Bettina Völter, 'Generationenforschung und "transgenerationale Weitergabe" aus biografietheoretischer Perspektive', in: Radebold, Bohleber und Zinnecker, Hg., *Transgenerationale Weitergabe kriegsbelasteter Kindheiten*, S. 95-106 (hier: S. 103). Völter geht demgegenüber von einem intergenerationellen 'Multilog' (ebd., S. 103) aus, in dem nicht nur Generationserfahrungen wechselseitig hergestellt werden, sondern auch das, was weitergegeben wird, in einem 'lebenslangen, komplexen Prozess biografischer Arbeit' (ebd., S. 104) verhandelt und immer wieder neu in sich aufschichtende Erfahrungen eingebettet wird.

[22] Ebd.

[23] Die hohe kulturelle Anschlussfähigkeit dieses Erinnerungsnarrativs zeigt sich darin, dass sich mittlerweile auch die Kinder und Enkel der Kriegskinder als Erinnerungskollektive erfinden, die unter den Folgen des Zweiten Weltkriegs zu leiden haben. Vgl. Sabine Bode, *Kriegsenkel: Die Erben der vergessenen Generation*, Stuttgart: Klett-Cotta, 2009; Anne-Ev Ustorf, *Wir Kinder der Kriegskinder: Die Generation im Schatten des Zweiten Weltkriegs*, Freiburg, Basel und Wien: Herder, 2008.

[24] Vgl. Klaus Eder und Willfried Spohn, Hg., *Collective Memory and European Identity: The Effects of Integration and Enlargement*, Aldershot: Ashgate, 2005; Helmut König, Julia Schmidt und Manfred Sicking, Hg., *Europas Gedächtnis. Das neue Europa zwischen nationalen Erinnerungen und gemeinsamer Identität*, Bielefeld: transcript, 2008.

[25] Für eine theoretische Ausarbeitung dieses Gedankens siehe Daniel Levy, Michael Heinlein and Lars Breuer, 'Reflexive Particularism and Cosmopolitanization: The Reconfiguration of the National in Europe', *Global Networks* (2010), im Erscheinen.

[26] Hartmut Radebold, 'Kriegskindheiten in Deutschland – damals und heute', in: Hartmut Radebold, Gereon Heuft und Insa Fooken, Hg., *Kindheiten im Zweiten Weltkrieg: Kriegserfahrungen und deren Folgen aus psychohistorischer Perspektive*, Weinheim und München: Juventa, 2006, S. 15-25 (hier: S. 25).

[27] Insa Fooken, 'Kriegskinder aus europäischer Perspektive – eine kurze Bestandsaufnahme', in: Radebold, Heuft und Fooken, Hg., *Kindheiten im Zweiten Weltkrieg*, S. 149-158 (hier: S. 150).

[28] Bode, 2004, a.a.O., S. 263.

[29] Ebd., S. 263f.

[30] Interview mit Dr. med. Helga Spranger, 1. Vorsitzende des Vereins kriegskind.de vom 2 November 2005, Z. 661-77. Das Interview wurde im Rahmen meiner Dissertation über die Konstruktion der Erinnerung an deutsche Kriegskindheiten geführt. Siehe Heinlein 2010, a.a.O.

[31] Daniel Levy und Natan Sznaider, 'Memories of Universal Victimhood: The Case of Ethnic German Expellees', *German Politics and Society*, 23:2 (2005a), 1-27 (hier: S. 3).

[32] Daniel Levy und Natan Sznaider, 'The politics of commemoration: The Holocaust, memory and trauma', in: Gerard Delanty, ed., *Handbook of Contemporary European Social Theory*, London und New York: Routledge, 2005, S. 289-97 (hier: S. 289).

[33] Ebd., S. 292.

[34] Dieses Zitat ist dem vorderen Klappentext von Frei 2005 entnommen.

[35] Kansteiner 2004, a.a.O., S. 193.

[36] Vgl. Harald Welzer, 'Die Nachhaltigkeit historischer Erfahrungen. Eine sozialpsychologische Perspektive', in: Radebold, Bohleber und Zinnecker, Hg., *Transgenerationale Weitergabe kriegsbelasteter Kindheiten*, S. 75-93.

[37] Micha Brumlik, 'Holocaust und Vertreibung: Das ambivalente Gedenken der Kriegskindergeneration', *Blätter für deutsche und internationale Politik*, 5 (2005), 549-63 (hier: S. 551f.).

Cathy S. Gelbin

Double Visions: Queer Femininity and Holocaust Film[1]

This chapter argues for a complex consideration of queer iconographies across Holocaust perpetrators, victims, bystanders, and resisters. Looking at the construction of same-sex sexual conduct in Holocaust memoirs, this article proposes sexual manifestations as an important issue in power relations between women during the Holocaust. I argue that, while invocations of queer femininity initially assisted in drawing attention to the extreme perversity of Nazism, post-1980s lesbian-feminist films draw on the lesbian to rewrite women into victims and resisters.

'she had favourites, always one of the young ones who was weak and delicate, and she [...] took care of them and fed them better, and in the evenings she had them brought to her.'

Bernhard Schlink, *The Reader*[2]

Since the opening of the concentration camps, images of queer femininity have played an important role in Holocaust representation, serving to both highlight the supreme perversity of Nazi crimes and construct agencies of innocence, i.e. sites of non-pollution by the Nazi menace. Where Schlink's portrayal of Hanna alludes to the real-life overseer Irma Grese with her exceptional beauty, meticulous cruelty and sexual proclivity for women, Max Färberböck's film *Aimée & Jaguar* draws on the figure of the lesbian to absolve the German private sphere from its implication in Nazism.

As part of a larger project on strategies of sexualisation and queer representation in visual culture on the Holocaust, this article on lesbian visuality and the Holocaust argues for a complex consideration of queer iconographies during the period of National Socialism. By stressing the gendered and sexualised dimensions of persecution and annihilation, the chapter proposes that same-sex sexual manifestations during the Holocaust go beyond the clear-cut constellations of victims, perpetrators, and bystanders. Moving from the early post-war discourse on the gendered and moral perversity of perpetrators and their accessories, the destabilisation of moral certainties in post-1960s art house cinema are explored. From there the argument will turn to a new filmic discourse which emerged in the 1980s and forms the centrepiece of this article. Coming to full fruition in Färberböck's work, this body of lesbian-feminist films draws on the modes of queer representation from the 1960s, only to perform a double normalisation: to domesticate the lesbian against the notion of perversion and make all women during the Holocaust into victims. In doing so, this chapter contributes to our still sketchy understanding of same-sex sexual manifestations during the Holocaust and theorise their discursive reconfiguration in post-1945 popular culture.

Pornographic troping of the female body, doubled in lesbian encounters, highlights the general problem of sexualised images of the Holocaust, which manifest Adorno's observations on the problematic aspects of Holocaust art. As Adorno argued in his 1962 essay 'Engagement', the artistic representation of suffering provides pleasure in the act of aesthetic appreciation, thus further denigrating the victims of the Holocaust.[3] Consequently, many critics have looked askance at the possibility of making art from the Holocaust. Sexual imagery, through its potential of evoking pleasure, ranged among the highly problematic narrative strands, and critics thus tended to condemn sexualised images of Nazism and the Holocaust as inappropriate. Alvin Rosenfeld, for example, insists that general depravation dulled sexual desires in camp inmates and that therefore 'one of the characteristics of Holocaust writings at their most authentic is that they are peculiarly and predominantly sexless'.[4]

Yet Rosenfeld's assertion is only partially true since a number of survivor memoirs, particularly by Jewish women and child survivors, feature graphic descriptions of sexuality. These include the public display of hetero- and homosexual acts, the witnessing of prostitution and experiences of sexual assault by other internees of both sexes. Such reports indicate how sexual acts under the constant threat of annihilation cannot be viewed in terms of intimacy and autonomous self-expression. This is not to say that sexual desire ceased to exist; on the contrary, some reports indicate, it continued to play an important role in the camps.[5] However, sexual expressions became so entangled in the need for physical preservation among less privileged groups of inmates that sexual acts were difficult to separate from sexual violence and broader forms of power within the camps. While this dynamic in no way characterises homosexual encounters alone, many survivor memoirs attribute to female and male homosexuals a particularly exploitative nature. One case in point is the overseer Irma Grese, whose surpassing beauty, sadistic brutality and apparent sexual interest in women[6] pervade narratives by female Auschwitz survivors.[7]

In her seminal historiography on the persecution of lesbians under Nazism, Claudia Schoppmann debunks the post-1980s lesbian-feminist parallels drawn between the Nazis' anti-lesbian persecution and the annihilation of European Jewry.[8] While many camp memoirs relate incidences of lesbianism among German women wearing the Black Triangle, a category marking 'asocials' which technically included lesbians, Schoppmann argues that it is unclear whether these inmates had engaged in same-sex relationships prior to their internment. Indeed, Schoppmann demonstrates that most traceable cases show no evidence that women were deported and assigned the Black Triangle because of lesbianism. Nonetheless, the Black Triangle has served for two diametrically opposed discourses: one found in a body of writings by former inmates asserting a special relationship between Nazism and sexual perversion on the one hand, and another in the 1980s lesbian-feminist reclamation of the Black Triangle to construct lesbians as victims. However, even where lesbian love may have occurred in the camp, its circumstance of struggle for sheer physical survival eludes conventional conceptualisations of romance and desire. Reality is inevitably more ambiguous, since same-sex sexual acts were obviously found across the constellations of agency and positionality during the Holocaust.

Whether narrative cinema can adequately approach the complexity of sexual acts under extreme duress remains to be seen. Adorno's observations on the representational problems of Holocaust art, particularly its ability to invoke pleasure, are especially salient for film, which Laura Mulvey has shown as structurally invested in manipulating pleasure through the figure of the woman.[9] Intersecting filmic constructions of femininity and the Nazi atrocities thus highlight the problems of both Holocaust and female representation, and it is no coincidence that works such as Alan J. Pakula's *Sophie's Choice* and Steven Spielberg's *Schindler's List* have come under fire for sexualising and trivialising the Holocaust through their female protagonists.[10] Cinematic portrayals of lesbianism during the Holo-caust would seem to exacerbate this conundrum, not least due to the particular pornographic coding of lesbian sex.

Although Mulvey elides a discussion of lesbian representation and spectatorial desire, her discussion is nonetheless useful for outlining some implications of lesbian visuality in narrative cinema. Where lesbian representation on screen would, on the one hand, amplify the vision of the female body as a site of pleasure, on the other hand the phallic lesbian, imbued with the ability to satisfy another woman, turns into a castrating figure thwarting male desire for her voyeuristic control of the female image.[11] Following patriarchal logic, the queer woman becomes the target of narrative punishment per se should the patriarchal and heterosexist logic of conventional narrative cinema be reinstated.

Holocaust film has traditionally used the disruptive implications of the queer figure to undermine historical narratives of power, although to very different ends. Here, the queer figure mediates the visual invocation of pleasure and displeasure to align viewer identification with particular positionalities and constellations of agency during the Holocaust. Where early socialist films, such as Wanda Jakubowska's *Ostatni Etap* and Andrzej Munk's *Pasazerka* contrast feminised political inmates with the masculinised Kapo figures and the harsher contours and dark uniforms of the female guards to catalyse sympathy and identification with the socialist cause,[12] art house cinema during the 1960s and 1970s developed a postmodern style of Holocaust signification employing sexual and particularly queer imagery as a historical and cultural agent. The strength of this latter body of films, which is exemplified by works such as Luchino Visconti's *The Damned*, Liliana Cavani's *Il portiere di notte* and Pier Paolo Pasolini's *Salò o le 120 giornate di Sodoma*, lies in their self-reflexive style to convey the deep disturbance of all moral and aesthetic values after Auschwitz.[13] These strategies, however, fail to fully account for the intersections and discordances produced by the racialised, sexualised and gendered dimensions of the Holocaust.

The self-reflexive moments of art house cinema were largely lost in a new body of Holocaust films emerging in the 1980s that were set among female protagonists. Here the key word of sisterhood would ultimately hamper a feminist consideration of women's complex positionalities during the Holocaust.[14] Although a differentiated feminist historiography is now well underway, feminist film, with the most recent example of Margarete von Trotta's *Rosenstraße*, perpetuates the model of female solidarity inspired by female resisters in socialist films.[15] In this sense, the mainstream 1980s discourse on women during the Holocaust owed much to the socialist paradigm of history from which it ostensibly tried to break by establishing 'the female question' as central rather than secondary.

The German context in particular saw heated discussions about the role of German women under Nazism. In a self-exculpatory move, German feminist debates tended to construct women as a category beyond the concepts of Holocaust perpetrators and bystanders. A typical argument asserted instead that patriarchy had culminated in Nazism and women were its victims.[16] The construct of women as Nazi victims found its culmination in the alleged Holocaust perpetrated on lesbians. The popularity of the Black Triangle as a signifier of lesbian identity only diminished in the 1990s when rainbow flags gradually replaced the Pink and Black Triangle as dominant symbols of the gay and lesbian movements. Alongside the feminist assertion that the private is political, lesbian-feminist configurations of the Holocaust can be read as an attempt to mediate the wider political issues surrounding the Holocaust, patriarchal culture and the question of race. Where earlier films had queered the Nazis as a strategy of disturbance, feminist film sought to normalise the lesbian in the private sphere, thus relativising the roles of women and bystanders more generally. Through the dual meanings of visual displeasure and pleasure present in the image of the lesbian, lesbian-feminist cinema reclaimed the queer woman to disrupt the patriarchal logic of Nazism, while offering her up for lesbian-feminist viewer identification. The interracial romance played a prominent role in absolving women from the charge of Nazi racism and constructing a universalised category of women as victims. Yet 'fascinating fascism' has not completely disappeared and is now translated into the period facets of the private sphere. Liliana Cavani's German-Italian co-production *Leidenschaften*, Alexandra von Grote's *Novembermond* and Max Färberböck's *Aimée & Jaguar* emphasise the spectacle of lesbian femininity through stylised women's fashion of the 1930s and 1940s, enhanced by the sepia-toned settings of Nazi-era Berlin and Paris.[17] Away from the atrocities, which nonetheless form the implicit or explicit tragic backdrop of the interracial love affair, the timeless elegance of period detail conjures the Nazi era itself nostalgically and rescues the private realm, and with it the generation of the mothers, from implication.

Liliana Cavani's *Leidenschaften* opened a sequence of films which located in the German private sphere a site of female resistance to Nazi ideology. At the centre of the plot stands the love affair between

the German housewife Louise von Hollendorf, who is married to a
high-ranking Nazi diplomat, and Mitsuko Matsugae, the daughter of
the Japanese ambassador in Berlin. Unlike her brother-in-law Wolf,
who hunts down homosexuals for the Nazi regime, Louise evinces
neither racist nor homophobic apprehensions about her attraction to
Mitsuko, although she is told that she is committing 'Rassenschande'
(race defilement).[18] As Chantal Nadeau has argued, the theme of
racial difference in the film undermines the notion of mimetic
sameness often associated with lesbianism, a stereotype ironically
signified in the film by the construction of both Louise and Mitsuko as
the 'idealised *Femme*'.[19] However, Nadeau fails to critically explore
the ways in which this construction implies a fetishism of race eliding
or even inverting the racialised structures of social power under
National Socialism. Such an exploration is, however, crucial to
understanding the historical references of the film. The
sadomasochistic affair between Louise and Mitsuko can be read as an
exploration of the fascist subject, which reenacts its authoritarian
conditioning in the private realm of relationships. The Japanese
woman epitomises the destructive aspects of the authoritarian regime
in her own fear 'of Buddha and Lord Husband' and her sadistic
cruelty, which seduces both Louise and her husband Heinz into a
threesome love affair and final suicide plot. The ethnic spectacle of
Mitsuko performing, as Nadeau has argued, 'with meticulous excess
the Japanese woman: kimono, geisha, low voice, porcelain skin […]'
and kamikaze impulses' cites and racialises the uses of gender drag as
fascist spectacle from Visconti to Pasolini. Epitomising fascism, the
figure of Mitsuko invokes the narrative of Hitler's seduction of
ordinary Germans and the suicidal outcome of his regime. This
reading of history places Germans at the centre of a discourse of
victimisation or at least configures them as one group of victims
alongside others. The German couple's downfall at the hands of a
beautiful stranger oddly anticipates the soon ensuing debate among
historians with Ernst Nolte's 1986 assertion of the Nazi crimes as an
'Asiatic deed'.[20] At the same time, the scheming, lying and hyper-
sexual Mitsuko invokes the psychopathology of the Jew in the
antisemitic imagination and the film thus implicitly repeats the Nazis'
configuration of Germans as victims of the racially alien Jews. The
film engages in an ambivalent discourse about the otherness of the
lesbian, which is both referred to in the racialised difference of the

seductress Mitsuko and paradoxically disavowed in the women's sadomasochistic encounter with its interchangeable subject positions. Obviously following a Reichian reading of fascism as a sexually repressive regime,[21] the film foregrounds sexual pleasure in all its facets as a sphere of resistance, and the Nazis thus arrest Louise's former literature professor for his frank novelistic depictions of sexuality.

Alexandra von Grote's *Novembermond*, which largely takes place in Paris, returns to the model of romantic love, with the lesbian relationship signifying the German-Jewish constellation. *November-mond* stresses the essential difference between male and female agency by linking the former to aggression and adventure ranging from Nazism to its opponents, and associating the latter with solidarity and resistance. When the Frenchman Laurent relates that he joined the Spanish Interbrigades because he, too, was seeking adventure, the German-Jewish refugee November retorts that the Nazis themselves made claims on the male proclivity for adventure. Nazism and the resistance as public acts of male violence and heroism contrast with the quiet help extended to the persecuted Jews by French women like the restaurant owner Chantal or Laurent's sister Férial. Female solidarity is highlighted in the lesbian encounter between Férial and November. As the Nazis march in, the narrative relegates the Jewish woman to complete passivity in her hideout beneath Férial's sofa, from where she occasionally emerges like Nosferatu raising the lid of his coffin. The camera's frequent focus on November's prominent nose in profile further highlights the antisemitic iconographies underlying the film. November's role as the masochistic and passive Jew finds its most salient expression when the hunted November, her gaze now submissive, cries uncontrollably as Férial washes her feet, an image invoking Maria Magdalene and Christian compassion.

November stands in for Grote's construction of Nazism as the culmination of patriarchy, the feminist paradigm gendering the Marxist conception of Nazism as the epitome of bourgeois society. During her arrest, November is raped by the SS and placed in a brothel, a memory revisiting her in the sound of marching boots, images of flames and the phallic symbol of a tattooing iron, as well as the hiss of singeing flesh. November's escape from the brothel in an SS jacket and red dress suggests her physical and ideological contamination by the perpetrators. The camera continues this misogynist and racist logic by showing November's buttocks in her red dress as she falls to the ground during her escape, a shot which invites the sexual violation of the Jewish woman. As in Cavani's *Il portiere di notte*, the victim's association with gender drag and Nazi spectacle in this sequence signifies the sexual exploitation of the woman in a heterosexual encounter, which is epitomised by the Holocaust. Yet where Cavani undermines the notion of the normal itself, Grote's film distinguishes the non-Jewish lesbian as symbolising romantic love and resistance from the heterosexual realm of violence. Implicit in her bearing the Nazi insignia is how the Jew November becomes a dubious figure, while Férial's plight as helper assumes the symbolism of the persecuted Jews. To deflect attention from her hidden Jewish lover, Férial prostitutes herself to the collaborator Marcel, a self-sacrifice reversing her fortunes after liberation when a French mob drags her out on the street and shaves her head. The final shot of the film contrasts the ravaged Férial and November, her hair still long, in an embrace obscuring November's tattooed camp number.

In its attempts to normalise the figure of the lesbian, Grote's film returns to essentialising concepts of gender and female sexuality. Gender drag and Nazi spectacle demarcate the contaminating sphere of Nazi masculinity, which contrasts the private realm of women. Drawing on the visual tropes of earlier sadomasochistic configurations of the Holocaust, Grote ultimately relegates the problem of Nazism to a select elite of men and the Jewish woman as a site of pollution. The theme of sadomasochism, however, no longer serves as a self-reflective strategy underlining the exploitative potential of Holocaust imagery. Instead, the sadomasochistic structure functions within the contingent setting of the plot, thereby locking the sexualised Jewish protagonist into a narrative of control. Despite the film's lesbian-feminist theme, Grote constructs female agency by resorting to the narrative sadism that Mulvey observed in the punishment of the female protagonist in conventional feature films. Epitomising the figure of the bluestocking, the lesbian must be punished, usually by dying or losing her partner. Grote's filmic treatment of the interracial lesbian romance perpetuates this structure with its Jewish lesbian and the way she heightens associations of death. In this sense, the new trope of the interracial romance during the Holocaust can be read as a variant of a highly successful genre of lesbian films, from Leontine

Sagan's *Mädchen in Uniform* to Larry and Andy Wachowski's *Bound* (1995), which link lesbianism to forms of confinement and bondage.[22]

Max Färberböck's *Aimée & Jaguar* highlights the problem of lesbian representation through the German-Jewish romance during the Holocaust.[23] Here, the Jewish woman Felice embodies the sadomasochistic split, since she exerts sexual control over her non-Jewish lover Lilly until she reveals herself to be Jewish. At this point the plot produces a sexual and emotional balance between the two protagonists which masks the Jewish woman's total dependence on her helper, even as it reverses the sadomasochistic constellation of both figures within the narrative. Whereas the Jew as a sadistic figure signals a German-Jewish sexual encounter as a form of racialised pornography, with Germans as victims of Jews,[24] transforming Felice and Lilly's sadomasochism into the romance of gendered equality allows Germans to become victims. As in *Novembermond*, the narrative focuses on the non-Jewish women in Lilly's pitiful circumstances after Felice's deportation and her life-long mourning for the absent Jewish lover. These elements contrast the film's concluding image of the vibrant Felice, which renders Lilly's desolation all the more tragic. The excessive uses of drag and costuming that Sieg has observed in the film's protagonists,[25] ranging in Felice's case from a stylised men's suit and cylinder to kimono top, further equalise the protagonists and map the fluid roles of butch and femme over the protagonists' positional differences with regard to race.

Queer imagery again supports a narrative absolving the private sphere from its implication within Nazi atrocities. Where Erica Fischer's book created a divide between Lilly Wust's story of romantic love across racial boundaries and the unforgiving voices of Felice's surviving friends, Färberböck's film constructs a generic category of women beyond the realm of Nazi ideology.[26] The only hostile female figure is that of the woman selling overpriced food stamps to Felice and her terrified friends in the toilet at the Hotel am Zoo, yet even she does so without the looming consequences of betrayal and death. Whether engaging in the rhetoric of the left, right or simply uttering nonsense, German men such as Lilly's lover Lieutenant Biermösl, her father or the neighbour Herr Krause talk about politics. Throughout the narrative, the apolitical women associated with them, be it Lilly, her mother or Krause's fiancé Frau Jäger, control the potentially catastrophic effects of such talk. The contrast between Ilse and her father epitomises the film's privileging of the feminised, private realm as a viable alternative to the male realm of politics: where Ilse shelters Felice without adhering to a particular ideology, her communist father evicts the Jewish woman when he finds out that she is a lesbian.

Färberböck's lesbian transforms historical racial divides into a queer utopia. Felice's circle of friends conveys a postmodern fluidity of ethnic categories as well as gender and sexual identities, which remain understated or even unclear in the film's supporting roles. This strategy characterises, for example, the appearance of Désirée Nick as the hairdresser Erika, whose androgynous artificiality in turn cites and plays with the longstanding rumours which posit the female Nick as a transvestite gay man. In the film, this postmodern playfulness of gender and sexuality ultimately signifies how essentialising discourses of the past have been overcome. In the opening sequence, a gender-ambiguous figure moving across the frame relates the old-new vision of Berlin as a centre of European culture. Queer subjectivities thus serve to stress the vision of Berlin as a permissive and utopian space liberated from the inhumane ideologies of the Nazi past. The city's final release from this history is symbolised by Lilly's physical removal, as she sits defiantly in a dark corner. Heterogeneous and fluid expressions of gender and sexuality, now part of the public narrative of the New Germany, stand in for the pre-war period's destroyed ethnic and cultural diversity, which the film does not refigure in its present dimension.

Conclusion

Where earlier Holocaust film tended to associate the queer woman with complicity or relegate her to the narrative margin, lesbian-feminist film has invoked the Holocaust to bring lesbian figures of victimisation and empathy into the discursive centre. Normalising female bystanders and losing sight of the perpetrators, this strategy again elided the complexity of queer histories during the Holocaust. The post-1960s linking of Nazism and sexual perversion itself did not facilitate a deeper understanding of varying positionalities and responses to Nazism across sexual and gender difference during the Holocaust. Does this mean, however, that Holocaust film should abstain altogether from depicting sexually charged images? Against such blanket prohibition, Barbie Zelizer argues that visual culture is still in the process of developing a language to approach atrocity.[27] The need to account for sexual manifestations as an essential aspect of individual human experience and because of the Nazis' anti-homosexual policies makes the problem of visual Holocaust representation all the more intricate. The interaction between gender, sexuality, and race in Holocaust film demands strategies of undermining viewer identification, especially in the German context, in order to counter the current tendency to identify with victims and absolve bystanders, while assigning the perpetrators a marginal space of otherness in the narrative.

In many ways, drawing on Cavani's *Il portiere di notte*, Tanya Ury's video artwork *Hotel Chelsea – Köln* attempts to formulate these multiple layers within the postwar German-Jewish encounter.[28] *Hotel Chelsea – Köln* assembles its images of a Jewish woman's lovemaking with a transgendered German through empty frames and jump cuts, which conjure a disjointed German-Jewish dyad, while the voiceover describes her encounters with German men and women filled with physical and verbal abuse. In one episode, a woman sexually assaults the female narrator, while insisting that she quite likely would have been a camp overseer; in another, a non-Jewish woman sharing a mirror with the voiceover speaker slips into anti-semitic speech. By juxtaposing on-screen lovemaking and off-screen narration, and through lapses of silence in the verbal and visual language, Ury shows the history of violence underlying images of a German-Jewish romance. Ury's piece acknowledges the sexual dimension of human experience, while exposing its historical and cultural conditioning, thus producing the double vision needed for a fuller appreciation of varying positional differences and political responses characterising women during the Holocaust. If female sisterhood indeed exists, it must examine the Greses who also loom in the mirror.

Notes

[1] Adapted from an article 'Double Visions: Queer Feminity and Holocaust Film from *Ostatni Etap to Aimée & Jaguar*', appearing in *Women in German Yearbook*, volume 23, published by the University of Nebraska Press. © 2007 by the Board of Regents

of the University of Nebraska. I thank the University of Nebraska Press for the kind permission to reprint this shortened version of the article.

[2] Bernhard Schlink, *The Reader*, London: Phoenix Paperback, 1997, p. 115.

[3] Theodor W. Adorno, 'Engagement', in: Petra Kiedaisch, ed., Lyrik *nach Auschwitz? Adorno und die Dichter*, Stuttgart: Reclam, 1995, pp. 53-5.

[4] Alvin H. Rosenfeld, *A Double Dying. Reflections on Holocaust Literature.* Bloomington, IN: Indiana University Press, 1988, p. 164.

[5] One of the earliest Auschwitz memoirs, Gisella Perl's 1948 *I Was a Doctor in Auschwitz* (North Stratford, NH: Ayer Company Publishers Inc., 2006) refutes in moralising tone the assertion that exhaustion and constant hunger cancelled out sexual desires: 'Sexual desire was still one of the strongest instincts and there were many who lacked the moral stamina to discipline themselves', p. 78.

[6] A number of survivor reports refer to Grese as bisexual, recounting both her sadistic attraction to female inmates and her rumored involvement with male SS. Historiographical research has established Grese's involvement with at least one male SS guard, SS *Oberscharführer* Franz Wolfgang Hatzinger, at her last post in Bergen-Belsen. See Daniel Patrick Brown, *The Beautiful Beast. The Life & Crimes of SS-Aufseherin Irma Grese*, Ventura, CA: Golden West Historical Publications, 2004, p. 64. Grese's liaison with SS doctor Josef Mengele at Auschwitz is said to have ended when Mengele heard about Grese's sexual conduct with women (ibid., 49f). Although he does not specifically mention Grese, Rudolf Höß, the former camp commander of Auschwitz, relates in his memoirs that he was repeatedly informed of sexual relations between female overseers and interned women. See Rudolf Höß, *Kommandant in Auschwitz. Autobiographische Aufzeichnungen*, Munich: dtv, 1996, p. 179.

[7] See, for example, Olga Lengyel, *Five Chimneys*, New York: Granada, 1980, p. 193; Gisella Perl, *I Was a Doctor in Auschwitz*, p. 62; Judith Dribben, *A Girl Called Judith Strick*, New York: Cowles Book Company Inc., 1970, pp. 205-7 and Isabella Leitner, *From Auschwitz to Freedom*, New York: Anchor Books, 1994, pp. 52-6.

[8] Claudia Schoppmann, *Nationalsozialistische Sexualpolitik und weibliche Homosexualität*, Pfaffenhofen: Centaurus, 1991.

[9] Laura Mulvey, 'Visual Pleasure and Narrative Cinema', in: Joanne Hollows et al., eds., *The Film Studies Reader*, London: Arnold, 2000, pp. 238-48.

[10] Alan J. Pakula, *Sophie's Choice*, USA, 1982; Steven Spielberg, *Schindler's List*, USA, 1994.

[11] I disagree here with Mandy Merck that the figure of the lesbian in art cinema has merely intensified the visual coding of the woman as a sexual object. See Mandy

Merck, '*Lianna* and the Lesbians of Art Cinema', in: *Perversions: Deviant Readings*, London: Virago Press, 1993, pp. 162-76. Following Mulvey (2000), this figure's associations with displeasure and its resistance to fetishistic scopophilia equally deserve attention and will be highlighted in my section on lesbian-feminist film.
[12] Wanda Jakubowska, *Ostatni Etap* (The Last Stage), Poland, 1948; Andrzej Munk, *Pasazerka* (Passenger), Poland, 1961.

[13] Luchino Visconti, *The Damned*, Italy, 1969; Liliana Cavani, *Il portiere di notte* (*The Night Porter*), Italy, 1974; Pier Paolo Pasolini, *Salò o le 120 giornate di Sodoma* (Salò or the 120 Days of Sodom), Italy, 1975. See also the discussion on these films in Saul Friedlander, *Reflections of Nazism. An Essay on Kitsch and Death*, New York: Harper & Row, 1984, and Susan Sontag, 'Fascinating Fascism', in: *Under the Sign of Saturn*, New York: Picador, 2002, pp. 71-105.

[14] While feminist scholarship had been, since the 1980s, broaching women's place in the constellations of victims, perpetrators and bystanders (see, among others, Claudia Koonz, *Mothers in the Fatherland*, New York: St. Martin's Press, 1986; Theresa Wobbe, *Nach Osten. Verdeckte Spuren nationalsozialistischer Verbrechen*, Frankfurt/M.: Verlag Neue Kritik, 1992; and Barbara Distel, *Frauen im Holocaust*, Gerlingen: Bleicher Verlag, 2001), discussions in the mainstream lesbian-feminist public show that these texts had not extended beyond the academic realm.

[15] Margarethe von Trotta, *Rosenstraße*, Germany, 2003.

[16] For a consideration of the broader discursive context of this feminist debate in Germany see Susannah Heschel, 'Konfigurationen des Patriarchats, des Judentums und des Nazismus im deutschen feministischen Denken', in: Charlotte Kohn-Ley and Ilse Koroton, eds., *Der feministische "Sündenfall"? Antisemitische Vorurteile in der Frauenbewegung*, Vienna: Picus Verlag, 1994, and Cathy Gelbin, 'Die jüdische Thematik im (multi)kulturellen Diskurs der Bundesrepublik', in: Cathy Gelbin et al., eds., *Aufbrüche. Kulturelle Produktionen von Migrantinnen, Schwarzen und jüdischen Frauen in Deutschland*, Königstein/Taunus: Ulrike Helmer Verlag, pp. 87-111.

[17] Liliana Cavani, *Leidenschaften (The Berlin Affair)*, Italy / FRG, 1985; Alexandra von Grote, *Novembermond* (November Moon), FRG, 1985; Max Färberböck, *Aimée & Jaguar*, Germany, 1998.

[18] This construction is, of course, historically inaccurate since the Nazis' racial persecution did not extend to their Japanese allies. In fact, the 1935 Nuremberg laws distinguished between 'Jews' and those 'of German blood' after the Japanese protested against the initial term 'non-Aryan', which potentially included them. See Uwe Dietrich Adam, *Judenpolitik im Dritten Reich*, Düsseldorf: Droste Verlag, 1972, p. 136.

[19] Chantal Nadeau, 'Girls on a Wired Screen. Cavani's Cinema and Lesbian S/M', in: Elizabeth Grosz and Elspeth Probyn, eds., *Sexy Bodies. The Strange Carnalities of Feminism*, London: Routledge, 1995, pp. 211-30 (here: p. 222).

[20] Ernst Nolte, 'Vergangenheit, die nicht vergehen will', in: *Historikerstreit. Die Dokumentation der Kontroverse um die Einzigartigkeit der nationalsozialistischen Judenvernichtung*, Munich: Piper, 1995, pp. 39-47 (here: 45).

[21] Wilhelm Reich, *The Mass Psychology of Fascism*, New York: Farrar, Strauss & Giroux, 1970.

[22] Leontine Sagan, *Mädchen in Uniform*, Germany, 1931; Larry and Andy Wachowski, *Bound*, USA, 1996.

[23] On the possible elements of prostitutions and exploitation in the real-life relationship between Felice Schragenheim and Lilly Wust, which formed the inspiration for the film, see Esther Dischereit, 'Aimee und Jaguar', *Mit Eichmann an der Börse. In jüdischen und anderen Angelegenheiten*, Berlin: Ullstein, 2001, pp. 62-72, and Katharina Sperber, 'Schmerzhafte Erinnerungen einer Überlebenden. Elenai Predski-Kramer, mit der im KZ ermordeten Felice Schragenheim befreundet, erzählte eine andere Version von Aimee und Jaguar', in: *Frankfurter Rundschau*, 7 January 2003, p. 7.

[24] In his article 'Reframing the Past: Heritage Cinema and Holocaust in the 1990s', in: *New German Critique*, 87 (Autumn 2002), Special Issue on Postwall Cinema, pp. 47-82, Lutz Koepnick has explored the influence of Veit Harlan's Nazi propaganda film *Jud Süß* (1940) on *Aimée & Jaguar*, arguing that Felice invokes Harlan's construction of the Jew as a suave sexual predator.

[25] Katrin Sieg, 'Sexual Desire and Social Transformation in Aimée & Jaguar', in: *Signs*, 28:1 (2002), 303-30.

[26] Erica Fischer, *Aimée & Jaguar. Eine Liebesgeschichte*, Berlin 1943, Cologne: Kiepenheuer & Witsch, 1996. On Färberböck's exoneration of "ordinary" Germans through the figure of Lilly, see Stuart Taberner, 'Philo-Semitism in Recent German Film: *Aimée und Jaguar, Rosenstraße* and *Das Wunder von Bern*', in: *German Life and Letters*, 58:3 (July 2005), 357-72 (here: pp. 362-64).

[27] Barbie Zelizer, 'Introduction: On Visualizing the Holocaust', in: Barbie Zelizer, ed., *Visual Culture and the Holocaust*, London: The Athlone Press, 2001, pp. 1-10 (here: p. 1).

[28] Tanya Ury, *Hotel Chelsea – Köln*, Germany, 1995. I thank Tanya Ury for making a copy of this piece available to me for this article.

Helmut Schmitz

Foundational Traumas: On a Figure of Thought in Recent German Literature on Wartime Suffering

The chapter explores the status of wartime trauma as a foundational narrative in texts by Hanns-Josef Ortheil, Dieter Forte, Jörg Friedrich and Günter Grass. Beginning with an elaboration of the Holocaust as 'negative myth of origin' of the present, the chapter argues that in the texts discussed here this understanding of the Holocaust is replaced by a concept of traumatic wartime experience.

One of the tropes of post-Holocaust thought is that of Auschwitz as a radical rupture, a break in historical continuity. Originating in Adorno's conception of Auschwitz as the culmination of enlightenment rationality, the trope of the Holocaust as break in Western civilisation is inscribed into the discourses of philosophy, social theory and Holocaust historioraphy. Both the French philosopher Jean-Francois Lyotard and the social theorist Zygmunt Bauman follow Adorno in the stipulation of Auschwitz as a liminal event that necessitates the re-thinking of the methodologies of their respective disciplines.[1] Historian Dan Diner maintains that 'der in Auschwitz verwirklichte Zivilisationsbruch [wird] zum eigentlichen universalistischen Ausgangspunkt von dem aus die weltgeschichtliche Bedeutung des Nationalsozialismus zu ermessen wäre'.[2]

The idea of a break in civilisation is inseparable from that of a radical re-orientation. Auschwitz becomes the birthplace of a present that is separated from a past prior to the Holocaust by an unbridgeable gulf. According to Adorno, the Holocaust has 'den Menschen [...] einen neuen kategorischen Imperativ aufgezwungen: ihr Denken und Handeln so einzurichten, dass Auschwitz nicht sich wiederhole [...]'.[3] If Kant's categorical imperative marks the foundation of the bourgeois age, Adorno's categorical stipulation can be regarded as the foundational claim for a post-Holocaust world. The conception of Auschwitz as the origin of a post-Holocaust universe is also central to a number of canonical works by Holocaust survivors. In *If this is a Man*, Primo Levi describes the stories of his fellow inmates at Auschwitz as 'stories of a new bible'.[4] In his 1960 Büchner Prize Speech 'Der Meridian', Paul Celan marks 20 January (1942), the date of the infamous Wannsee Conference where the Nazi 'Final Solution' was decided, as the point of origin of poetry after Auschwitz: 'Vielleicht darf man sagen, dass jedem Gedicht sein "20 Jänner" eingeschrieben bleibt. [...] Aber schreiben wir uns nicht alle von solchen Daten her?'[5] This experience of an unhealable break is also inscribed into the *magnum opus* of the early Federal Republic, Günter Grass's *Die Blechtrommel*, there pre-dated to the pogrom night of 9 November 1938. With a reference to Schiller's remark on beautiful art as a toy for mankind, Grass's protagonist Oskar Matzerath comments on the suicide of the Jewish toy shop owner Sigismund Markus as ultimate loss of innocence: 'Es war einmal ein Spielzeughänder, der hieß Markus und nahm mit sich alles Spielzeug aus dieser Welt.'[6] Avishai Margalit and Gabriel Motzkin have described the slow awakening of public consciousness to the dimensions and implications of the Holocaust in the 1950s and 1960s as the turning of Auschitz into a 'negative myth of origin' of the West, a foundational narrative of a post-Holocaust universe.[7]

A parallel can be drawn between public consciousness with respect to the Holocaust as foundational moment of the post-war West and the notion of survivor trauma in individual psychology. In 'Trauma and Reintegration', Bruno Bettelheim develops a typology for the process of coming to terms with extreme traumatisation in which survivors of the Holocaust serve as prime examples. The extreme traumatic experience of the withdrawal of the entire social and spiritual basis in the camp and the simultaneous terror, humiliation and continuous threat to one's life result in a total destruction of a person's social existence.[8] This presents survivors with the problem of 'maintaining integration in the face of the effects of past disintegration'.[9] Bettelheim connects the successful re-integration after the experience of trauma to the coming to terms with the radically accidental nature of survival. This confronts survivors with an unsolvable problem: 'As for the question "Why was I saved?", it is as unanswerable as the question "Why was I born?"'[10] Bettelheim distinguishes roughly between three types of survivor: one group that is destroyed by the traumatic experience, another that attempt to reconstruct their lives prior to the traumatic experience by means of repression and a third which makes the destroyed integration into the starting point of a new existence. One point in Bettelheim's typology seems central for the interpretation of the Holocaust as a break in civilisation: Bettelheim's parallelisation of survival and birth makes clear that the price for a successful re-integration is the re-dating of the survivor's birthday onto the moment of trauma.[11] In a wider sense, something similar happens in the cultural paradigm shift after the Holocaust.[12] Over the course of the 1990s the Holocaust increasingly becomes the point of origin for the self-description not only of Germany but of Europe and the West.[13]

The debate about German wartime suffering and victimhood that gripped the German media roughly since the turn of the millennium was marked by a conspicuous repetition of implicit and explicit comparisons with the Holocaust, in both images and rhetorical tropes.[14] To a certain extent this is a legacy of the 'settling of accounts' mentality of the 1950s and 1960s, a defence mechanism that seeks to exculpate German responsibility for the Holocaust by evoking Germany's own suffering.[15] A remnant of this mentality can still be seen in the explicit modelling of the 'Zentrum gegen Vertreibungen', initiated by the *Bund der Vertriebenen*, on the Washington Holocaust Memorial Museum.[16] However, implicit comparisons with the Holocaust or rhetorical figures implying the 'commonality of victim status linking Germans and Jews'[17] can also be observed in works that otherwise have no revisionist agenda or make direct comparisons between Jewish and German suffering. The *tertium comparationis* that makes the Holocaust comparable with German wartime experience, in this case is the concept of trauma. Particularly arguments about the intensity of traumatic experience in the bombings or on the flight from the East contain open or implicit comparisons with the death camps and frequently seek to achieve their rhetorical legitimacy via these implications.[18] Rather than being in competition with the Holocaust, these works operate with a concept of German suffering that exists *alongside* the Holocaust with a comparable status of traumatic rupture. One of the central topics in the discourse of German wartime trauma over the last decade is the notion of transgenerational traumatic heritage that animates a series of fictional and non-fictional works.[19]

Over the next pages a number of texts will be discussed that operate with the trope of a traumatic break in civilisation as origin of the present, a trope that is re-directed from the Holocaust to the traumatic horrors of the war. The issue of traumatic rupture is central to Dieter Forte's *Der Junge mit den blutigen Schuhen*[20] and Jörg

Friedrich's *Brandstätten*,[21] as well as Günter Grass's *Im Krebsgang*.[22]
However, as Hanns-Josef Ortheil's novels *Hecke* (1983)[23] and
Abschied von den Kriegsteilnehmern (1992)[24] were the first narratives
in which this re-direction of focus from the Holocaust to traumatic
German memories of the war were central to the issue of
Vergangenheitsbewältigung, the chapter will begin with a discussion
of Ortheil. Following this, the foundational narratives of Grass, Forte
and Friedrich will be problematised with respect to questions of
individual and collective coming to terms as well as the claimed taboo
on memory and empathy. One of the central questions will be to what
extent the memory of German suffering is facilitated by a metonymic
shift of the trope of trauma from the Holocaust to the German
collective and to what extent these two contradictory forms of
memory are set in context with each other. The chapter will focus on a
central motif that all of these texts have in common.

Hanns-Josef Ortheil and Transgenerational Trauma as Origin of the Present

It was Hanns-Josef Ortheil, whose sensitive narrative exploration of
the long-term effect of parental wartime trauma in his novels *Hecke*
and *Abschied von den Kriegsteilnehmern* anticipated the paradigm
shift in German memory culture towards German suffering and thus
posed anew the question of German memory of the war. In Ortheil's
Hecke, the narrator carries out a paradigmatic re-orientation of
perspective with respect to the time of National Socialism:

> Ich begriff diese Zeit nur von ihrem Ende her. Ich hatte die Bilder der verwüsteten
> Städte, der Toten, der Vergasten gesehen. Ich selbst empfand mich als einen
> Fremden, der in die Städte eines Landes versetzt worden war, in dem Barbaren
> gehaust, gemordet, vernichtet hatten. (H, 37)

This understanding of Nazism from the perspective of its decline and
aftermath prevents any empathetic engagement with the time and thus
any insight into the long-term effects of the Nazi period:

> Ich selbst sollte ein Sohn, ein Enkel dieses mordenden Geschlechts sein? [...]
> Nein, ich wollte mit dieser Zeit nichts zu tun haben. Der Krieg – das war die Zeit
> vor meiner Geburt, eine andere Zeit, die zu dem, was ich erlebte in keinem
> Verhältnis und in keiner Beziehung stand. (H, 37)

The novel itself is the deconstruction of this perspective through the narrator's slow and painful re-telling of his mother's and his entire family's deep traumatisation in the war. Ortheil's re-orientation of perspective from a judgemental post-war perspective to an empathetic form of 'witnessing' is analogous to Martin Broszat's demands for a 'historisation' of National Socialism which would detach the period from a moralising attitude towards it.[25] This re-orientation that moves the Third Reich into a historicist context in order to facilitate an emotional closeness is the pre-condition for the approach of Ortheil's narrator as well as Broszat's history of the everyday in the Third Reich.[26]

Both *Hecke* and *Abschied von den Kriegsteilnehmern* describe the parental experiences in the war and the resulting traumatisation as origin of the mental situation of the post-war generation(s). In both texts the narrator's investigation of family history leads him back to his post-war childhood which is lived in the shadow of the destroyed desires of his traumatised parents.[27] The conclusion of Ortheil's novels is that the parents unconsciously transmit their traumatic damage onto their child. Both novels are the attempt to read the traumatic parental war experiences, the bombings for the mother and the Eastern front for the father, as the origin and mental horizon of the post-war generation(s) and to historicise them as such. Ortheil's novels narrativise the issue of transgenerational trauma two decades before it becomes a cultural explanatory model.

Simultaneously, *Abschied von den Kriegsteilnehmern* explicitly connects the parental trauma with the son's own 'Traumatisierung durch die Judenvernichtung als Geschichtserbe'.[28] Ortheil historicises the intergenerational conflict of the student movement in juxtaposing the father who insists on his status as victim of the war and his adolescent son for whom the Holocaust is more central than the father's experiences. This deadlock and the son's hate of his father's 'Zeitzeugenschaft' (AK, 107) is only released after the father's death and the son's work of mourning which enables him to accept the self-description of his father as victim.

Ortheil's narrators thus carry out a belated form of empathy with the suffering of the parents. Central to both texts is the retrospective re-dating of the narrator's own origin onto the parental trauma, something that attains symbolic collective weight in both novels. The belated acceptance of the parents' claim to victim status is a condition for the successful work of mourning, resulting in an acceptance of historical facticity. In his 1989 essay 'Weiterschreiben' Ortheil explains what has prevented him from accepting the parents' status as victim with recourse to the double meaning of the term as both victim and sacrifice:

> Der Faschismus, der meine Familie entstellt hatte, war [...] an dieser Familie nicht ursächlich schuldig geworden. [...] Eben an diesem Gedanken scheiterte die Vorstellung von Opfern, denn ich verstand das Wort Opfer in einem positiven Sinn, als Hingabe, als Weggabe des Eigenen zur Aufhebung des Schuld-zusammenhangs. Diesen Zusammenhang aber, der Trauer gerechtfertigt hätte, konnte ich in den ununterbrochenen Trauergesten um mich herum nicht erkennen [...].[29]

At the end of *Abschied von den Kriegsteilnehmern* both meanings of the German term *Opfer* are merged into one. The narrator symbolically carries his dead family members Eastwards 'um sie hier, in der fernen Weite, zu begraben für immer...' (AK, 412). The acceptance of the family's status as victim is implicitly contained in the 'Weggabe des Eigenen zur Aufhebung des Schuldzusammen-hangs'. This acceptance implies a shift from the Holocaust to German war experience as the determining origin of the present. *Abschied von den Kriegsteilnehmern* refers explicitly to Adorno's understanding of Auschwitz as historical rupture:

> [...] in schlimmen Augenblicken war es mir sogar so vorgekommen, als sei die menschliche Geschichte mit diesen Verfolgungen an ein Ende gelangt. So hatte ich einen Neubeginn des Lebens nach diesen Verfolgungen und Morden oft für etwas nicht nur Verlogenes, sondern für etwas Unmögliches gehalten, [...]. (AK, 107)[30]

The shift from the Holocaust to parental war trauma as origin of the present makes possible the integration of that which previously could not be integrated. The son's acknowledgement of the parents' trauma as origin of himself is explicitly connected to the history of the nation in the connection of the son's coming to terms with the father's death with the fall of the wall in 1989. The integration of the parents' trauma into a collective history opens up the possibility of genealogy and tradition in the son's explicit re-connection to his father: 'Ich habe die Arme meines Vaters, [...]. Ich habe die Hände und Finger meines Vaters, [...] Ich habe das Lachen meines Vaters, [...].' (AK, 294)[31]

Transgenerational Trauma as Origin of the Present: Grass's *Im Krebsgang*

Grass's novella *Im Krebsgang* is also animated by a constellation of inner-familial trauma similar to that in Ortheil's novels. The focus will be exclusively on the issue of transgenerational trauma as it pertains to the argument.[32] *Im Krebsgang* schematically combines three generations and three forms of German memory. Tulla Pokriefke, heavily traumatised survivor of the sinking of the *Wilhelm Gustloff*, brings up her son Paul, born during the sinking of the ship, to write down her experiences: 'Ech leb nur noch dafier, daß main Sohn aines Tages mecht Zeugnis ablegen.' (K, 19) Tulla bears all signs of severe trauma from the stereotypical and repetitive way she talks about her experience to the employment of her only child to alleviate her trauma, a motif that is also central to Ortheil's novels and that frequently recurs in narratives of transgenerational trauma. Like Ortheil's narrators, Paul grows up with a non-negotiable task to compensate the parental trauma.

Helm Stierlin has described this 'recruitment' of children by their traumatised parents as 'delegation: 'many children were expected to fulfil their mothers' hopes and expectations [...].' [33] The parental task can rarely be modified or negotiated by the children and parents refuse to acknowledge the childrens' achievements. 'But this causes a vicious circle: The children who feel themselves exploited, betrayed and unrecognised "fail" sooner or later in one way or another. [...] Finally they turn in despair and fury against their parents [...]'.[34]

Tulla and Paul are supposed to represent two aspects of the post-war German discourse on suffering. While the 'experiential generation' is exclusively focused on its trauma, the children refuse all engagement with it and rebel against the parents' version of history. Paul, plagued by latent self-hate as a result of his birth on the *Gustloff*, is characterised by the extensively documented latent melancholia of the 'second generation.'[35] In contrast to Ortheil's successful performance of *Vergangenheitsbewältigung*, *Im Krebsgang* is characterised by the return of the repressed, as the latent history of repression becomes manifest in the third generation. Having been stuffed with 'Flüchtlingsgeschichten, Greuelgeschichten, Vergewaltigungsgeschichten' by his grandmother (K, 100), Paul's son Konrad develops an unhealthy obsession with the *Gustloff* which he lives out on his internet site *blutzeuge.de*. Konrad's obsession with the apparently repressed history of German suffering leads to the shooting of his apparently Jewish chat-room partner 'David', in parallel to the historical murder of Wilhelm Gustloff by the Jewish David Frankfurter. Konrad's murder of 'David' is a kind of reverse acting out of the repressed historical substance; its function is to underscore the narrative's central premise of the return of the repressed, in analogy to Grass's *Blechtrommel*: 'Nichts ist vorbei, alles kommt wieder.'[36] The difference is that here, in *Im Krebsgang*, the repressed is the story of German suffering, in particular the flight from the East, symbolised in the ship *Wilhelm Gustloff*.

The trauma, obsession for the first generation and repressed by the second, returns in the third in the form of violence. On a psycho-analytical level, Grass's novella corresponds to Tilmann Moser's thesis 'die Schicht der neuen demokratischen Erziehung schob sich wie frische, geologische Sedimente über das Unbewältigte, erlaubte nicht Transformierung, individuelle Aneignung, Betrachtung, Integration.' The consequence is that

> tief unterirdisch, und weit außerhalb der bewußtseinsbildenden Sprache seelische Gewaltsamkeit und unverarbeitete Traumata weitergegeben werden: als Lebensstile, unerledigte Aufgaben, Geheimnisse, Mythen, Aufträge, Verleugnungen.[37]

All three generations in the novella fit into this pattern. Paul's own repression is not only visible in the admission that despite his demonstrative left-liberal convictions he is 'insgeheim rechtsgewickelt' (K, 75). Above all, his entire existence is determined by the withdrawal of empathy from the conditions of his own existence, in the vehement rejection of his orw birth: 'All die Jahre lang […] gelang es mir, die Umstände meiner Geburt auszusparen.' (K, 32)

It is only in the writing down of the *Gustloff* story, complete with the history of the entire ship that Paul can acknowledge his birth in the moment of traumatic suffering. Similarly to Ortheil's *Hecke* where the son re-connects himself to family history through the empathetic re-telling of his mother's story, Paul is able to connect his own existence with the death of the drowning Gustloff passengers in the act of storytelling: '[…] worauf sich der Schrei der Zigtausend mit meinem ersten Schrei mischte.' (K, 177) Since Paul symbolically represents the post-war generation, this has to be read as his acknowledgement of the birth of post-war Germany from wartime suffering.[38] Like Ortheil's novels before, *Im Krebsgang* is also engaged in a re-dating of the origins of the present to the traumatic experience of the war. However, Grass does this without presenting the conflicts of memory discourse as resolvable or resolved. The final words of the novella are: 'Das hört nicht auf. Das hört nie auf.' (K, 216)

The 'Luftkrieg' as origin of the present: Dieter Forte and Jörg Friedrich

Both Dieter Forte's *Der Junge mit den blutigen Schuhen* and Jörg Friedrich's book of photographs *Brandstätten. Der Anblick des Bombenkrieges* centrally operate with an image of the 'Luftkrieg' as traumatic origin of the present.

Forte's autobiographical novel on his experiences during the bombing of Düsseldorf is the third part of the tetralogy *Das Haus auf meinen Schultern*. The novel is characterised by a double perspective of innocence: on the one hand the perspective of the eight-year-old protagonist, on the other that of the ethnically diverse personnel of the whole novel, inhabitants of the heavily idealised working-class quarter Oberbilk, for which National Socialism arrives in form of an invasion. Forte's novel is an attempt to inscribe the period of Nazism and the bombings into cultural memory, which he sees threatened by forgetting. Forte ascribes to literature a similar power as W.G. Sebald who in *Luftkrieg und Literatur* had claimed that German literature had failed to inscribe the experience of the air war into collective memory:[39]

> Wir bilden uns ein, alles aufschreiben, alles festhalten zu können, damit wir es weitergeben können. Ich glaube, das ist ein Irrtum. Wenn es nicht durch verdichtendes Erzählen von Generation zu Generation weitergegeben wird, sich tief einprägend, so daß es zum unvergessenen Schreckensbild im Erzählen wird, ist es für die Nachkommen verloren.[40]

Forte's struggle for 'verdichtendes Erzählen' has doubtful consequences. The narrative increasingly amalgamates the autobiographical perspective of the eight-year old boy with a language reminiscent of legend and chronicle which is characterised by an unmistakeable function to be memory-constitutive:

> Menschen verschwanden. Die Zurückgebliebenen hielten den Atem an, verstummten, schwiegen, flüchteten sich in Ahnungslosigkeit, beherrscht von einer unbestimmten, unbenennbaren Angst. Man hörte Grauenhaftes und vergaß es vor Entsetzen, obwohl es einem eindrücklich geschildert worden war. Man blickte gebannt auf irritierende Vorgänge und hatte sie doch nicht gesehen, konnte sich

nicht an sie erinnern. Die Menschen versteinerten wie Vögel, auf die ein
Raubvogel herabstößt, sich bewegungslos duckend, stellten sich tot, starrten mit
aufgerissenen Augen auf das Opfer neben sich, sahen zu, wie der Raubvogel tötet
und den getöteten Körper zerreißt. Menschen verschwanden. (JbS, 75)

Forte's narrative *Gestus* moves the historical events into an almost
mythical distance which levels all action and responsibility. The
distancing tone is part of Forte's narrative programme to preserve the
historical experience in a lasting form: 'Ich habe versucht, aus einer
distanzierten Nähe zu beschreiben, fast ikonenhafte Bilder zu finden,
Sprachbilder, die meines Erachtens gültiger sind und dauerhafter.'[41]
Forte's narrative programme conflates the mode of autobiographical
writing with the desire to write collective memory. The result is that
the novel levels the differences between victims and perpetrators and
that the Germans appear, as Stefan Braese has observed, as double
victims: those of Hitler and of the Allies:[42]

und es gab ja auch kaum noch Menschen. […] Das ganze Volk war durchnum-
meriert und durchorganisiert, vom Führer bis zur deutschen Hausfrau […] Die
Menschen verloren ihr Gedächtnis und warteten ergeben auf den Befehl des
Führers, standen bereit in ihren Uniformen, und auch die, die verschwunden waren, trugen nun die verschiedensten Uniformen mit den verschiedensten Zeichen,
so daß der Uniformierte, der sie bewachte, an der Uniform und an dem Zeichen
und an der eintätowierten Nummer den Gefangenen erkannte […]. (JbS, 87)

This parallelisation of victims and perpetrators has been heavily
criticised.[43] Forte's narrative style is characterised by what Martin
Broszat has referred to with respect to Jewish memory of the Holocaust as 'mythical' memory or 'coarsening of history'. Broszat explicitly connects this form of memory with the status as victim, a status
which in Broszat's view is legitimised by the narrative form itself.[44]
    In an interview with Volker Hage, Forte maintains that the German
repression of memory does not originate in the post-war reconstruction but in the war itself: 'Man mußte ja schon während des Krieges
darüber schweigen. Schon im Krieg entstand dieses Schweigen, die
Verdrängung des Geschehenen.'[45] The hectic reconstruction of
German cities after the war thus represents a second forgetting for
Forte. In *Der Junge mit den blutigen Schuhen*, the destructions by the
Allied bombings are described as the origin of a new network of
memory, 'ein Geflecht von Gedenkstätten, Tabuzonen, Vergangen-
heitsgeschichten, das sich über die Straßennamen legte, eine neue
Orientierungsebene bildete' (JbS, 195). This new memory space is

eradicated in the reconstruction. Here, Forte is in agreement with Sebald's assessment in *Luftkrieg und Literatur* that the post-war reconstruction marks a radical overwriting of the traumatic experience of the bombings with a narrative of triumphant 'Wiederaufbau'.[46] Forte's novel is thus an attempt to re-constitute the repressed memory of war and post-war reconstruction and to install it in cultural memory. In contrast to Sebald, however, who stresses a causal nexus between the aerial bombing and the silence about the Holocaust, Forte disentangles both aspects.

Forte's *Der Junge mit den blutigen Schuhen* is essentially a foundational narrative in the sense of Jan Assmann's definition of cultural memory as mythical foundational narrative of the collective:

> Man könnte auch sagen, daß im kulturellen Gedächtnis faktische Geschichte in erinnerte und damit in Mythos transformiert wird. Mythos ist eine fundierende Geschichte, eine Geschichte, die erzählt wird, um eine Gegenwart vom Ursprung her zu erzählen.[47]

Forte's description of the result of the 'Luftkrieg' as 'totaler Zivilisationsbruch' raises the bombings to the same foundational level as the interpretation of the Holocaust as radical historical rupture.[48] *Der Junge mit den blutigen Schuhen* can thus be read as an attempt to interpret the 'Luftkrieg' as the original German trauma in the explicit extrapolation from individual to collective traumatisation. Forte explicitly stresses that the writing of the novel was accompanied by nervous breakdowns, triggered by the encounter with the repressed trauma, repeating Wolf Biermann's assessment of his experience during the Hamburg firestorm: 'Meine Lebensuhr ist damals auch stehengeblieben, und alles, was danach kam war nicht sehr wichtig und nicht sehr wesentlich. [...] Also ich empfinde mein Leben als zerstört.'[49] The historical fatalism that characterises Forte's *Der Junge mit den blutigen Schuhen*, and the accidental nature of survival corresponds to Bruno Bettelheim's observation regarding the survivors of extreme trauma, that re-integration happens on the ruins of destruction and depends on an acceptance of the facticity of this destruction.[50]

Friedrich's book of photographs, *Brandstätten*, likewise operates with a framing narrative of the continuity of trauma, the origin of which is the 'Luftkrieg'. The book opens with a section titled 'Früher' that features photographs of the 'whole' German cities of Pforzheim,

Hamburg, Halberstadt, Würzburg and others with their scenic old centres. This is contrasted with a section titled 'Heute' at the end of the book which juxtaposes old city centres and old buildings with their contemporary counterparts. The juxtaposition of medieval, renaissance or baroque splendor with the post-modern non-spaces that make up contemporary city centres wilfully obscures the history of city planning between 1950 and 1990 and stages the air war as the sole origin of the contemporary lack of spatial identity. The rhetorical function of Friedrich's positioning of the photographs is, again, to eschew the triumphant narrative of 'Wiederaufbau' that according to Sebald is characteristic for Germany's suppression of any engagement with the trauma of the 'Luftkrieg'.[51] Rather than being triumphant documents of post-war reconstruction, Friedrich's photographs of contemporary German cities, set against their pre-war 'wholeness', testify to the continuity of trauma. The book's afterword spells out the visual lesson of the photographs, that the ugly inner cities of contemporary Germany are the symbolic expression of the state of the collective German spirit become concrete: 'Das Narbengewebe, das die Brache des Luftkriegs bedeckt, ist auch der Überzug der deutschen Seelenlandschaft' (BS, 225).

The traumatic origin of contemporary dislocated city space is to be found in the gruesome photographs of charred and disfigured bodies of the section 'Bergung' at the heart of Friedrich's book. In contrast to the visual memory of the Holocaust which is dominated by bodies, either skeletal dead bodies in mass graves or emasculated survivors, the visual memory of the bombings is determined by pictures of destroyed cities. There are probably a number of reasons for this, not least the tight control that the Nazis exerted over who was allowed to photograph bombing sites.[52] The purpose of the shocking photographs in the section 'Bergung' are an attempt to re-cathect the visual memory of the air war with photographs of dead and burned corpses, to reinsert the corpses, so to speak, into collective memory.[53] Friedrich's unmediated focus on images of disfigured and charred bodies in *Brandstätten* is, therefore, an attempt to affectively cathect these images with the traumatic intensity that produces a sense of rupture in the present.[54] Their ultimate reference is, as Heinz-Peter Preußer has argued, Holocaust imagery.[55] The purpose of Friedrich's photos is to produce a reaction analogous to concentration camp photographs, in order for the viewer to 'bear witness to the air war', as Brad Prager asserts.[56] The horrific photographs of the human victims of the bombings are thus an essential prerequisite for *Brandstätten*'s argument of a continuing trauma in the German people. Prager argues that Friedrich wishes to shift the terms from 'divine violence to mythic or Greek violence', i.e., from the post-war idea that the bombings in their apocalyptic dimension were akin to the divine destruction of Gomorrah as a form of punishment for sin, to a war of mythical and historical dimension which 'calls for witnesses, in both text and image.'[57] This is correct inasmuch as mythical narratives are by their very nature foundational.[58] The story Friedrich tells in *Der Brand* and *Brandstätten* is that of a foundational trauma, a rupture of German history that has not yet healed but one that can be captured in narration: 'Die erinnerten Szenen überliefern eine Folter, die nicht auf immer unaussprechlich sein wird.'[59]

Conclusion – From Individual to Collective Trauma

Saul Friedländer remarked in the context of the notorious Walser-Bubis-debate, which for the first time exposed the gap between public memory of Nazi crimes and private memory of suffering, that, unlike other nations, Germany as a nation is characterised by a collective memory of the victims of its politics, rather than by a memory of its victims.[60] The origin of this public memory discourse is the realisation of the crimes committed under National Socialism. The centrality of the Holocaust for a public memory of National Socialism rests on an understanding of Auschwitz as the essence and centre of Nazism. This results in a privileging of the victims' perspective as the true experience of the Third Reich. Dan Diner insists:

> Der Zugang, der sich an der Opferperspektive orientiert, stellt keineswegs eine bloß subjektive oder komplementierende Sichtweise dar. Vielmehr ist sie die umfassendere, der Totalität der Ereignisse angemessenere Perspektive und dies, weil sie vom *absoluten Extremfall* ausgeht.[61]

The texts discussed here construe another 'extreme case' which implicitly is in analogy to the Holocaust, if only with respect to the destructive force of trauma on the level of individual experience.[62] This is not to belittle the real historical traumatisation of the experiential generation or of Dieter Forte himself or to stipulate a one-dimensional focus on Nazi crimes as the only valid memory of National Socialism. My argument is that Ortheil's, Forte's, Friedrich's and Grass's texts are characterised by an explicit extrapolation from individual trauma onto a collective level. All texts discussed here operate with the implicit or explicit transposition of individual trauma onto a symbolic level that denotes the collective as a whole. This extrapolation lifts the dimension of individual trauma in all its excess onto the level of an explanatory model for the state of the nation. It is this symbolic level of their texts that creates the implicit analogy with the Holocaust as origin of the collective present. While Forte and Friedrich focus on the war experience as traumatic origin, Ortheil's and Grass's transgenerational narratives symbolically draw out the continuity of trauma across the generations.

Ortheil, Grass, Forte and Friedrich are engaged in the project of articulating traumatic war experience as foundational moment in cultural memory. Their texts are foundational narratves in Jan Assmann's sense of a transformation of history into mythical memory: 'Für das kulturelle Gedächtnis zählt nicht faktische, sondern nur erinnerte Geschichte. [...] Durch Erinnerung wird Geschichte zum Mythos.'[63] A brief reference to Hans-Ulrich Treichel's *Der Verlorene*, another narrative of transgenerational traumatisation, will illustrate this point further. The nameless narrator of *Der Verlorene* is another distant relative of Ortheil's protagonists. He grows up neglected by his parents who are traumatised by their flight from the East during which the mother is raped by the Russians and loses her first-born son Arnold. Treichel's novel is characterised by the same constellation that animates Ortheil's novels and Grass's *Im Krebsgang*, the transmission of parental trauma onto the next generation by educational practices and the emotional employment of the children in their parents' inability to deal with their trauma. Similarly to Ortheil's narrators, who grow up knowing that they have to make good for the lost lives of their dead brothers, Treichel's narrator grows up in the knowledge of being an insufficient substitute for Arnold: 'Denn erst jetzt begann ich zu begreifen, dass Arnold, der untote Bruder, die Hauptrolle in der Familie spielte und mir eine Nebenrolle zugewiesen hatte.'[64] In contrast to Grass and Ortheil, however, Treichel's novel resists the collectivisation of individual fate, but instead subtly contrasts the parents' traumatisation with the persistent and uncanny presence of remnants of the unacknowledged Nazi past in the 1950s.[65] Treichel thus presents a sensitive narrative about the issue of the transmission of trauma, suffering and pain across the generations without turning it into a foundational narrative.[66] It is thus by no means a structural characteristic of narratives of transgenerational trauma that they elevate the traumatic family situation to the level of a cultural signifier.[67]

All texts discussed here are engaged in a process of 'narrating the nation', of producing self-conscious contributions to collective memory. Operating with a concept of trauma as foundational experience for the present state of the collective, they are engaged in the transposition of concrete traumatic experience onto a symbolic level, thus elevating the trauma to a cultural explanatory model. While the concept of Auschwitz as historic rupture ultimately questions and undermines the crealtion of collective meaning, and certainly questions the constitution of homogeneous memory collectives, the idea of a collective German trauma does precisely the opposite, it founds a memory collective on the experience of historic rupture.

Notes

[1] For Lyotard, Auschwitz divides the concept of universal humanity into the divided collectives of victims and perpetrators. The impermeability of these collectives in Nazi racial thought, simultaneous with the total heteronomy of the victim collective results in a categorical separation of these collectives. See Jeff Bennington, *Lyotard. Writing the Event*, Manchester: Manchester University Press, 1988, pp. 150-2. For Zygmunt Bauman, the Holocaust confronts western civilisation with its self-deception regarding its own barbaric potential, something which necessitates the revision of sociological methodologies: 'The Holocaust says more about the condition of Sociology than Sociology in its current state can say about the Holocaust'. Bauman, *Modernity and the Holocaust*, Cambridge: Polity Press, 1989, p. 3.

[2] Dan Diner, 'Zwischen Aporie und Apologie. Über Grenzen der Historisierbarkeit des Nationalsozialismus', in: Diner, ed., *Ist der Nationalsozialismus Geschichte?*, Frankfurt/M.: Fischer, 1987, pp. 62-73 (here: pp. 71-2).

[3] Theodor W. Adorno, *Negative Dialektik*, Gesammelte Schriften, vol. 6, Frankfurt/M.: Suhrkamp, 1997, p. 358.

[4] Primo Levi, *If this is a Man*, London: Abacus, 1987, p. 72.

[5] Paul Celan, 'Der Meridian', in: *Büchner-Preis-Reden 1951-1971*, Stuttgart: Reclam, 1972, pp. 88-102 (here: p. 96).

[6] Günter Grass, *Die Blechtrommel*, Werkausgabe in 10 Bänden, vol. II, ed. Volker Neuhaus, Darmstadt: Luchterhand, 1987, p. 247. Cf.: Schiller: 'der Mensch soll mit

der Schönheit nur *spielen* und er soll *nur mit der Schönheit spielen*. Denn, um es endlich auf einmal herauszusagen, der Mensch spielt nur, wo er in voller Bedeutung des Worts Mensch ist, *und er ist nur da ganz Mensch, wo er spielt.*' Friedrich Schiller, *Über die ästhetische Erziehung des Menschen in einer Reihe von Briefen*, 15. Brief. In: Schiller, Werke in 3 Bänden, vol. II, Munich: Carl Hanser, 1966, p. 481, italics in original. Oskar's comment signifies the realisation of the end of the utopian value of art in the Holocaust, stipulated by Adorno.

[7] Avishai Margalit, Gabriel Motzkin, 'Der Holocaust. Zur Einzigartigkeit eines historischen Geschehens', *lettre international*, 35:4 (1996), 23-7 (here: p. 27).

[8] See Bruno Bettelheim, 'Trauma and Reintegration', in: Bettelheim, *Surviving and other Essays*, London: Thames & Hudson, 1979, pp. 19-37 (here: p. 25).

[9] Ibid.

[10] Ibid., p. 35.

[11] See Christian Schneider, 'Geschichtliches zu einem methodischen Modeartikel. Das Interview als sozialwissenschaftliches Forschungsmittel', *mittelweg 36*, 5 (1996), 73-89 and 6 (1996), 20-37.

[12] Eric L.Santner e.g. argues that Paul deMan's method of deconstruction is a praxis-oriented form of atoning for guilt, the origin of which is the shock of the Holocaust. DeMan had collaborated during the occupation of Belgium with the Nazi occupying forces. See Santner, *Stranded Objects. Mourning, Memory and Film in Post-War Germany*, Ithaca/NY and London: Cornell University Press, 1990, pp 1-30.

[13] See Lothar Probst, 'Der Holocaust – eine neue Zivilreligion für Europa?' in: Wolfgang Bergem, ed., *Die NS-Diktatur im deutschen Erinnerungsdiskurs*, Opladen: Leske und Budrich, 2003, pp. 227-39.

[14] See my 'The Birth of the Collective from the Spirit of Empathy: From the Historians' Debate to German Suffering', in: Bill Niven, ed., *Germans as Victims: Remembering the Past in Contemporary Germany*, London: Palgrave, 2006, pp. 93-108. See also Heinz-Peter Preußer, 'Regarding and Imagining. Contrived Immediacy of the Allied Bombing Campaign in Photography, Novel and Historiography', in: Helmut Schmitz, ed., *A Nation of Victims? Representations of German Wartime Suffering from 1945 to the Present*, Amsterdam: Rodopi, 2007, pp. 141-60.

[15] Marcel Atze shows, for example, that the public debate that arose around the Frankfurt Auschwitz trial of 1963-65 was awash with explicit comparisons of Auschwitz with Dresden. See Marcel Atze, '"...und wer spricht über Dresden?" Der Luftkrieg als öffentliches und literarisches Thema in der Zeit des Frankfurter Auschwitz-Prozesses 1963-1965', in: Marcel Atze and Franz Loquai, eds., *Sebald. Lektüren*, Eggingen: Edition Isele, 2005, pp. 105-15.

[16] On the 'Zentrum gegen Vertreibungen' see Bill Niven, 'Implicit Equations in Constructions of German Suffering', in: Schmitz, ed., *A Nation of Victims?*, pp. 105-23.

[17] Bill Niven, 'Introduction', in: Niven, ed., *Germans as Victims*, pp. 1-25 (here: p. 13).

[18] This is especially visible in Jörg Friedrich's *Der Brand* (Munich: Propyläen, 2002) Although Friedrich explicitly rejects any comparison between the Allied bombing and the Holocaust in his argument, his language is littered with vocabulary that implicitly produces an analogy between the two. The bombings are apostrophised as 'Massaker' (pp. 176, 187, 234), the cellars turn into 'Krematorien' (p. 195) where the German victims are 'vergast' (p. 387) etc.

[19] See the chapter by Michael Heinlein in this volume. On transgenerational trauma see for example Sigrid Weigel 'Telescopage im Unbewussten. Zum Verhältnis von Literatur, Geschichtsbegriff und Literatur', in: Elisabeth Bronfen, Birgit R. Erdle, Sigrid Weigel, eds., *Trauma. Zwischen Psychoanalyse & kulturellem Deutungsmuster*, Cologne, Weimar, Vienna: Böhlau, 1999, pp. 51-76. See also the volume by Jörn Rüsen und Jürgen Straub, eds., *Die dunkle Spur der Vergangenheit. Psychoanalytische Zugänge zum Geschichtsbewusstsein*, Frankfurt/M.: Suhrkamp, 1998.

[20] Dieter Forte, *Der Junge mit den blutigen Schuhen*, Frankfurt/M.: Fischer, 1995. All page references in the text as (JbS, page number).

[21] Jörg Friedrich, *Brandstätten. Der Anblick des Bombenkrieges*, Munich: Propyläen, 2003. All references in the text as (BS, page number).

[22] Günter Grass, *Im Krebsgang*, Göttingen: Steidl, 2002. All page references in the text as (K, page number).

[23] Hanns-Josef Ortheil, *Hecke*, Frankfurt/M.: Fischer, 1983. All page references in the text as (H, page number).

[24] Hanns-Josef Ortheil, *Abschied von den Kriegsteilnehmern*, Munich: Piper, 1992. All page references in the text as (AK, page number).

[25] See Martin Broszat, 'Plädoyer für eine Historisierung des Nationalsozialismus', *Merkur*, 39 (1985), 373-85.

[26] See Martin Broszat/Saul Friedländer. 'Um die "Historisierung" des Nationalsozialismus. Ein Briefwechsel', *Vierteljahrshefte für Zeitgeschichte*, 36 (1988), 339-73. On the issue of historicism with respect to the issue of German suffering see my 'Historicism, Sentimentality and the Problem of Empathy', in: Schmitz, ed., *A Nation of Victims?*, pp. 197-222.

[27] See the chapter on Ortheil in my *On their Own Terms. The Legacy of National Socialism in Post-1990 German Fiction*, Birmingham: University of Birmingham Press, 2004, pp. 27-53.

[28] Volker Wehdeking, 'Ortheils *Abschied von den Kriegsteilnehmern* als Generationenkonflikt und Geschichtslektion', in: Martin Durzak and Hartmut Steinecke, eds., *Hanns-Josef Ortheil. Im Innern seiner Texte*, Munich: Piper, 1995, pp. 148-66 (here: p. 158).

[29] Hanns-Josef Ortheil, 'Weiterschreiben', in: Ortheil, *Schauprozesse. Beiträge zur Kultur der 80er Jahre*, Munich: Piper, 1990, pp. 89-102 (here: p. 96-7).

[30] This is a paraphrase of Adorno's question whether one can go on living after Auschwitz: 'Nicht falsch aber ist die minder kulturelle Frage, ob nach Auschwitz noch sich leben lasse, [...]', *Negative Dialektik*, p. 355.

[31] On the issue of genealogy and heritage in narratives of transgenerational trauma see my '"Ich bin der einzige Erbe." Family, Heritage and German Wartime Suffering in Hanns-Josef Ortheil, Stephan Wackwitz, Thomas Medicus, Dagmar Leupold and Uwe Timm', in: Stuart Taberner and Karina Berger, eds., *Germans as Victims in the Literary Fiction of the Berlin Republic*, Rochester, NY: Camden House, 2009, pp. 70-85.

[32] For a wider discussion of this issue see the chapter on *Im Krebsgang* in my *On their Own Terms*, pp. 263-86.

[33] See Helm Stierlin, 'The Dialogue between the Generations about the Nazi era', in: Barbara Heimannsberg and Christoph J. Schmidt, eds., *The Collective Silence. German Identity and the Legacy of Shame*, San Francisco: Jossey-Bass, 1993, pp. 143-61, (here: p.147).

[34] Ibid., p. 154.

[35] On the latent melancholia of the student generation see Michael Schneider, 'Väter und Söhne Posthum', in: Schneider, *Den Kopf verkehrt aufgesetzt, oder Die melancholische Linke*, Darmstadt: Luchterhand, 1980, pp. 1-65. Paul's shift of conviction from Springer journalist to 'ziemlich links' (K, 21) reminds one of Bernward Versper who until the mid-1960s tried in vain to publish the collected works of his father Will, Hitler's favourite poet, before founding the (radically) left-wing 'Voltaire Flugschriften'.

[36] Grass, *Die Blechtrommel*, p. 582.

[37] Tilmann Moser, 'Motive und Ziele der Rechtsradikalen', in: Moser, *Politik und seelischer Untergrund*, Frankfurt/M.: Suhrkamp, 1993, pp. 143-56 (here: pp. 145-6).

[38] See Stuart Taberner, '"Normalisation", the new Consensus on the Nazi Past and the Problem of German Wartime Suffering', *Oxford German Studies*, 31 (2002), 161-86 (here: p. 179)

[39] See W.G. Sebald, *Luftkrieg und Literatur*, Munich: Carl Hanser, 1999. References are to the paperback edition, Frankfurt/M.: Fischer, 2001.

[40] Dieter Forte, 'Luftkrieg im Literaturseminar', in: Forte, *Schweigen oder sprechen*, Frankfurt/M.: Fischer, 2002, pp. 31-36 (here: p. 33).

[41] Dieter Forte, '"Alles vorherige war nur ein Umweg"'. Interview with Volker Hage, in: Forte, *Schweigen oder sprechen*, pp. 45-68 (here: p. 46).

[42] See Stefan Braese, 'Bombenkrieg und literarische Gegenwart', m*ittelweg 36*, 1 (2002), pp. 2-24 (esp. pp. 12-13).

[43] See Braese, ibid. It is worth noting that the quoted scene takes place before the war. I know of no case where inmates of concentration camps, prior to the erection of the death camps in Poland, received a tattoo on their arm. The scene is thus a metonymy which ascribes to the non-Jewish Nazi victims the same status as to the Jews.

[44] See Martin Broszat/Saul Friedländer. 'Um die "Historisierung" des National-sozialismus', p. 343.

[45] 'Forte, '"Alles Vorherige war nur ein Umweg"', p. 49.

[46] Cf. Sebald, *Luftkrieg und Literatur*, p. 16.

[47] Jan Assmann, *Das kulturelle Gedächtnis*, Munich: Beck, 1997, p. 52.

[48] Forte, '"Alles Vorherige war nur ein Umweg"', p. 62.

[49] Ibid., p. 63 and p. 57.

[50] 'A precondition for a new integration is acceptance of how severely one has been traumatized, and what the nature of the trauma has been.' Bettelheim, 'Trauma and Reintegration', p. 34-5.

[51] See Sebald, *Luftkrieg und Literatur*, p. 16.

[52] See Christian Groh's chapter in this volume.

[53] See my 'Catastrophic History, Trauma and Mourning in W.G. Sebald and Jörg Friedrich', in: Christine Anton and Frank Pilipp, eds., *Beyond Political Correctness. Remapping German Sensibilities in the 21st Century*, Amsterdam: Rodopi, 2010, pp. 27-50.

[54] It is a frequently repeated trope that any confrontation with Holocaust photographs ruptures or arrests the flow of time. See for example Susan Sontag, *On Photography*, New York: Doubleday, 1989, pp. 19-20. See also Martin Walser's insistence: 'Seit Auschwitz ist noch kein Tag vergangen' (Martin Walser, 'Auschwitz und kein Ende', in: Walser, *Deutsche Sorgen*, Frankfurt/M.: Suhrkamp, 1997, pp. 228-34 [here: p. 228]).

[55] See Preußer, 'Regarding and Imagining', p. 146.

[56] Brad Prager, 'A Collection of Damages: Critiquing the Violence of the Air War', *Forum for Modern Language Studies*, 41:3 (2005), 308-19 (here: p. 317).

[57] Ibid, p. 317.

[58] See Assmann, *Das kulturelle Gedächtnis*, pp. 75-8.

[59] Jörg Friedrich, *Der Brand*, Munich: Propyläen, 2002, quoted from the paperback edition Berlin: Ullstein, 2002, p. 505.

[60] See Saul Friedlander, 'Die Metapher des Bösen', *Die Zeit*, 26 November 1998.

[61] Diner, 'Zwischen Aporie und Apologie', p. 71.

[62] Cf. Forte: 'Und nun zur Schuld dieses Volkes: Das eine ist ohne das andere nicht zu denken. […] Man muß nicht auch noch sagen: "Es gab da Auschwitz." Das setze ich doch voraus, das ist doch selbstverständlich.' Forte, '"Alles vorherige war nur ein Umweg"', p. 67.

[63] See Assmann, *Das kulturelle Gedächtnis*, p. 52.

[64] See Hans-Ulrich Treichel, *Der Verlorene*, Frankfurt/M.: Suhrkamp, 1998, p. 17.

[65] For an illuminating comparison between Treichel's and Grass's texts see Martina Ölke, '"Flucht und Vertreibung" in Hans-Ulrich Treichels *Der Verlorene* und Günter Grass' *Im Krebsgang*', *Seminar*, 2 (May 2007), pp. 115-33.

[66] See Stuart Taberner. 'Hans-Ulrich Treichel's *Der Verlorene* and the Problem of German Wartime Suffering', *Modern Language Review*, 97:1 (2002), 123-34.

[67] See for example Uwe Timm's *Am Beispiel meines Bruders* and Dagmar Leupold's *Nach den Kriegen* which, like Treichel's *Der Verlorene*, are transgenerational narratives that eschew the reading of family trauma on a collective level. See my '"Ich bin der einzige Erbe." in: Taberner and Berger, eds., *'Germans as Victims' in The Literary Fiction of the Berlin Republic*, pp. 70-85.

Bill Niven

German Victimhood Discourse
in Comparative Perspective

Analyses of German victimhood discourse have tended to focus on national questions such as whether or not the subject of German wartime suffering was long 'taboo' in Germany, whether generational changes impacted on its reception, or whether domestic political changes have brought about a greater empathy for German victimhood. By contrast, this article seeks to contextualise the reinvigoration of interest in German historical suffering within wider European, and particularly Eastern European trends. To what extent is Germany's case not so much unique, as symptomatic?

Sometimes those who research the way Germany remembers its problematic past fall into the trap of imagining that only Germany has such a past to face. We often consider Germany in terms of a 'unique' national history, as reflected for instance in the horrific perpetration of the Holocaust, the process of division and unification, its own particular inflection of the Cold War, and the ongoing legacy of a 'double past' of National Socialism and Stalinism. However, if we consider developments in Germany's culture of memory largely in national terms, we run the risk of overlooking the fact that other European countries are also grappling with difficult pasts character-ised by forms of fascism and socialism. This essay is based on the premise that opening out the discursive framework beyond Germany's boundaries may help us to understand to what extent Germany's present confrontation with its past is typical of a wider European trend, and to what extent this confrontation takes distinctive forms. The first half of this essay provides a *tour d'horizon* of recent 'memory struggles', particularly in Eastern Europe, where, it can be argued the greatest similarities to the German case can be found (Developments in the Russian Federation, which represents something of a different case, will, however, not be discussed). The concluding part of this discussion will ask: how different is Germany really?

The collapse of communism towards the end of the last century was accompanied throughout Eastern Europe by a wave of iconoclasm. Arguably, this iconoclasm had been anticipated by the destruction and defacement of images of Stalin or Lenin during the

Hungarian and Prague uprisings of 1956 and 1968 respectively. Arguably, too, in the last few years there has been a second post-communist wave of iconoclasm in Eastern Europe.[1] The recent removal of the Soviet Bronze Soldier memorial in Tallinn is the most obvious and widely publicised example.[2] Less well known, perhaps, is the fact that Poland's then President Lech Kaczynski in 2009 approved legislation imposing a ban on displaying communist symbols. This will not just affect any existing memorials or buildings: it will effectively criminalize the possession or distribution of motifs such as the hammer and sickle. The law also applies to fascist symbols, and President Kaczynski's twin brother Jaroslaw – head of Poland's Law and Justice Party – had no hesitation in declaring communism a 'genocidal system' whose symbols 'should be compared to German Nazism'.[3] A similar ban has been in place in Hungary since 2003.[4] Those tributes to communism and the Red Army which survived the first wave of destruction or removal following the break-up of the Soviet Union are unlikely to survive the second. If not destroyed or dumped, they will live on in comical memorial theme parks such as those in Lithuania (Grutas Park) and Hungary (Szobor Park), a form of old folks' home for decrepit and unwanted stone citizens.[5]

But it has not all been about destruction and removal. At the same time, Eastern European countries since the end of communism have been creating a new focus for memorialisation and commemoration: the victims of communism. In the newly institutionalised historical narratives underpinning such developments, the Soviets appear not as liberators, but as the bringers of (repeated) totalitarian oppression. In December 2009, a Monument to the Victims of Communism, 1918-89, was unveiled in Lodz in central Poland; it is dedicated, for instance, to the victims of the Soviet invasions of 1919-20 and 1939, and to those Solidarity activists persecuted in the early 1980s.[6] In October 2009, a memorial to the victims of communism was unveiled in Trencin in Slovakia.[7] Major memorial-cum-documentation centres commemorating either the victims of communism, or both the victims of communism and National Socialism, have sprung up throughout Eastern Europe. These include the Memorial to the Victims of Communism and of the Resistance in Sighet, Romania (initiated in 1997);[8] Latvia's Museum of Occupation in Riga (since 1993);[9] Hungary's House of Terror in Budapest (since 2002);[10] and the

Museum of Genocide Victims in Vilnius, Lithuania (established in 1992), which, contrary to what one might expect, is focused mainly on Lithuanian victims of Soviet persecution, not on Jewish or even non-Jewish Lithuanian victims of National Socialism.[11] It is certainly true that, increasingly, post-communist Eastern Europe is also constructing memorials and exhibitions to Jewish victims of the Holocaust. The website of the Holocaust Task Force – among whose members are former communist-run states such as the Czech Republic, Estonia, Hungary, Poland, Romania and Slovakia – provides evidence of processes of Holocaust memorialisation in all member states, including the Eastern European ones.[12] Thus Slovakia has unveiled some 100 memorials and memorial plaques to Holocaust victims since 1992, including the Central Memorial to the Holocaust of Slovakian Jews in Bratislava (1997).[13] To a degree, too, post-war anti-Semitism in Eastern Europe is also now memorialised. In 2006, for instance, Poland marked the 60th anniversary of the infamous Kielce massacre by unveiling a monument to the pogrom's victims.[14] The end of the communist era with its anti-Semitic purges and reluctance to confront the suffering of the Holocaust has given way to a belated attempt in Eastern Europe to acknowledge Jewish victimhood.

Nevertheless, one might question the extent of this commitment. The Holocaust Task Force's website references Latvia's Museum and Documentation Centre 'Jews in Latvia' – yet this was the product of a private initiative dating back to 1990, and still lacks state funding.[15] The Latvian government did support the construction of a monument (dedicated in 2007) in honour of Zanis Lipke and other Latvians who saved the lives of Jews during World War Two.[16] But there is little preparedness to confront Latvian collaboration with Nazism. During the Nazi occupation, the notorious Latvian Auxiliary Police actively participated in the murder of Jews, Roma and mental patients. Subsequently, tens of thousands of Latvians served in Hitler's Waffen-SS. How many of the latter were volunteers, or participated in atrocities, is still a matter of debate. Yet in 2005, Latvian SS veterans were allowed to parade through the streets of Riga. The Latvian Foreign Ministry's website rather suggests that it is quite legitimate to honour Waffen-SS veterans because these were 'soldiers who fought against the Soviet Union in World War II'.[17] Estonia's government has shown more willingness to take a stand against trends to glorify Estonians who fought in Hitler's army and the Waffen-SS. A memorial to the latter, erected in Parnu, was removed by the authorities in 1992. At the time, Estonia's prime minister seemed more concerned about the memorial jeopardising Estonia's efforts to join the EU than he was about its transformation of Estonian collaborators into anti-Soviet patriots fighting for Estonian independence and a 'free Europe'.[18]

Officially, Eastern European states since the fall of communism – outside of the Russian Federation – are basing their re-emerging national collective memory on a narrative of victimhood at the hands of two totalitarian regimes. Thus Latvia's Museum of Occupation in Riga seeks to 'provide information about Latvia and its people under two occupying totalitarian regimes from 1940 to 1991'.[19] It also aims to 'remind the world of the wrongdoings committed by foreign powers against the state and the people of Latvia'. Hungary's House of Terror, opened in 2002, likewise focuses on the two dictatorships of fascism and communism. 'Having survived two terror regimes', the exhibition's website declares, 'it was felt that the time had come for Hungary to erect a fitting memorial to the victims, and at the same time to present a picture of what life was like for Hungarians in those times'.[20] Yet of the two totalitarian regimes, it seems clear, to Eastern Europeans, that Soviet communism was the worse. If the Nazis practised genocide against Jews, then the Soviets, according to the narrative, practised it against Eastern Europeans. As already indicated, Lithuania's Museum of Genocide Victims in Vilnius, symbolically set up in a former KGB prison, is largely about Soviet persecution of Lithuanian nationals. When the Soviet deportation of Latvians from Tornakalns station in June 1941 to Siberian labour camps was commemorated in Latvia in 2004, the Latvian Ministry of Foreign Affairs declared on its website that 'Communist genocide victims' had been commemorated.[21] Arguably, it is precisely this anti-Russian animus which has made the work of the 'Volksbund Deutscher Kriegsgräberfürsorge' easier than might have been expected. Since 1990, the VDK has embarked upon tending and developing German soldiers' graves and cemeteries in Eastern Europe. At a military cemetery near Wroclaw in 2002, the bodies of some of those Germans who defended Breslau against the Russian advance in 1945 were buried with the blessing of high-ranking Polish priests. Here, it seems, the Germans are not remembered as occupiers, but as a determined if ultimately unsuccessful bulwark against bolshevism.

There are, of course, many obvious reasons why the Soviet Union should be remembered as the key aggressor. Post-war communist rule, imposed by and maintained to varying degrees by the Soviets, dominated in Eastern Europe from 1945 through to the late 1980s or early 1990s – for a far longer period than Nazi rule (and countries such as Romania and Hungary, as collaborators, long escaped the direct hand of Nazi control). The Baltic states, and Poland, endured Soviet control both prior to and subsequent to Nazism. Moreover, the memory of communism is far fresher in the minds of Eastern Europeans than the memory of Nazism. Confronting communist crime – through, for instance, the Czech Republic's Office for the Documentation and Investigation of the Crimes of Communism[22] – was a very real necessity after the collapse of communism. Confronting the legacy of Nazism or fascism generally was hardly as pressing. Anti-Soviet iconoclasm and the construction of anti-Soviet national victimhood narratives also served and serve to keep Eastern European countries at a distance to post-communist Russia, while echoing longstanding anti-communist feeling in western Europe – a way of demonstrating a desire and suitability for western integration. Focusing more on memory of Nazi crime, moreover, might risk alienating Germany, a key player in the EU's expansion into Eastern Europe. The rush to join the western club is not simply driven, though, by economic and political interests: there is still a genuine fear of Russia in some Eastern European countries, and the Soviet-critical thrust of memory expresses this fear.

But one can be critical of this memory trend. The Russian philosopher Boris Groys, in a recent interview, points to growing nationalism in Eastern Europe; by example of Estonia and Poland, Groys argues that the communist past of Eastern European countries is being understood increasingly in terms of an 'occupation', a view formulated in terms of ethnic conflict. For Groys, the motive behind this 'ethnicisation of communism', mostly, is self-exculpation.[23] In other words: communism is projected back onto the Soviet Union, with Eastern European countries denying responsibility for it. (The more Eastern Europeans seek to disown their communist past and project communism back onto Russia, the more, of course, Russia will feel inclined to strengthen rather than critically confront the tradition of celebrating the 'Great Patriotic War'.)[24] Collaboration with communism is recognised in former Eastern bloc countries, but there is a tendency to single out individuals for blame, resulting in scapegoating rather than an awareness of widespread collusion. If collusion with Nazism appears even harder to face, then because, for several states, this would mean accepting that they had installed their own authoritarian, fascist or clerico-fascist regimes (one thinks of Tiso's Slovakia, Pavelic's Croatia, or Antonescu's Romania). It would also mean, for several states, accepting the part they, or groups of their citizens had played in the Holocaust and other ethnic atrocities. One of the advantages of the totalitarian narrative, according to which Eastern Europeans were twentieth century victims, is that it erases questions of differing levels and extents of autonomous responsibility and collaboration.

It might seem as if Eastern European countries are attempting to achieve *synchronically* what western European countries achieved *diachronically*. There is substantial evidence that in northern and western Europe the narratives of victimhood and *résistance* so central to national memories in the 1950s, 1960s, 1970s and even 1980s are gradually shifting towards a self-critical focus on the Holocaust. This can be illustrated by the example of France. In February 2009, France's top judicial body, the Council of State, acknowledged the French government's responsibility for the deportation of thousands of Jews during World War II.[25] Throughout the first decade of the new millennium, in fact, France has made significant moves towards memorialising and commemorating the Holocaust generally and the deportations specifically – a sign, perhaps, that the 'Vichy syndrome', i.e. the self-obsessed focus on the trauma of occupation is not as dominant as it was.[26] Given that memory of the Second World War was frozen into set formulae for decades in the former Soviet bloc – Soviets as heroes and liberators – the end of the Cold War has prompted a veritable eruption of suppressed victimhood narratives in Eastern Europe, while opening towards the West has necessitated a confrontation with the Holocaust. Denied the gradualist evolution of memory over time characteristic of the West, Eastern Europe has seen the simultaneous and consequently rather fraught emergence of – for want of better terms – 'self-focused' and 'others-focused' memory narratives. Tensions between them are currently being defused by means of the totalitarian paradigm, according to which Eastern Europeans and Jews were all victims of comparable repression and even genocide.

This is not to say that the more self-critical memory which is evolving in the West does not have its pitfalls. One can certainly see in the Europeanisation or even globalisation of Holocaust memory a well-motivated attempt to increase awareness of this genocide in order to foster a sense of historical conscience and to activate social concern in the present.[27] But the rhetoric of acknowledgement can soon dissipate into a collection of rather vapid and formulaic assertions and avowals in which concrete acknowledgement of national responsibility for involvement in the Holocaust is either absent or watered-down. Where it is present, its actual sincerity might be questioned. It is arguably easier for nations to remember their entanglement in the destructive web of fascism, racism and genocide when they simultaneously claim to have learnt lessons from the past and indeed to be applying these in the present. It is also easier when memory of collaboration can be shared with other countries; the burden of memory is denationalised. 'We were not the only ones, and we have moved on since' often seems to be the message.

Furthermore, it would be wrong to maintain that taking leave of well-worn myths is proving easy for all northern or western European countries. Having hosted a hugely significant and influential international Holocaust conference in 2000, Sweden has established itself as a pioneer of Holocaust memory in the new millennium. Yet it was not until 2001 and 2002 that Swedish historians and journalists such as Bosse Schön began to challenge seriously what Schön has sarcastically called the 'Pippi Langstrumpf Idyll' which had long characterised Swedish memory of Sweden's role in the war.[28] Historian Tobias Hübinette claims that some 60,000 to 100,000 Swedes sympathised with Nazism.[29] Revelation of collaboration often prompts angry and indignant responses in the public realm. In 2002, Finland became embroiled in a long-running debate about the Finnish philosopher Georg Henrik von Wright after a Finnish television team discovered documents demonstrating Wright's sympathy for Nazism.[30] In Italy, Mimmo Franzinelli's book on the readiness of some Italians during the fascist era to denounce Jews and partisans (*Delatori* [*Denouncers*], 2001) also prompted much debate.[31] Usually it has been journalists and historians who have paved the way to a more self-critical memory. But not always. The Mattéoli Report ('Mission Mattéoli'), for instance, published by the official Mattéoli commission in France in 2000, has done much to reveal the degree of

French participation in and profit from Aryanisation in wartime France.[32] Other pasts, too, are coming back to haunt. Spain's political establishment cannot continue to deny the sufferings of Republican forces during the Spanish Civil War, or to ensure their elision from public memory, especially as this past has literally been disinterred in recent years, prompting a flood of media debates on the subject.[33]

And what of Germany? Like other western countries, Germany has been taking leave of myths in recent years: the myth of the 'clean' Wehrmacht, for instance, was surely shattered by the long-running exhibition 'Vernichtungskrieg: Verbrechen der Wehrmacht 1941-1944' (1995-99).[34] The same could be said for the view that 'ordinary Germans' were by and large not involved in the Nazi government's anti-Semitic ideology and praxis. This view was left in tatters after the intense media debate which accompanied the publication in Germany of Goldhagen's *Hitler's Willing Executioners*.[35] Germany could also be seen to have embraced memory of the Holocaust as a central element of public and political commemoration through the construction and dedication of Berlin's Memorial to the Murdered Jews of Europe (2005).[36] Yet it would not be appropriate to seek to explain memory trends in Germany only with reference to *western* Europe. One of the main foci of public memory in Germany, certainly since 1998, is past national victimhood – as great a preoccupation, perhaps, as past national crime or levels of participation in that crime. This (from a western perspective) reinvigoration of sentiments of national victimhood, a reinvigoration of considerable intensity, can surely best be explained by seeing it in the context of the memory trends typical of *Eastern* European countries outlined above. Germany's current preoccupation with national victimhood may have more in common with national memory trends in a country such as Latvia or Lithuania than it does with memory trends in France or Holland.

In some respects, of course, Germany is a unique case. Unification in 1990, while often seen as involving simply the integration and 'westernisation' of Eastern Germany, was in fact – at least in terms of memory – a complex fusion, with resulting tensions, between a country which had 'grown up' with western European post-war traditions of memory, and one which had been shaped by Eastern European ones. In contrast to the situation in Eastern Europe after 1990, where a public culture of Holocaust memory needed to be developed, such a public culture – albeit still contested – existed in

West Germany prior to unification with the GDR.[37] It could therefore be 'transferred' to the new Länder. From one perspective, one might argue that the traditionally anti-communist character of West Germany smoothed the passage towards a judicial, social and ethical confrontation with the legacies of the GDR in united Germany. From another, one could maintain that united Germany started life on a much stronger democratic base than the newly emancipated Eastern European states, and was thus more thorough, rigorous and forceful in its process of lustration. In contrast to the situation in *western* Europe, Germany after 1990 was the only western country which had to confront the fact that a significant part of its territory had been in the grip of Soviet-style socialism for half a century. It was the only country that had to find a way of mediating between two radically different memory traditions according to which the Second World War was won either by socialist-inspired antifascism (the GDR view) or by western democracy with some help from Stalin (the FRG view).

That said, similarities between united Germany and contemporary Eastern Europe need to be highlighted. After all, a substantial portion of Germany *was* part of the Eastern European bloc until 1990. The GDR was as much, indeed even more of a Soviet satellite state than other Eastern bloc countries. The opening of the Stasi files, the removal of compromised individuals from the civil service, the trials of former border-guards and the politicians behind the border regime – all of these measures bear a resemblance to processes of lustration and judicial proceedings against former communists in other Eastern European countries. At some of Berlin's memorial sites, the critical memorialisation of the communist persecution of dissidents at the hands of the Stasi and SED parallels the critical memory of communism characteristic of contemporary Eastern European countries.[38] That Germany sees itself in relation to Eastern European countries is certainly borne out by a project currently being undertaken by the 'Stiftung zur Aufarbeitung der DDR-Diktatur' – itself comparable to the various institutions set up in Eastern Europe to examine and help to overcome the legacy of state socialism. So far, the 'Stiftung' has largely focused on its immediate remit. Thus in 2004, it commissioned the publication of a book charting the sites of memory of socialist dictatorship in Germany.[39] More recently, however, it has become engaged in compiling a topography of memory which will document all European sites commemorating the victims of 20th-century communism. According to what the Foundation calls a 'cautious estimate', some seven to eight thousand of these have sprung up since the fall of communism.[40]

We also need to see to understand the current reinvigoration of interest in German wartime and post-war suffering in this context. Germans, freed on the one hand from the constrictions of Ostpolitik and on the other from the obligation to unquestioningly celebrate the historical role of the Soviet Union, can give voice to a sense of historical grievance. For the Soviets not only defeated Hitler; they raped a huge number of German women, carted off German civilians for forced labour, set up post-war internment camps in which tens of thousands of (in many cases, innocent) Germans died, played an instrumental role in the expulsion of Germans, annexed German territory and supported its annexation by Poland and Czechoslovakia, and set up a dictatorial order in Eastern Germany.[41] Similar injustices, *mutatis mutandis*, were visited upon a number of Eastern European countries by the Soviets between 1939 and 1950 (and subsequently). That these countries can now recall the suffering of, say, Polish, Czech and Baltic states' nationals at the hands of the Soviets feeds into a discourse of self-identification as historical victim – a discourse which parallels and perhaps influenced that in Germany.

Of course the 'Germans as victims' discourse encompasses much more, in its condemnatory dimension, than criticism of the Soviets. Germans at the end of the war were expelled by Poles and Czechs; Germans suffered injustice, too, at the hands of other Eastern European countries, such as Romania and Yugoslavia. Thus while Poland and Germany certainly share a critical view of the Soviets, they differ radically in their views of responsibility for expulsion. The Poles, and to a lesser extent the Czechs, take the view that the expulsions were a regrettable but nevertheless understandable response to the savage occupation of their countries by the Nazis. Many Germans, by contrast, point also to aggressive, opportunistic Polish and Czech ethnic nationalism[42] – and to indiscriminate brutality towards old men, women and children innocent of any role in Nazism. Germany and Poland, particularly, are locked into an ongoing saga of competitive victimhood which current plans to build a 'visible sign' to expulsions in Berlin are not doing anything to bring to an end – despite the German government's will to acknowledge the criminal role of Nazism, and the suffering through expulsion of other nations.[43]

Yet the 'cross-border' bickering over historical responsibility between Poland and Germany is by no means unique. Other Eastern European countries have been and are enmeshed in heated debates about the past and its relationship to the present. Only recently (2009), a dispute broke out between Slovakia and Hungary. The Hungarian minority in Slovakia, having constructed a memorial to Hungarian King Stephen I (c 970-1038), invited Hungarian State President Solyom to attend its unveiling; the Slovakian government responded by denying Solyom entry to the country.[44] Sensitivities deriving from the ceding of Hungarian territory to Czechoslovakia after World War I – territory which was to change hands again in 1938 and yet again in 1945, accompanied by expulsions and the creation of ethnic minorities – erupted with some vehemence. Competitive victimhood played its part here, too: building national identity on a sense of grievance only really works if the grievances of others against you can be made to appear smaller or even unjustified. Fear of territorial revisions and the claims of renascent ethnic nationalism – unthinkable during Soviet times – also play their part. They do in the case of the tensions between Germany and Poland, too. The constant redrawing of borders in the 20th century across Eastern Europe had deep psychological effects whose ongoing legacy it would be wrong to play down, for all the talk of European unity.[45]

There are, then, clear parallels between post-communist memory trends in Germany and Eastern Europe. But we must sound a note of caution. Parallels should not lead us to overlook problems of comparison, or differences in approach and intention. While the self-conceptualisation as historical victim in most Eastern European countries is based, for all its tendentiousness and blind spots, on the very real experience of two imposed dictatorships, for Germany to imagine itself as a victim of a 'double past' would be particularly questionable, given that Germany was responsible for Nazism, the Third Reich and the Second World War. Yet there are examples of precisely such 'double victimhood' constructions in recent German memorialisation – most notoriously, the *Neue Wache* in Berlin, the memorial brainchild of Helmut Kohl, which clearly brands Germans as victims of Nazism and communism.[46] Equations between Nazism and GDR socialism are not uncommon in post-unification Germany. This serves the purpose of simultaneously playing down Nazism and exaggerating the (nevertheless considerable) severity of repression in the GDR. Some fear, even, that memorialisation in Germany may be shifting too much towards memory of socialist crime – at the expense of an awareness of the singular criminality of Nazism, and of the particular nature of German responsibility. In 1997, the Association of Concentration Camp Memorial Sites in the Federal Republic objected to planned revisions to the Federal Strategy for Memorial Sites not least because of the danger that the significance of National Socialism for German history would be rendered 'unclear'.[47] The objections of the association – and the fact that the Federal Strategy was revised in the light of these criticisms – indicate, though, that many German historians, politicians and memorial site representatives are quick to resist attempts to shift the central focus of German memorial culture away from National Socialism. As it currently stands, the Federal Strategy for Memorial Sites certainly explicitly points out the differences in severity between Nazism and socialism, and begins with a clear acknowledgement of the inhumanity of National Socialism.[48]

In contrast to Eastern Europe, then, the place of Nazism in German memory arguably remains greater than that of socialism – despite developments towards focusing more on the latter in recent years. Germans remain acutely aware of the need to remember their own crimes, another point of contrast. Furthermore, while there is an 'anti-totalitarian consensus' in Germany, there is less agreement on how the GDR past should be approached. Just as there are criticisms of ostensibly over-negative portrayals of the GDR, so there are objections to portrayals perceived to be too 'soft'. When an official commission of experts made a set of recommendations on how best to work through the past of the SED dictatorship, it was immediately accused of such a 'soft' approach because it recommended more research into the everyday life of the GDR (in addition to further research into issues of state criminality, collaboration and resis-tance).[49] For all the recognition in Germany that GDR socialism was oppressive, the trend of 'Ostalgie' – surely without parallel elsewhere in Eastern Europe – remains. While it may have a variety of roots, one is certainly the perception among some east Germans that unification represents a western-style takeover of the Eastern Länder. In contrast to Eastern Europe, where western-style liberalism was (and still is being) recreated from below, in Germany it could be grafted onto the former GDR from the FRG, leading to charges of triumphalism where the import process was seen to be accompanied by a systematic demontage of GDR traditions (such as antifascism) and by the denigration of east Germans to second-class citizens. The west-east tensions within Germany on top of party-political differences mean that coming to terms with the past is in some respects more complex than in Eastern Europe.

In conclusion, while Germany's current interest in its own historical victimhood has many causes, some of which have been discussed in this volume, one is certainly its embedment in processes triggered by the end of communism throughout Eastern Europe. While I recently argued that it was the very depoliticisation of discourse surrounding German victimhood in the late 1990s which enabled the explosion of interest in the theme in the public realm,[50] more recently the discourse has arrived back on the political stage. Discussions surrounding the government-backed Foundation 'Flucht, Vertreibung, Versöhnung' are clear evidence of this.[51] One view might be that Germany, by riding the waves of contemporary European memory trends, can see an opportunity to finally cast off the pariah role of European perpetrator *per se*. If the Holocaust – indeed the Second World War as a whole – and communism are remembered (in whatever relation) throughout Europe and as European phenomena, then such an opportunity is certainly there. But while it seems clear that Germany is participating in the international cult of self-pity, the degree and nature of its politicisation within Germany remains unclear. Without doubt, mourning the expellees, or SED victims, was not possible in the GDR, while in West Germany, as Andreas Kossert has shown, expellees and expellee themes were often treated with disdain.[52] One thing that is certainly happening, then, is that suppressed themes are, as it were, coming up for air – which is hardly a political agenda. Moreover, the government's 'visible sign' to the expulsions is surely designed to counterbalance the arguably tendentious centre against expulsions idea proposed by the 'Bund der Vertriebenen'.[53] We shall have to await the outcome of developments in the next years before we will know whether Germany's participation in the international discourse of historical suffering results in a reshaping, or partial reshaping of German national identity around concepts of victimhood.

Notes

[1] See Sonja Zekri, 'Stalin als Seifenoper' (interview with Boris Groys), *Süddeutsche Zeitung*, 11 May 2007 (at http://www.sueddeutsche.de/kultur/386/406163/text/ (accessed 15 January 2010)). According to Zekri, 'wir erleben einen zweiten post-kommunistischen Bildersturz'.

[2] See 'Tallinn's "Bronze Soldier" Involved in a New Conflict', http://www.tallinn-life.com/news/news/42-Tallinn's_'Bronze_Soldier'_Involved_in_a_New_Conflict (accessed 15 January 2010).

[3] See http://www.spiegel.de/international/europe/0,1518,663154,00.html (accessed 1 January 2010).

[4] Ibid.

[5] See Paul Williams, 'The Afterlife of Communist Statuary: Hungary's Szoborpark and Lithuania's Grutas Park', *Forum for Modern Language Studies* (Special Issue on Representations of the Past in European Memorials), ed. Bill Niven, 44:2 (2008), 185-98.

[6] See http://www.thenews.pl/national/artykul121845_monument-to-communist-victims-unveiled.html (accessed 13 January 2010).

[7] See http://www.trencin.sk/en/index.php?s-cv-contentID=12288&s-cv-embeddedID =52101 (accessed 8 January 2010).

[8] See http://www.memorialsighet.ro/index.php?lang=ro (accessed 15 January 2010).

[9] See http://www.occupationmuseum.lv/ (accessed 3 January 2010).

[10] See http://www.terrorhaza.hu/en/index_2.html (accessed 12 January 2010).

[11] See http://www.genocid.lt/muziejus (accessed 15 January 2010).

[12] See http://www.holocausttaskforce.org/memberstates.html (accessed 15 January 2010).

[13] See http://www.holocausttaskforce.org/memberstates/member-slovakrepublic.html (accessed 13 January 2010).

[14] See http://kieltzer.org/memorials.html#60th (accessed 14 January 2010).

[15] See http://vip.latnet.lv/LPRA/ebr_muz.htm (accessed 15 January 2010).

[16] See http://www.holocausttaskforce.org/memberstates/member-latvia.html (accessed 15 January 2010).

[17] See http://www.li.lv/index.php?option=content&task=view&id=139 (accessed 10 January 2010).

[18] See http://news.bbc.co.uk/1/hi/world/europe/2148732.stm (accessed 10 January 2010).

[19] See http://www.omf.lv/index.php?lang=english (accessed 14 January 2010).

[20] See http://www.terrorhaza.hu/en/index_2.html (accessed 13 January 2010).

[21] See http://www.am.gov.lv/en/latvia/news/archive/news/?pg=4992 (accessed 15 January 2010).

[22] Other examples are Poland's Institute for National Remembrance and Romania's Presidential Commission for the Study of the Communist Dictatorship in Romania.

[23] See Zekri, 'Stalin als Seifenoper'. See also Tony Judt, *Postwar: A History of Europe since 1945*, London: William Heinemann, 2005, pp. 820-31.

[24] The Soviet Union, in the countries it occupied after the Second World War, built or encouraged the building of grand memorials to the 'Great Patriotic War' as a means of legitimising the Soviet right to implement communist regimes. Nowadays, the celebration of the Soviet victory – evident for instance in the massive extension to the memorial complex on Poklonnaya Hill in Moscow, inaugurated in 1995 – rather has the function of defending Russian sensitivities against anti-communist feeling in former Eastern bloc countries.

[25] See 'French Holocaust Role Recognised', *BBC News*, at http://news.bbc.co.uk/1/hi/7893127.stm (accessed 26 January 2010).

[26] This term was coined by Henry Rousso, see Henry Rousso, *The Vichy Syndrome: History and Memory in France since 1944*, Cambridge/Mass.: Harvard University Press, 1991.

[27] See Daniel Levy and Natan Sznaider, *The Holocaust and Memory in the Global Age*, Philadelphia: Temple University Press, 2005.

[28] See Bosse Schön, *Hitlers svenska soldater*, Stockholm: Pocky AB, 2005.

[29] In Gerhard Fischer, 'Der Mythos von Schwedens Unschuld', *Süddeutsche Zeitung*, 17/18 August 2002. See also Tobias Hübinette, *Nationalsocialismen i Sverige. Medlemmar och sympatisörer 1931-45*, Stockholm: Carlssons, 2002.

[30] See http://www2.hs.fi/english/archive/news.asp?id=20021112IE8 (accessed 12 January 2010).

[31] See Mimmo Franzinelli, *Delatori: Spie e confidente anonimi: l'arma segreta del regime fascista*, Milan: Mondadori, 2001. Franzinelli's work mirrors research done by Gellately and Johnson into levels of denunciation by 'ordinary Germans' during the Third Reich. See Robert Gellately, *Backing Hitler: Consent and Coercion in Nazi Germany*, Oxford: Oxford University Press, 2001, and Eric Johnson, *Nazi Terror: Gestapo, Jews and Ordinary Germans*, London: John Murray, 2000.

[32] Its official French title is 'Mission d'étude sur la spoliation des Juifs de France'. For an online version of the report, see http://www.ladocumentationfrancaise.fr/rapports-publics/984000110/index.shtml (accessed 14 January 2010).

[33] The recent (unsuccessful) efforts to find and exhume the remains of Spanish poet Federico   Garcia   Lorca   were   particularly   controversial.   See http://www.telegraph.co.uk/news/worldnews/europe/spain/6826532/Lorcas-civil-war-grave-found-empty.html (accessed 13 January 2010).

[34] See Hannes Heer and Klaus Naumann, eds., *Vernichtungskrieg: Verbrechen der Wehrmacht, 1941-1944*, Hamburg: Hamburger Edition, 1998 [2nd ed.].

[35] In German translation as: Daniel Jonah Goldhagen, *Hitlers willige Vollstrecker*, Berlin: Siedler, 1996.

[36] For an interesting discussion of Berlin's Holocaust Memorial, see Claus Leggewie and Erik Meyer, *Ein Ort, an den man gerne geht*, Munich: Hanser, 2005.

[37] This is not to suggest that the GDR had not moved towards greater acknowledgement of the Holocaust; as I have shown elsewhere, by the mid-1980s, to a degree it had (see Bill Niven, 'Remembering Nazi Anti-Semitism in the GDR', in: Bill Niven and Chloe Paver, eds., *Memorialization in Germany since 1945*, Basingstoke: Palgrave Macmillan, 2010, pp. 205-13). But without doubt, West Germany had moved much further in this regard. See Jeffrey Herf, *Divided Memory: The Nazi Past in the two Germanies*, Harvard: Harvard University Press, 1999.

[38] Such critical memorialisation can be found, for instance, at the Berlin-Hohenschönhausen Memorial (http://en.stiftung-hsh.de/), and the Berlin Wall Documentation Centre (http://www.berliner-mauer-dokumentationszentrum.de/eng/index_dokz.html (accessed 15 January 2010)).

[39] See Anne Kaminsky, *Orte des Erinnerns. Gedenkzeichen, Gedenkstätten und Museen zur Diktatur in SBZ und DDR*, Leipzig: Forum Verlag, 2004.

[40] See www.stiftung-aufarbeitung.de/downloads/pdf/conceptIGOF.pdf (accessed 15 January 2010).

[41] For a highly critical view of the Soviet role at the end of the Second World War and subsequently, see Hubertus Knabe, *Tag der Befreiung? Das Kriegsende in Deutschland*, Berlin: Propyläen, 2005.

[42] For a good discussion of the complex relationship between nationalism and communism in post-war Poland, see Michael Fleming, *Communism, Nationalism and Ethnicity in Poland, 1944-1950*, London: Routledge, 2009. The biggest problem with the plans for the 'visible sign' at present is the issue of the inclusion or non-inclusion on the board of directors of the head of Germany's League of Expellees, Erika Steinbach, who is regarded by the Poles as a revisionist because of her reluctance after 1990 to recognise the Oder-Neisse line as Germany's Eastern border with Poland – a reluctance she subsequently overcame.

[43] See http://www.bundesregierung.de/Content/DE/Pressemitteilungen/BPA/2009/04/ 2009-04-08-bkm-stiftung-flucht-vertreibung-versoehnung.html (accessed 15 January 2010).

[44] See http://news.bbc.co.uk/1/hi/world/europe/8215220.stm (accessed 15 January 2010).

[45] Though it would be wrong to claim that such anxieties are restricted to Eastern Europe. There have been sensitive reactions in Italy to groups in Austrian Tyrol who regularly commemorate the historical loss of parts of Tyrol to Italy by organising processions in which crowns of thorns are held high – symbolising South Tyrolean German 'suffering' at the hands of Italy. See Michael Frank, 'Freiheitsheld oder Alpen-Taliban', *Süddeutsche Zeitung*, 19/20 September 2009.

[46] For a controversial perspective, see Thomas Schmidt et al., eds., *Nationaler Totenkult. Die Neue Wache. Eine Streitschrift zur zentralen deutschen Gedenkstätte*, Berlin: Karin Kramer Verlag, 1999.

[47] See Volkhard Knigge, 'Stellungnahme zur *Fortschreibung der Gedenkstätten-konzeption durch den Beauftragten der Bundesregierung für Kultur und Medien vom 22. Juni 2007* für die Anhörung des Ausschusses für Kultur und Medien des Deutschen Bundestages am 7. November 2007', at http://www.gedenkstaettenforum .de/nc/gedenkstaetten-rundbrief/rundbrief/?tx_ttnews%5Btt_news%5D=31299 (accessed 5 August 2010).

[48] See http://www.bundesregierung.de/nsc_true/Content/DE/__Anlagen/BKM/2008- 06-18-fortschreibung-gedenkstaettenkonzepion-barrierefrei,property=publicationFile .pdf/2008-06-18-fortschreibung-gedenkstaettenkonzepion-barrierefrei (accessed 15 January 2010).

[49] See Martin Sabrow et. al., eds., *Wohin treibt die DDR-Erinnerung? Dokumentation einer Debatte,* Göttingen: Vandenhoeck & Ruprecht, 2007.

[50] Bill Niven, 'Introduction: German Victimhood at the Turn of the Millennium', in: Bill Niven, ed., *Germans as Victims*, Basingstoke: Palgrave Macmillan, 2006, pp. 1- 25.

[51] See http://www.bundesregierung.de/Content/DE/Pressemitteilungen/BPA/2009/04/
2009-04-08-bkm-stiftung-flucht-vertreibung-versoehnung.html (accessed 15 January
2010).

[52] Andreas Kossert, *Kalte Heimat: Die Geschichte der Deutschen Vertriebenen nach
1945*, Munich: Siedler, 2008.

[53] For a discussion of the League's point of view, which arguably plays down German
responsibility for the processes which led to the expulsions, see Bill Niven, 'Implicit
Equations in Constructions of German Suffering', in: Helmut Schmitz, ed., *A Nation
of Victims? Representations of German Wartime Suffering since 1945 to the Present*,
Amsterdam: Rodopi, 2007, pp. 105-24.

Krijn Thijs

Holland and the German Point of View: On the Dutch Reactions to German Victimhood

The chapter analyses the reception of the discourse of German suffering in the Netherlands, one of the countries occupied by Nazi Germany. After a brief overview of memory discourses in Holland, the chapter examines reasons for the lack of controversy in Holland with regard to the issue of German suffering, before discussing the representation of German suffering in two Dutch novels.

As German history debates in recent years have shown, the shift to commemoration of Germans as victims was in many respects a controversial one. This is largely so because of the international consequences of this memory shift. When Germans represent themselves as victims of the Second World War, this implies that others must have been perpetrators. It is thus not surprising that German memory debates in the past decade have been eagerly watched by many neighbouring countries, for example Poland and the Czech Republic, which firmly objected to the revival of German expulsion stories as well as the supposedly revisionist 'Zentrum gegen Vertreibungen'. Another example is the defensive British reactions to Jörg Friedrichs *Der Brand*, which represents the Allies as war criminals and German civilians as victims of 'mass destruction'. Thus, this discourse clearly has European dimensions – it might even be seen as an effect of a specific German approach to Europeanising the history of the Second World War.

Despite their European context, the discussions about the intermingling of perpetrator and victim experiences and about guilt, vengeance and war crimes have mainly remained debates between the larger nations among the former belligerents. But how do the smaller and occupied Western European countries fit into these changing stories? Does the reorganising of German war narratives have any consequences for their national memory cultures? Why do their voices remain silent in current memory debates, which seem to redefine European history of the 20th century? This paper will address these questions based on the case of the Netherlands. It will start with a short overview of Dutch public memory culture since the Second

World War. Secondly, it will formulate two reasons why the topic of German wartime suffering has generally *not* been a very controversial or even important part of the Second World War from the Dutch point of view. The third part of this paper will consider two exceptions to this overall picture, which are to be found in Dutch literature. Fourth and finally, the paper will focus on a period of change in Dutch memory culture in the mid-1990s. Since then, German points of view concerning the experiences of World War II have been acknowledged more widely in the Netherlands.

I. Stories of 'Good' and 'Bad' in Dutch memory

Following a long national tradition, the Netherlands remained neutral in the 1930s. With the important exception of various colonial wars far away, the last armed conflicts were the skirmishes with Belgium in 1830. World War I had passed the Netherlands by. So the Nazi attack on 10 May 1940 took Holland by surprise. The Dutch army was old-fashioned and poorly equipped and capitulated after an unequal battle of no more than five days, forced to do so by the bombing of Rotterdam on 14 May. The queen and government fled to London, where they tried to keep in touch with the resistance. What followed were five years of Nazi occupation, which are still seen as a major landmark in Dutch collective memory.

The main narrative that post-war Holland used to tell about these years emerges from an influential national television series *The Occupation*, which was broadcast between 1960 and 1965, the storyline of which was later summarised as follows:

> The Occupation is the history of the assault on an innocent and ignorant people which, however, due to its mental strength and indomitability, and under the inspiring leadership of its queen, defeats evil and in fact emerges unbroken and purified from this struggle. The costs are high, but justice triumphs.[1]

This was for a long time the Dutch master narrative of 'the War', as the Dutch call the Second World War, and the storyline smoothly fits into a long tradition in Dutch popular memory. The self-image of 'small but brave' is a founding myth of the Dutch Republic since its struggle for independence against Spain in the 16th century, and it also fits later battles against England and France – according to this self-image, small Holland always stood for the love of liberty and freedom, courage and the willingness to resist.[2]

The perspective of resistance also provided post-war society with its main categories of moral judgement: namely 'good' and 'bad'. This very polarised scheme between 'good' and 'bad' is typical for the Dutch memory landscape, especially the particular meaning of 'bad', or even 'wrong' or 'false'. The word 'fout' in Dutch has gained an entire new dimension of meaning since 'the War', politically as well as morally. It refers not so much to the German aggressors, but instead to the Dutch collaborators, who made 'wrong' choices during occupation. The Dutch National Socialists, never a major force in politics (up to 50,000 members in 1935, up to 10% regionally at elections), belong to this category, as well as all other Dutch collaborators. Attributing to them the adjective 'fout' excluded these Dutchmen symbolically from the national community after 1945. Because of this very polarised black-and-white scheme of remembering, bystanders, accommodators or non-acting people for a long time could simply identify with the heroic 'good' part of the nation, and it is only since the 1970s and 1980s that this majority of Dutchmen and their passive behaviour received more critical attention. The Germans, of course, represented in this view the un-Dutch evil that came from outside. This plot is also the narrative backbone of Dutch historiography, exemplified in the huge work of the Dutch historian Lou de Jong, whose *History of the Kingdom of the Netherlands During the Second World War* (14 volumes, 29 books, published between 1969 and 1991) is a kind of 'official' and state-sponsored history of the war, interspersed with clear moral judgements by the author.[3]

This storyline also was – and perhaps still is – the master narrative to be contested by different story types. In the post-war years, alternative versions of the past were primarily formulated in arts and literature. In academia, the dominating categories of 'good' and 'bad' in historiography were openly questioned since the 1970s, most visibly in an influential inaugural lecture in 1983 by Hans Blom, who, among other things, imported the views expressed in Martin Broszat's project on the 'Alltagsgeschichte' of the Bavarians into the Netherlands.[4] His lecture in favour of a more analytic perspective on the Occupation has informed much research since then, and it might today still be read as the dominant academic paradigm. But as Blom was retiring in April 2007, he stated that the spell of 'good and bad' still dominates the *public* memory of the war.[5] Indeed, as Ian Buruma has demonstrated for the debates around Pim Fortuyn and after the murder

of Theo van Gogh, Dutch national identity is – especially in crises –
still deeply rooted in Occupation stories, with their clear moral
frontlines.[6]

II. Germans and *their* suffering?
Let us now turn to the perceptions of the Germans in this *milieu de
memoire*, and to the question of how *their* wartime suffering has been
perceived in the Netherlands, if at all. The topic is seen today by most
of the Dutch public as a very interesting part of the history of Second
World War, but *not* as a story that affects Dutch history very much.
'Germans as victims' will cause no big controversies in the Netherlands.[7] Although there are some important exceptions, to which this
part will turn in the next section, two reasons for this very low key
attention in the Netherlands will first be considered.

First of all, in the Netherlands – as in many other countries – the
topic of German wartime suffering does not fit into the overarching
narrative of the Second World War, as was outlined above. German
victim stories cannot be located on the dominant good-bad axis – they
even seem to question this important tool of moral judgment. And
besides that, the Dutch memory about 'the War' has for a long time
been very Holland-centric. From the moment that critical questions
about the years of occupation started to be discussed, these questions
were aimed at the Dutch role in the persecution of the Dutch Jews. As
is widely known today, in the Netherlands an abnormally high percentage of Jews did not survive the Nazi occupation: no less than
107,000 of the 140,000 Dutch Jews were deported, 102,000 of whom
were murdered in the 'Vernichtungslager' of the Third Reich. Since
the 1960s, as the Holocaust has emerged as the cornerstone of western
memory, the Dutch were subconsciously aware of these uncomfort-
able events – although up until today there never really has been a
large public debate on the background to this question. (There have
been some heated debates on other aspects of Occupation history,
which could be interpreted as substitute debates for this crucial moral
question.[8]) But it was not until the 1990s that much-needed comparative research on the Nazi Occupation was pushed forward in Holland,
and even in 1997 international specialists judged that 'the historiography of the persecution of the Jews in the Netherlands has remained
primarily a domestic issue'.[9] In public memory, Anne Frank for
example had been remembered since the 1950s and 1960s as a

'symbol of national innocence', a symbol in which 'the fate of the Dutch and the Jewish people were unified'.[10] Of course, everybody knew that she was hidden by Dutchmen and murdered by Germans, but the truth that she also was betrayed by a Dutchman was publicly treated as a kind of 'subversive fact', which, as the one well-known exception to the rule, rather seemed to confirm the covering narratives of general Dutch resistance, victimhood, or passiveness. At best, the persecution of the Dutch Jews was traditionally conceived to be a matter between the Jews and the Germans, with the Dutchman in a not so very favourable position of non-acting bystander.[11]

Of course, this heroic and naïve story of the occupation years has also been thoroughly criticised since the end of the war. Jacques Pressers *Ondergang*, about the 'destruction of Dutch Jewry', caused a first shock in Dutch memory in 1965.[12] Since the 1980s, research programmes on different forms of collaboration, accommodation, profits etc. have been firmly pushed forward everywhere in Europe, and Holland was no exception. (Although, typically enough, one of the first profound works on Dutch collaboration under Nazi occupation other than De Jong's was presented abroad, by the German historian Gerhard Hirschfeld in 1984.[13]) Today, critical research has been published about Dutch police and bureaucracy, the fleeing Queen, the bitter consequences of the famous February strike of 1941, etc. The polarising 'goed' and 'fout' categories have again been forcefully attacked in a celebrated but controversial bestseller synthesis *Grijs Verleden* ('grey past') in 2001 by Chris van der Heijden.[14] Moreover, the myth of the resistance has lost much of its aura – so much so that it even appears to be an almost neglected field of research today.

And yet these examples show one thing: from the moment that the clear division between good and bad became muddy, this had consequences in the first place for the 'good' side of the spectrum, in that question marks were placed over the assumption that most Dutch people had been heroic resistance fighters who had resolutely helped the Jews in their catastrophic situation. At the other end of the moral spectrum the Dutch National Socialist movement to be sure became a well-researched area of the history of the War, but still it seemed to belong to a certain 'Other', to the forces of the unquestioned 'bad'. It is only in recent projects and debates that 'bad' Dutchmen, their motives, and their experiences have been treated with new academic and public curiosity. And compared to the Dutch National Socialist

Movement, the German occupiers were even more remote from the true national community of the Netherlands. They came from abroad, and their experiences, stories and feelings seemed to belong to a foreign world that brought all the Nazi calamities over innocent Holland. For a very long time after 1945 Germans still encountered coldness and open hostility in the Netherlands.[15] Until well into the 1990s, and with only few exceptions, the Dutch showed no particular interest in the German side of the history of the War. Typically, there is no monograph on the experiences of the occupation army in the Netherlands, let alone a broad interest in the experiences of 'normal Germans' during the war.

Next to this very national scope and the traditionally German-sceptical outline of Dutch memory, there is of course a second reason why German wartime suffering was never seen in the Netherlands as an urgent theme. This second reason lies in the Dutch (near-)non-participation in the armed battles in Europe and the liberation after World War II, at least on the Allied side. The role of mad and blood-thirsty enemies in various German victim stories may be played by raping Russians, by bombing British and Americans or by vengeful Czechs and Poles, but not by the Dutch, who had hardly caused the German 'Volksgemeinschaft' any harm. They did not liberate them-selves in a bloody battle for freedom. Except for some individual adventurers, Dutch forces had not joined the Allied armies in their march on Berlin. Dutch acts of revenge for the Occupation traumas were not taken out on Germans, but instead mostly on Dutch colla-borators – and especially Dutch girls who had dated German soldiers. In 1945, there were no German colonists in the Netherlands to expel; there were no conquered German territories to burn, and there was little German property to steal. All this meant that the Dutch seemed not to be involved in the debates on supposed Allied war crimes or German wartime suffering.

To go even further, the Dutch themselves seemed not really to have experienced any substantial war crimes that might be compared to the German experiences, and which could perhaps have evoked some understanding for the German war stories. No continuous bombing had taken place in the Netherlands, no Dutchmen – except for Dutch colonial populations in the Far East and, of course, the Jews – had been permanently expelled from their homelands, no large-scale rapes had been committed by the German enemy. So even from this point of view many of the 'typical' wartime suffering experiences from the German discourse were completely foreign to most of the Dutch. Even the bombing of Rotterdam, with about 800 dead civilians, was hardly comparable to the continuous bombing and firestorms in German cities – although the pure shock of the unexpected bomb attack in May 1940 caused deep wounds in Dutch memory.

So for a long time, the Germans could not count on Dutch understanding, recognition or even interest for those unfamiliar types of suffering 'in their own war' – suffering to which the Dutch themselves had delivered no contribution at all. This is the main reason for the long-lasting Dutch ignorance on this topic: It simply did not seem to concern the Dutch.

There are two exceptions to make to this overall picture. First, there had been quite a few Dutchmen that had witnessed German suffering themselves. 'Bad' Dutchmen were among them, for example Dutch Wehrmacht- or Waffen-SS soldiers who fought for Hitler. But their stories, experiences and testimonies had not been very popular in post-war Holland, to say the least. Other Dutch eyewitnesses of German wartime suffering were of course the approximately half a million forced labourers who had been working in the war industry in the Third Reich. But their often more differentiated stories about everyday life in wartime Germany never resonated either. In fact, their status in the Netherlands after 1945 was, for the majority of the nation remembering the war, still pretty suspect – what had they been doing in the enemy's country, had they tried hard enough to hide and escape, or did they perhaps like working for Hitler? – and they had not shared the nation-renewing fate of the last years of occupation. Still, it was often these voices from long neglected eye-witnesses that encountered the recent German victim discourse with understanding.

Another exception to this low-key interest in 'Germans as victims' by many Dutchmen is their often upset reaction to the *indirect* consequences of this storyline. First of all, Dutch observers protested strongly against any equation of German and Jewish victims, who are clearly considered to be more deserving of victim status. Further protest came in response to the reverse side of the 'Germans as victims' story, which is to represent the Allies as war criminals. Although the Dutch themselves were not implicated in this charge, in recent debates many of them nevertheless declared immediate solidarity, especially with the British and Americans. The sound of flying bombers crossing occupied Holland to attack cities in the Third Reich is remembered by older Dutchmen as the sound of hope and expectation. Moreover, the military history of the battles, the strategy and the frontlines of the Second World War have of course always been read by most Dutchmen from a Western Allied point of view, and Winston Churchill for this generation was a straightforward hero. The charge that these Allies may have been war criminals concerns many much more than the claim that Germans have been victims.

This argument even goes for some leftist groups in the Netherlands, which clung very strongly to the image of the Red Army as liberators. These Dutchmen did consider the stories about Russian revenge and rape as a threat to the reputation of communism – although anti-totalitarian rejection of the Soviet Union and its Red Army of course prevailed in Cold War Holland. Perhaps because of this context, the small Dutch Communist Party deliberately suppressed stories about the awful behaviour of many Russian soldiers. This happened, for instance, when some former Dutch inmates of the concentration camp of Ravensbrück in 1983 claimed to have witnessed how Red Army soldiers raped and abused women detained in the camp. The executive of the Dutch Communist Party more or less censored the story. To prevent the inversion of the image of the victorious liberators into inhuman war criminals was more important for the communist party than compassion with the victims or even curiosity about the historical truth. This episode, which was uncovered by sociologist Jolande Withuis in the early 1990s, was again brought to public attention in 1998 by conservative Dutch politician Frits Bolkestein – better known as a former EU Commissioner – in order to blame the communists for their crimes and for their falsification of history thereafter as well. But again, this debate was caused not by the question of 'Germans as victims', but of 'Soviets as perpetrators'. The victims in this case were antifascist women in Ravensbrück, some of them Dutch, not 'ordinary Germans'.[16]

To sum up, questions of German wartime suffering never were autonomous or urgent themes in Holland's historical memory, for two reasons: a very powerful national master narrative that sharply polarised between right and wrong behaviour and that concentrated on the Dutch context on the one hand, and the nearly total absence of the Dutch as potential perpetrators against German victims on the other.

The last two sections will consider some exceptions to this overall picture.

III. The German Point of View in Dutch Literature

The first and foremost exceptions to the overall low key treatment of the German point of view in Dutch memory are two novels by well known Dutch writers. *Het stenen Bruidsbed* (*The Stone Bridal Bed*) by Harry Mulisch (1959) and *De Tweeling* (*The Twins*) by Tessa de Loo (1993) were widely read books. Mulisch's *Het stenen Bruidsbed* is known as one of the first literary reflections on the bombing of Dresden.[17] It is a complex, multi-layered and partly philosophical, but very tempting book, full of mysterious references. In the novel, the American dentist Norman Corinth visits Dresden for a professional congress in 1956, over ten years after his first visit to the city as an aerial gunner of one of the bombers in February 1945. Mulisch tells both events, the stories of which constantly intertwine, metaphorically and semantically. In 1956, Corinth has a short affair with East German Hella, he meets witnesses of the bombing, and walks through the ruined cityscape, which is also visible from his hotel on a hill across the Elbe. Mulisch parallels the city and war with the woman and love: Corinth first captures and destroys Dresden, then captures and abuses Hella. Both events are narrated in similar terms.

Mulisch creates a very explicit ancient context for his story, by using many Trojan metaphors (Destruction of the city, names like Corinth and Hella, Corinth calls himself 'a Greek, slain under Agamemnon, but still alive' (78)), by using epic forms and verses and, as often mentioned, by using Homeric language. The author elaborates especially on the figure of the perpetrator, since Corinth turns out to have been one of the mysterious *Tiefflieger* at the Elbe, who, according to popular memory, consciously killed fleeing civilians on the river banks. In the story, this 'meaningless' crime puts him on the same level as other big war-criminals of history, such as Attila, Genghis Kahn, Hitler and Mao. In this way, the novel creates a universal and timeless setting:

> The city was dead before it died; the houses and churches stood erect in space but they were no longer standing on the earth: something was missing, it was not 1945, it was beyond history, it was a hundred thousand years before Christ. (61-2)

Mulisch even gives Corinth (Hegelian) philosophical thoughts about history in general, in which the Dresden bombing, as a senseless and meaningless event, without any consequences in the cause of history, is located outside of this history, 'as if the bombing never happened':

> Corinth closed his eyes even tighter and thought, it never *did* happen. Damn it. It never happened because it might as well not have happened: it was not part of a strategic plan, of the Second World War, like the massacres of other cities. The others had a purpose, and demonstrable results – like the massacre of Carthage, and Hiroshima; these pointed beyond themselves, as the battle of Troy was not about Troy but about Helen. Dresden was not like that. (…) He thought, there are two histories. (…) He thought, one is the history of the *spirit*, bloody but spiritual, with a purpose and results: Alexander, Caesar, Napoleon – Battle of Marathon, Battle of Dresden, Bombardment of Berlin, Hamburg. That is time, evolution. But beside it, under it, there is an anti-history in the stillness of death, and at certain intervals history sinks away in it. At such times the anti-history of Mao Dun Tanhu, Attila, Tamerlane, Genghis Kahn, Hitler, prevails. Then there is no more thought, no purpose, no result – only nothingness. There is no lapse of time between the massacres of the Huns and the concentration camps of Hitler. They lie side by side at the bottom of eternity. He thought, *and there lies Dresden.* Massacre of Aquilea, Massacre of Auschwitz – Massacre of Dresden. We smashed up Dresden because it was Dresden, just as the Jews were slaughtered because they were Jews. (95-6)

And with this last parallel, the book contains the controversial and so often debated equation between Allied and Nazi crimes, an equation to which Mulisch's character comes by universal historical reasoning. In this respect, and seen from the perspective of current German debates on German wartime suffering, the book is more interested in timeless perpetrators than in specific, individual German victims of the Dresden events.

Nevertheless, the story contains some impressive literary accounts on the events of 13 February 1945, formulated retrospectively by eye-witnesses, who trelated their memories to Mulisch when he visited Dresden in 1956. As Mulisch told Volker Hage:

> Da haben Leute in der Elbe gestanden, unter ihnen eine Frau mit einem Kind auf dem Arm, und das Kind ist tot. Solche Geschichten habe ich mir berichten lassen, ich habe mit vielen Menschen in Dresden gesprochen. Nein, ich hatte überhaupt keine Scham, das zu erzählen.[18]

These parts recall the tropes currently so popular in Germany, where mostly women and children are depicted, in order to stress the innocence of German victims. One of the contemporaries in *Het stenen Bruidsbed* tells about his wife:

> She wrapped the child in her skirts and began to run between walls of fire. Everything was on fire, the whole city, the streets had changed into ovens, but you could hardly see the flames for the smoke. In half a minute her hair and her clothes were scorched off her body and she was almost choked in the smoke, because the fire consumed all the oxygen. She said there was a smell of roast meat everywhere. In a square she found a tea-cosy which she put on her head and she recovered a little there until she had to run for cover from the bombs that came down amongst the refugees from Bohemia, crawling on top of each other like bleeding worms. (64)

But, apart from some contemporary stories, Mulisch didn't dwell on these reports: 'Ich wusste, von solchen schrecklichen Szenen brauche ich nur ganz wenige.'[19]

Because Harry Mulisch was already a well known writer in 1959, his *Het stenen Bruidsbed* received much attention from literary critics. Initially, many of their voices expressed mixed feelings, quite a few of them being rather sceptical, due to the unusual style and plot of the book. Some anti-communist authors rejected the book with political arguments: they accused Mulisch of reproducing the GDR point of view on the bombing of Dresden. Only a very few reviewers blamed Mulisch for the fact that he 'was concerned about the harm that the Germans in World War II had suffered, instead of caused'.[20] But this theme of German wartime suffering did not at all dominate the reception of the book.

However when, almost 35 years later, Tessa de Loo published her novel *De Tweeling* in 1993 the issue of German wartime suffering was central to the book's reception.[21] In the following debates, the two words 'German' and 'victim' were for the first time consciously coupled in Dutch public discourse, and the book provoked a new kind of autonomous interest for the German side of the story of the War. De Loo composes a story of German-born twins who are separated from each other when they are seven years old in 1923: The one girl, Anna, grows up in a traditional German farmer's family, the other, Lotte, grows up in an upper-class family in the Netherlands. The story of their parallel but opposite lives is framed as a backward-looking conversation between Anna and Lotte, who coincidently meet again at the end of their lives in the Belgian health resort of Spa. Whereas German Anna is happy to see her long missed sister again, Dutch

Lotte keeps her distance and rejects Anna, because she is German. Over a couple of days, the two sisters tell each other their stories, full of reproaches and mutual misunderstandings.

In contrast to Mulisch's *Het stenen Bruidsbed, De Tweeling* is a very clear and transparent story without philosophical claims. In the retrospective form of the storytelling of two older ladies, the book recognises the importance of the past in present culture and makes 'remembering' its central theme. The dialogues between Anna and Lotte become a kind of conversation between the Netherlands and Germany: the German Anna on the one hand, asking for understanding and recognition, telling the suffering of her life (including a bad education, a marriage with a German SS soldier who died at the front, no children and hard work); and the Dutch Lotte, whose future Jewish bridegroom had been deported and murdered, on the other hand, being proud, rejecting her sister and her stories as apologies. Lotte openly blames her sister for the War and the death of her boyfriend:

> 'At least you had a grave you could go to', said Lotte coolly. She was disinclined to get carried away by the story of Anna's pilgrimage to the grave of her SS officer. Lost in thought, Anna looked at her. 'How do you mean?' 'There was no cemetery at Mauthausen.' (360)

Understanding rather than forgiving or remembering is the main theme, and in this respect Lotte slightly develops throughout the novel. 'I do not believe', says Lotte to Anna, 'I need to understand. First, all of you people set fire to the world and on top of that you want us to go deeply into your motives.' (29) Although Lotte remains unconciliatory, her conscience pricks her later, as she thinks by herself: 'Would you ever have been able to say to her what she actually wanted to hear, which had become everything to her? Would you ever have succeeded in squeezing out those two words: "I understand..."?' (390) In short, Anna's German life story is told by De Loo more convincingly, and her character is more round and sympathetic than Lotte's.

Tessa de Loo afterwards explicitly admitted that she had written the book to confront the Dutch with their own unfair prejudices, and with the 'obvious truth', that most Germans had suffered 'as much' from National Socialism as the Dutchmen had done.[22] In the form of conversation, or even confrontation, the Dutch audience for the first time was directly faced with a German perspective on the events of National Socialism and the Second World War. *De Tweeling* in 1993 immediately became a huge commercial success in the Netherlands: it sold over 130.000 copies in the first year and won various prizes, for example the Dutch 'Publieksprijs 1994' (readership's prize). De Loo said she never received as many reactions from readers as she received after the publication of *De Tweeling*. But not all reactions were positive. Interestingly, many professional reviewers in different newspapers criticised the book, mainly because it was not a skilled masterwork of literary art, but a rather simple story. Very few of them acknowledged the supposed taboo-breaking issue. Instead, some reviewers were even hostile to De Loo's pedagogical purpose: 'The poor German people had been blinded, it says ... of all the nerve!'[23] Notwithstanding the success of De Loo's novel, such views still could count on major popular support in the Netherlands. To go even further, one of the main reasons for the huge interest in the novel might have been the sharp tension between De Loo's story, mainly the Anna part, and the public debates about Germany in the Dutch media of the early 1990s. After the publication of *De Tweeling* in November 1993 one of the newspapers wrote that it was 'heartbreaking to see how happy the staff of the Amsterdam Goethe Institut were about the fact that in the Netherlands finally a book was presented in which the Germans for a change were *not* the personification of evil'.[24]

Indeed, the publication of *De Tweeling* appeared right in the middle of a straightforward crisis in Dutch-German relations in the early 1990s. Anti-German feelings had increased heavily in Dutch public life after 1990 and they disturbed official bilateral politics. Some features of this short ice-age were, besides of course a series of symbolic national soccer games between 1988 and 1992, a general Dutch anxiety about a bigger Germany, some overheated Dutch reactions to neo-Nazis in the new 'Bundesländer' in 1993 (after the racists attacks in Solingen in May 1993, the Dutch media started a coordinated campaign, which resulted in no less than 1.2 million Dutch postcards with the text 'I am angry' arriving in the 'Kanzleramt' in Bonn), the German (and French) veto against Dutch politician Ruud Lubbers' application for President of the European Commission in 1994, and the discovery that the third Dutch generation after 'the War' had as strong or even stronger anti-German feelings than their parents and grandparents had.[25] In this climate, sceptical reactions to a novel like *De Tweeling* initially were almost natural. Some Dutchmen now did acknowledge the suffering of some 'good Germans' like Anna from *De Tweeling* – which she was not, by the way! – , but these 'good Germans' were conceptually separated from the supposed majority: 'Good Germans are not real Germans'.[26]

This is not the place to dwell on those Dutch-German relations, but it may be clear that the perception of Germany in the Netherlands played a major role in the willingness of the Dutch to acknowledge German war experiences. The unpopularity of Germany has decreased substantially since those mid-1990s. And without suggesting that the book *De Tweeling* played a major role in this process, it is true that its prize-winning story has reached a huge audience and had a great influence in public life, including public and partially self-critical debates about its content. The story was filmed in 2002 by Ben Sombogaart and the movie was even nominated for an Oscar. Now, the reactions were much more relaxed than ten years earlier, although some critics this time blamed the story – pretty up to date, in regard of academic debates on memory – for not presenting any guilty perpetrators anymore.

IV. Elements of Change

A turning point in Dutch public perceptions of German wartime stories – and of 'the War' in general – seems to have been, as in so many European societies, the commemoration year of 1995. Three events are particularly important in this respect.

First of all, the influence of wartime memory on present Dutch-German relations was explicitly debated with respect to the commemorations of May 1995. Dutch media and politicians discussed the idea of inviting German guests to the commemorations of the fiftieth anniversary of the end of the Occupation. The field was first explored on various local levels in the summer of 1994 in the south of the Netherlands, where the mayors of Maastricht – which was liberated in the autumn of 1944 – and Arnhem – where the Allied advance was blocked – proposed remembering those historical events together with neighbouring German communities across the border. However, they quickly withdrew the plan following angry reactions from their Dutch citizens. In the months that followed, a long and animated debate took place about the question of a joint commemoration on the national level, in order to demonstrate the reconciliation 50 years after 'the War'. In this debate negative stereotypes took turns with more differentiated positions. Dozens of readers wrote letters, the opinion pages of the newspapers were full of reactions, self-critical arguments about the typical good-and-bad pattern of Dutch memory, but also bad names and prejudices, and original stories and memories. The discussion seemed to be a pretty open introspection of Dutch identity and memory, and it deserves a more reliable study than can be delivered here. Even when the result of the debate was the rejection of the plan, the explicit debates contributed to a certain relaxation of Dutch-German relations, as well as of Dutch memory of 'the War'.[27]

This already became clear as, secondly, the commemoration year of 1995 began. In February the Dutch newspapers paid a lot of attention to the fiftieth anniversary of the bombing of Dresden. Partly, this coverage was due to the big German ceremonies: reports were written by correspondents in Germany, and Dutch 'news' now was just a function of German news. But on the other hand, some impressive independent stories appeared in Dutch media. Harry Mulisch was interviewed time and again about his old *Het stenen Bruidsbed*, and many commentators critically reflected on the Allied strategy of the bombing war. All in all, it seemed that during the commemorations of 1995 Dutch opinion on Germany had changed somewhat in favour of a less black-and-white scheme of memory.

Thirdly, considerable influence on these processes of normalisation was exercised through the conscious memory politics of the Dutch and German governments. Political leaders on both sides reacted to the bilateral tensions of the early 1990s with a concentrated programme of speeches and mutual visits, some of which were directly devoted to history. Thus, Queen Beatrix used her traditional Christmas address of 1994 to make some critical remarks concerning certain Dutch myths about the Occupation years and about the Resistance Movement. On the 5 May 1995 she expressed her respect for the open and critical ways in which Germany faced the Nazi past, which was a quite remarkable comment in an official commemoration speech on Dutch Liberation Day. Later that month, chancellor Helmut Kohl officially visited the Netherlands, where his tour was greatly appreciated because he succeeded in finding 'the right tone' in speaking to the Dutch people. According to Friso Wielenga these mutual government actions made the year 1995 a turning point in post-Wende bilateral relations between the Netherlands and Germany.[28]

Beneath the surface of such remarkable events in the 'memory year' lies of course a set of social and cultural developments which accompany the slow shift in the Dutch memory landscape in the 1990s. Among them we find some of the same factors that also pushed forward the victims debate in Germany, such as the end of the cold war order in Europe, including a certain depoliticisation and Europe-anisation of remembering, [29] and the well-known generational developments, including Norbert Frei's 'Abschied der Zeitgenossenschaft' and Jan Assmann's development of 'cultural' forms of memory.

Another force behind the 'opening up' of Dutch historical consciousness might have been the emergence of memory studies themselves. Since cultural and historical sciences everywhere in the Western world have turned to the memory paradigm, the different forms of collective remembering have moved to the centre of professional and public interest in the Netherlands, too. Since the 1990s, various comparative studies on Dutch historical culture and research into transnational memory processes have *historicised* the national scope of traditional Dutch war-memory as well as putting Dutch developments in an *international* context. Such reflexive projects in turn shape much of public debate and media output and this has resulted in a certain emancipation from national memory stories. For example, the old reactions to *De Tweeling* of 1993 had already turned into history ten years later, as Dutch newspaper *NRC* made them the object of journalistic retrospection themselves, thereby quasi-remembering its own earlier memory work. [30]

Thus, historicisation and internationalisation together have started to shape the Dutch wartime memory landscape since the mid-1990s. This has robbed the issue of German suffering of much of its potential to give offence, as the following examples might demonstrate. First, Paul Verhoeven's 2006 movie *Zwartboek* (*Black Book*) about the occupation years and Dutch resistance movement, is an explicit and therefore reflexive comment on his earlier and more heroic movie of *Soldaat van Oranje* (*Soldier of Orange*, 1977). *Black Book* even presents one German officer as a 'good' human being, who is unjustly shot, thus turning at least some German soldiers, who had been collectively evil in *Soldaat van Oranje*, into human victims of the war. Secondly, Dutch memory institutions and museums increasingly cooperate with international and especially German partners, thus exploring (and building) European patterns of remembering. Dutch-German memory confrontation is further reduced by such international networks, which seem to professionalise but also to synchronise 'official' European memory.[31] Thirdly, in academic history many memory projects are designed today from a comparative point of view. National divisions along former frontlines are less interesting. For example, the experiences of so-called 'war children', and their emergence as a public collective, are studied everywhere in Europe.[32]

Such varied perspectives demonstrate that the stories of German loss and mourning today are less offensive for Dutch identity than they were in the 1950s, the 1980s or the early 1990s. They even demonstrate that stories about German history today are less *important* for Dutch national identity, as the low-key reactions to recent German perceptions of their own victimhood have shown. Dutch debates on collective memory now seem to follow international developments and when talking about German history they simply respond to German events. The Goldhagen Debate, the 'Wehrmacht' exhibition or the building of the 'Denkmal für die ermordeten Juden Europas' were broadly covered in Dutch newspapers. Agenda setters are Dutch correspondents in Berlin as well as specialists at German Studies centres or universities. It might even be hard to distil a specific 'Dutch' view on such issues. In general, the strongest prejudices about Germans and their fate in 'their own war' have disappeared, it seems, although the Occupation years themselves still are at the core of Dutch cultural identity and although the traditional stories of 'good' and 'bad' are never far away.

Notes

[1] Frank Van Vree, *In de schaduw van Auschwitz. Herinneringen, beelden, geschiedenis*, Groningen: Historische Uitgeverij, 1995, p. 64, my translation. Van Vree's lines have been recycled in many useful studies, such as Friso Wielenga, 'Erinnerungskulturen im Vergleich. Deutsche und niederländische Rückblicke auf die NS-Zeit und den Zweiten Weltkrieg', and Frank van Vree, 'Denkmäler ohne Sockel. Der Zweite Weltkrieg und die Transformation der historischen Kultur in den Niederlanden', both in: *Jahrbuch des Zentrums für Niederlande-Studien*, 12 (2001), 11-30 and 59-80, as well as Hans Marks and Friederike Pfannkuche, 'Die Toleranz der Generationen. Wie gut und Böse in den Niederlanden unterschieden werden', in: Harald Welzer, ed., *Der Krieg der Erinnerung. Holocaust, Kollaboration und Widerstand im europäischen Gedächtnis*, Frankfurt/M.: Fischer, 2007, pp. 112-49.

[2] Wielenga, 'Erinnerungskulturen im Vergleich', p. 11.

[3] CF. Pieter Lagrou, *The Legacy of Nazi occupation. Patriotic memory and national recovery in Western Europe, 1945-1965*, Cambridge: Cambridge University Press, 2000.

[4] Hans Blom, 'In de ban van goed en fout? Wetenschappelijke geschiedschrijving over de bezettingstijd in Nederland', in: Blom, *In de ban van goed en fout. Geschiedschrijving over de bezettingstijd in Nederland*, Amsterdam: Boom, 2007, pp. 9-30.

[5] Hans Blom, 'Een kwart eeuw later. Nog altijd in de ban van goed en fout?', in: Blom, pp. 133-54

[6] Ian Buruma, *Murder in Amsterdam. The Death of Theo van Gogh and the Limits of Tolerance*, New York: The Penguin Press, 2006.

[7] Cf. Patrick Dassen, Ton Nijhuis and Krijn Thijs, eds., *Duitsers als slachtoffers. Het einde van een taboe?*, Amsterdam: Mets en Schilt, 2007.

[8] For example the debates in the 1970s about the treatment of war criminals (Hinke Piersma, *De Drie van Breda. Duitse oorlogsmisdadigers in Nederlandse gevangenschap, 1945-1989*, Amsterdam: Balans, 2005) or in the 1990s about the return of Jewish survivors after 1945 (Martin Bossenbroek, *De Meelstreep*, Amsterdam: Bakker, 2001).

[9] Bob Moore, *Victims and Survivors. The Nazi Persecution of the Jews in the Netherlands 1940-1945*, London a.o.: Arnold, 1997, p. 2. Wolfgang Seibel, 'The strength of perpetrators – The Holocaust in Western Europe, 1940-1944', *Governance* 15:2 (2002), 211-40.

[10] Van Vree, 'Denkmäler ohne Sockel', p. 71-2.

[11] Cf. Ido De Haan, *Na de ondergang. De herinnering aan de Jodenvervolging in Nederland 1945-1995*, Den Haag: SDU Uitgevers, 1997, p. 229.

[12] Translated as: J. Presser, *Ashes in the Wind. The destruction of Dutch Jewry*, London: Souvenir Press, 1968.

[13] Gerhard Hirschfeld, *Fremdherrschaft und Kollaboration. Die Niederlande unter deutscher Besatzung*, Stuttgart: Deutsche Verlags-Anstalt, 1984.

[14] Chris van der Heijden, *Grijs verleden. Nederland en de Tweede Wereldoorlog*, Amsterdam and Antwerp: Contact, 2001. Krijn Thijs, 'Kontroversen in Grau. Revision und Moralisierung der niederländischen Besatzungszeit', in: Nicole Colin, Matthias Lorenz und Joachim Umlauf, eds., *Täter und Tabu. Grenzen der Toleranz in deutschen und niederländischen Geschichtsdebatten*, Essen: Schriftenreihe der Bibliothek für Zeitgeschichte, 2011, forthcoming.

[15] Cf. Friso Wielenga, *Vom Feind zum Partner. Die Niederlande und Deutschland seit 1945*, Münster: Agenda, 2000, esp. pp. 297ff.

[16] Jolande Withuis, 'Het verlies van onschuld van het geheugen', in: Withuis, *De jurk van de kosmonaute. Over politiek, cultuur en psyche*, Amsterdam: Boom, 1995, pp. 32-59; Withuis, 'Ravensbruck en het gelijk van Bolkestein', *De volkskrant*, 22 November 1997; Withuis, 'Ina Brouwer en het stalinistisch geweten', *Trouw*, 14 February 1998; Elsbeth Etty, 'Ravensbrück', *NRC*, 14 February 1998.

[17] All quotes are from the English translation by Adrienne Dixon, London, New York and Toronto: Unknown Binding, 1962. See also: Volker Hage, *Zeugen der Zerstörung. Die Literaten und der Luftkrieg. Essays und Gespräche*, Frankfurt/M.: Fischer, 2003, pp. 223-34.

[18] Hage, *Zeugen der Zerstörung*, p. 230.

[19] Ibid., p. 230.

[20] See the 'Receptiegeschiedenis' by J. A. Dautzenberg, *De sleutel in de kast*, pp. 213-24, quote at p. 215.

[21] All quotes are from the English translation by Ruth Levitt, London: Soho Press, 2000.

[22] *NRC*, 5 November 1993.

[23] Hans Warren, quoted in: Pieter Steinz, 'Dubbellief en dubbelleed', *NRC*, 1 May 2004.

[24] 'Het verzet van Tessa de Loo tegen Na-oorlogs verzet', *Algemeen Dagblad*, 6 November 1993.

[25] See Wielenga, *Vom Feind zum Partner*, esp. p. 402, p. 408-12.

[26] Albert de Lange, 'Mogen wij nog anti-Duits zijn?', *Het Parool*, 6 November 1993.

[27] See Wielenga, 'Erinnerungskulturen im Vergleich', p. 29 and p. 30.

[28] Wielenga, *Vom Feind zum Partner*, pp. 411-13.

[29] For the influence of the Cold War on German memory see Bill Niven, *Facing the Nazi past*, London: Routledge, 2002, pp. 1-9 and on Dutch memory see Jolande Withuis, *Na het kamp. Vriendschap en politieke strijd*, Amsterdam: De Bezige Bij, 2005.

[30] Pieter Steinz, 'Dubbellief en dubbelleed', *NRC*, 1 May 2004.

[31] For some sceptical comments on this process, see my 'Vergleichen, Austauschen, Abstimmen? Tagungsbericht zum 39. Bundesweiten Gedenkstättenseminar', in: H-Soz-u-Kult, 11.06.2003, http://www.hsozkult.geschichte.hu-berlin.de/tagungsberichte/id=239.

[32] See Michael Heinlein's chapter in this volume. See also I. Tames, 'War experience of the children of Dutch Nazi-collaborators', in: M. Abbenhuis and S. Buttsworth, eds., *New Curtains on the Theatre of War: Non-Combatants and the impact of War in the Western World*, Basingstoke: Palgrave Macmillan, 2008.

Annette Seidel-Arpacı

The Miracle Workers: 'German Suffering', Israeli Masculinity, and the Feminised/Queered Nation as Redemptive in Eytan Fox's *Walk On Water*

This chapter traces representations and constructions of transgenerationally suffering Germans, here as grandchildren of perpetrators, of German and Israeli identities, and of redemptive queerness in *Walk On Water* (Eytan Fox, Israel 2004). It discusses how notions of gendered/queered national identities and the search for redemptive narratives can intertwine in cultural production and (in)form perspectives on young Germans as a traumatised generation which has nevertheless acquired a different access to and sense of fluid gendered identities presented in stark contrast to Israeli nationalist hyper-masculinity. The chapter suggests that in *Walk On Water* the new 'Germanness' has to be feminised and queered in order to establish a redemptive narrative and the possibility for a common ground between Germans and Israelis after the Holocaust.

A woman interviewed in Germany by the Israeli film-maker Asher Tlalim for his 1994 film *Don't Touch My Holocaust* recounts: 'My sister once said to my father "You are a murderer," and there he was, my poor father. He is a poor murderer.'[1] The empathy for the problematic relationships of Germans to parents who were perpetrators, fellow travellers or bystanders during National Socialism in Tlalim's filmic essay from 1994 is taken up, if in differently pronounced ways, ten years later by Eytan Fox in his feature film *Walk On Water.* Partly filmed in Berlin and subsequently celebrated at the 2004 *Internationale Filmfestspiele Berlin*, the movie achieved international acclaim and has won several awards. While *Walk On Water* may reflect debates about nationalist sexual politics and – albeit Eurocentric – queer masculinity in Israel, the same movie in a German context could be considered as a 'we-are-all-victims' narrative, feeding into the widespread claim to victimhood pertaining to WWII as well as post-1945 Germany,[2] and as a call for Germans to be(come) saviours, rescuing Israelis from their emotionally entrapped and violent selves. The German main characters are depicted as traumatised by their family's implication in the Holocaust, yet, as opposed to the Israeli main protagonist, they are empathetic to other people's plights. In *Walk On Water*, we see, for instance, encounters between Germans and Palestinians which are depicted as not possible between Jews and Palestinians – primarily due to the racism of Israeli Jews towards Arabs. However, there is no racism implied for the German lead characters. Rather they seem free from prejudice against any 'others'. The gendering/queering of the young Germans in the movie sets them in contrast to the nationalist heteronormative Israeli. Thus the following is also a critique of the idealising desire for a queer utopia.

This chapter argues, firstly, that despite the bridging of locales and the sideways glances towards 'other' histories, *Walk On Water* sidelines 'the Other' both within the German and the Israeli context. This move is the necessary ground upon which the relationships between the main characters are developed into a redemptive narrative. Secondly, this paper suggests that the German main characters, Axel and Pia, are presented as in touch with their emotions, able to empathise with 'the Other' and free from racist prejudices, and thus as queer and female protagonists set in stark contrast to the Israeli main character, the nationalist macho Eyal. The third point pertains to the movie's representation of suffering and trauma, and it is argued that *Walk On Water* is not only concerned with Eyal's trauma but also construes a second and third generation trauma for Axel and Pia. Yet, as opposed to Eyal, they are able to deal with their (family) history, and hence can give Eyal a way to open up and confront his violence and pain.

Walk On Water relates the story of Mossad agent Eyal – who is seen at the beginning of the movie killing a leader of Hamas in broad daylight in İstanbul – and his latest mission: the assassination of the Nazi Alfred Himmelmann. Himmelmann had been declared dead by his family but we later learn that he had been in hiding ever since 1945, with the help and support of his son and daughter-in-law. Eyal's task is to track him down, and for this purpose he has to get close to Himmelmann's granddaughter, Pia, who lives on a kibbutz in Israel. The Mossad has become aware of the upcoming visit of Pia's younger brother Axel to Israel. Eyal poses as a tour guide to find out what Pia and Axel know about the whereabouts of their grandfather, and he ends up spending a lot of time with both. It turns out that Axel has arrived to convince Pia to come to Berlin for their father's 70th birthday celebration.

Pia, however, had turned away from her parents after finding out that her grandfather was alive and in hiding. Axel knew nothing about it and is shocked that Pia did not tell him before. They both know that their grandfather is a wanted Nazi. Meanwhile, Eyal has to cope with the very recent suicide of his wife Iris, yet as a tough Israeli man he is not able to confront his pain and grief, and he refuses to go to therapy sessions. It is later suggested that Iris had killed herself precisely because of Eyal's line of work. In *Walk On Water* all the characters are haunted by the past, and Fox suggests that they can only confront their shared and divided pasts together and beyond what the movie presents as Israeli inability to deal with traumata. After befriending Pia and Axel in Israel, Eyal is invited by Axel to come to Berlin for a visit. This trip to Berlin is life-changing for Eyal: here he encounters a society that is not at all what he had expected. This surprise in the encounter with Germany takes various forms and after his arrival Eyal is being confronted with a Berlin that is far removed from the Israeli machismo he represents. Fox has Eyal enter into the new Berlin which is most notably a world of openness and diversity. While in Israel, Eyal was upset about the fact that Axel was gay, in Berlin he begins to open up even to the extent of inquiring about Axel's preferences for sex. Eyal accompanies Axel to the birthday celebration of the father. The Nazi Himmelmann arrives as a surprise for his son, and Eyal leaves to meet with his boss Menachem who is also in Berlin by now. Later, Eyal returns with the aim to kill Himmelmann in his sleep but finds himself unable to go through with it. Instead, Axel kills his grandfather, and at the end of the film, Pia and Eyal live together in Israel and have a child.

Bridging Waters, Bridging Languages

While *Walk On Water* attempts to bridge histories and contemporaneities via the inclusion of particular locales and references to 'other' histories and memories, the movie nevertheless sidelines 'the Other' within both the German and the Israeli context. On this basis the film develops its redemptive narrative. The movie's opening shots are set in İstanbul, taken from the perspective of passengers aboard one of the many boats regularly used for public transportation as well as by tourists exploring the city. The boat approaches Bosphorus bridge, and we see the first shots of the main character, Eyal, who seems to be relaxed, taking photos while smiling to a little boy in front of him.

Only a few minutes later, it becomes clear that Eyal's presence was not one of leisure pursuit but was rather aimed at assassinating a fellow passenger – the father of the boy – later identified as Abu-Ibrahim, a Hamas leader. After Eyal has injected an apparently deadly substance into Abu-Ibrahim while passing by, he falls to the ground, with his wife calling out his name, and – by inserting the word 'Habibi' – the director makes the audience aware of the family's Arab background. The little boy stands and watches Eyal quickly disappear by way of a waiting car; the boy's tears will be revisited in later sequences: his pain comes to stand in for human suffering in general, and specifically for the respective sufferings and traumata of Palestinians and Israelis. This link is alluded to in the repetition of the close-up of the boy's tear-streaked face in a later dream sequence – the boy's face fades out to be replaced by the face of Iris and her tears. The initial murder scene is the first glimpse of the suffering the emotionally hardened Israeli macho represents and causes, construed as redeemable by a queered national identity – and the scene will echo later in Eyal's attempt – and Axel's act – of killing Himmelmann.

In *Walk On Water* the city of İstanbul, with its many literal and figuratively construed bridges between histories, cultures, religions, comes to represent the first bridge between Israel's and Germany's varied and painfully interwoven present. But just as 'the Arabs' figure mainly at the sidelines of an essentially (Jewish) Israeli-German dilemma, so do 'the Turks'. Nicholas Baer argues that 'Turks are evoked both through the protagonists' professional work and through the inclusion of Istanbul among the film's geographical "stations" (alongside Jerusalem and Berlin)'.[3] After his arrival in Israel, Axel tells Eyal that he wanted to do something useful with his life, and so is working at an organisation that 'helps children of immigrants', such as the Turks. Apart from this reference to Turkish-Germans, the only other moment in the movie dealing with 'Turks', without any Turkish-Germans ever being present, occurs when Axel explains to Eyal that he had never been with 'a German', and amongst the nationalities of his lovers he also recounts 'Turks'. Apart from Eyal and Axel's chance meeting with a group of drag queens in Berlin, individuals from a non-white, not 'German-German' background are not present beyond Axel's mentioning of Turks as lovers and in the context of an earlier conversation with Eyal about circumcision in Europe. In particular during Axel's visit in Israel, his encounters with Eyal have a decidedly homoerotic air, yet the gap between the two locales and between the men can only be bridged after Eyal comes to Berlin and it becomes obvious that he speaks German, and after his hostility begins to make way for curiosity. While an earlier scene already alludes to a shared commonality – both men are covered from head to toe in mud at the Dead Sea – it is ultimately their shared language and openness to one another's experience that can provide the ground for a deeper commonality. According to Jacques Derrida, who asks whether there can be 'in one way or another, a scene of forgiveness without a shared language',

> this sharing is not only that of a national language or an idiom, but that of an agreement on the meanings of words, their connotations, rhetoric, the aim of a reference, etc. [...] when the victim and the guilty share no language, when nothing common and universal permits them to understand one another, forgiveness seems deprived of meaning.[4]

Eyal makes no such effort to find a shared language when it comes to Palestinians – and we are led to believe that this is true of his relationship with his wife, Iris, also. Upon leaving the Old City after Eyal forced Rafik's uncle to give most of the money back Axel had paid for a jacket,[5] Rafik knocks on the window of the car and asks Eyal whether he may say just one sentence. The comment turns out to be a critique of Jewish Israeli neglect of Palestinian suffering but is cut off mid-sentence by Eyal with the words 'that's already three sentences'.[6] At this point, switching from English which allows Pia and Axel into the conversation, Rafik addresses Eyal in Hebrew yet there is no common 'agreement on the meaning of words'. This fact is further amplified by Rafik's short last sentence – thanking Eyal for a lift from Tel Aviv to Jerusalem – which contains words in Arabic, Hebrew and English and is naturally perfectly understood by Eyal. Axel, Pia and Eyal, on the other hand, do have a wider language in common – if strongly patronising on Axel's part. In Berlin, when Eyal attempts to explain his previous behaviour and his pain, Axel responds with an empathic 'It's okay', and adds, 'eat your currywurst'.

In *Walk On Water*, racism of Israeli Jews against Arabs is represented. Yet there is no hint of potential prejudices the German characters might harbour. After Axel has spent the night with Rafik, Eyal is taken aback both by the very idea of gay sex and, additionally, by Rafik's ethnic background. *Walk On Water* repeatedly implies that

Eyal may be able to empathise with 'the Other' within the Israeli-Palestinian context if he softens his tough masculinity and moves towards reconciliation with his own German-Jewish heritage and trauma. The moving towards one another is facilitated by Axel and Pia who represent a new German generation. Yet, the new 'Germanness' remains safely – if queered – within national parameters and ethnicised boundaries and, just as the movie sidelines non-Ashkenazi or Palestinian queers and Arabs of all genders in general, even more so do 'other Germans' remain almost invisible and without voice.

Gent(i)le Touch
While the Israeli main protagonist is a nationalist and hyper-masculine Mossad agent, the German main characters, Axel and Pia, are presented as able to express emotions and empathise with 'the Other'. As queer and female protagonists they are set in stark contrast to the macho Eyal. The movies and TV series directed by Eytan Fox are part of Israeli new queer productions. Amongst several other feature films, Fox directed *Yossi and Jagger* (2002) which premiered at the Berlinale in 2003 while *Walk on Water* was being shot in Berlin. *Yossi and Jagger* is a movie about a secret love affair between two male soldiers in the Israeli army; it thus explores Israeli masculinity and gay relationships, issues at the heart of Fox's filmmaking.

But if the new queer cinema has stimulated questions about Israeli masculinity and gay relationships, it has done little to push forward Ashkenazi-Mizrahi ones. Queer cinema in Israel is dominated by, and thereby constructs and enforces, an Ashkenazi gay normative identity. According to Raz Yosef, this process functions not least through 'the repetition of a colonial fantasy that confines Mizrahi men to a rigid set of ethnic roles and identities'.[7] He points out that the 'exotic Oriental boy and the hyper-masculine Mizrahi male are major images through which Mizrahi men become visible in the Ashkenazi urban gay subculture'.[8] This orientalising gaze is also directed towards Palestinians and other Arabs, albeit in this case fraught with additional layers complicating the issue of queer and national positionalities. Yosef discusses and critiques several of Fox's productions, for instance for the avoidance of dealing with the specific experience of 'coming out' for Mizrahi queers, by representing a Mizrahi gay man as already 'out' – such as in the TV series *Florentin* by Fox.

In *Walk On Water,* this is also how Rafik, Axel's Palestinian lover, is constructed. His background merely matters in the context of Israeli/Jewish-German history and trauma. On the one hand, Fox points to precisely this problem in Jewish-Arab relations in Israel when he has Rafik address Eyal in Hebrew after the farewell scene with Pia and Axel. On the other hand, *Walk On Water* simultaneously repeats and perpetuates the invisibility of the particular conditions that non-Jewish Arab queers encounter. Rafik is apparently 'out' in Tel Aviv, where he works, but we do not learn whether this is true in his home in Beit Jalla near Jerusalem. The only space unambiguously permitting openness and fluidity we are presented with is the gay nightclub in Tel Aviv which Axel, Pia and, reluctantly, Eyal visit – yet this club also potentially suggests sameness of queer experience. In contrast to Eyal, the German siblings are depicted as perfectly comfortable with Palestinians and in queer spaces. The potentially orientalist gaze and desire on Axel's part appears only fleetingly in his patronising attitude towards Rafik and in a later comment about his lovers. Upon Eyal's outburst at Menachem's office after he had learned that Axel was gay, another Mossad agent makes fun of Eyal and his latest mission. Apart from Menachem, who has survived the Holocaust, all the other agents are younger and represent the masculine Sabra in the context of an Ashkenazi-dominated intelligence service. Jeffrey T. Richelson points out that the actor Lior Ashkenazi (Eyal),

> has been described as having 'the debonair subtlety and charisma of an Israeli Clive Owen', and as 'hawkishly handsome'. He also has 'the fearless flair of a thriller cop' and 'lightning physical reflexes' – as demonstrated in a fight scene in which he skillfully handles three German skinheads who had started beating a group of transvestites.[9]

When Axel asks him if he ever wonders why suicide bombers are willing to kill themselves, Eyal responds: 'What's to think? They're animals.' Later he complains to Menachem in a phone conversation that he is 'stuck with this pseudo-liberal who talks about suicide bombers' motives', and that Axel 'wants to see Palestinians. He's such a nudnik […]. I might drown him in the Dead Sea'. The pronounced contrast between the gentle Axel and a tough Eyal comes to the fore repeatedly. However, not unlike other representations of (usually male) Mossad agents in literature and film, Eyal is emotionally detached – a psychological state given physical form by a tear duct problem that prevents his shedding tears. But it is more than an inability to cry that results in his emotionless reaction when he returns from a mission to find that his wife has committed suicide.[10]

Thus, Eyal stands in for a whole traumatised Israeli generation that can only be redeemed through what will, towards the end of *Walk On Water*, appear like a miracle. While Pia and Axel dance a Hora at the kibbutz, Eyal sneaks into Pia's room and plants a surveillance device, and later – after having listened to the siblings' conversations – reports to Menachem that 'Hansel and Gretel' had been arguing all evening. Raz Yosef argues that Eyal's

> [l]istening in on Axel and Pia speaking in German constitutes a kind of symbolic reenactment of the primal scene in which the child eavesdrops on his parents' intimate secret. In this retroactive reconstruction of the traumatic scene of origin, Eyal witnesses the process of his own creation, his muted history, the unspoken Holocaust past that has constituted his subjectivity. Moreover, like Freud's 'Wolf Man' who disguised the primal scene in a children's fairy tale about wolves in order to facilitate a discussion of the event that had not been registered in his consciousness, so too does Eyal displace the trauma of his Holocaust-survivor parents to the legend of 'Hansel and Gretel', the German children who survived a trauma of physical abuse, in order to represent the unrepresentable.[11]

Yet, if we were to follow this reading further, not only does Eyal displace the trauma, he displaces it to a fairy tale which ends with the children's revenge: they burn the 'witch' who had imprisoned them. She is represented in the legend as woman who lives alone outside of a community, and as ugly, evil, and particularly preying on children. Thus the roles of the children and the 'witch' can in fact be read in reverse, since she is the outsider who has to be murdered for the German children to be safe. The German fairy tale is repeated in the movie, though with a considerable shift: 'Hansel and Gretel' are gay and female, and while Pia refuses to return to Germany to see her parents, both she and Axel represent the new German generation who now direct their desire for liberation from history and trauma no longer against 'the outsider-other' but rather 'the insider-other', the familial evil who had been preying on the (grand)children's psyche.

The misconception that suffering could or at least should morally elevate the victims is revisited twofold: through the idea that Israelis did not draw enough lessons from the trauma of the Holocaust and through the representations of younger Germans as 'gentle' precisely because they are seen attempting to deal with and learn – if unconsciously as it were in Axel's case – from the trauma of their grandparents' perpetration. While Axel is depicted as deeply affected by the history of the Holocaust but unaware of the existence and source of his trauma, Pia is conscious of their family's involvement in the Holocaust, and suffering because of it. The filmic narrative of the hyper-masculine Israeli versus the (German) feminised-queer gent(i)le potential for enabling a touch,[12] and entanglement that will change the lives of all the main characters – in fact, a redemptive touch rather than mere encounter[13] – must rely on the absence, or rather muteness, of Israeli women (and non-Palestinian queers). As Ella Shohat pointed out, 'the Arab woman' and the 'Oriental Jewish woman' are 'typically denied a voice in Israeli film'.[14] In *Walk On Water,* this extends to all the Israeli women: the Israeli lead characters are male; Israeli women appear very briefly and as either aggressive (regularly checking up on a Mossad agent's shooting practice) or mute (we only see the body of Eyal's wife, Iris, after she committed suicide, and later on she reappears – speech-less as it were – in Eyal's dream). Both women are linked to violence and death while Pia is the only woman of this generation in the film who is connected to life. Moreover, at the end of the movie she literally gives new life to Eyal, and thus Israel, in the form of a child.

Miracle Workers

Walk On Water is not only concerned with Eyal's trauma but also construes a second- and third generation trauma for Axel and Pia. Yet, as opposed to Eyal, and precisely because they are queer and female, the siblings are presented as able to deal with their (family) history, and help Eyal to confront his violence and pain. As Welzer *et al* convincingly pointed out, in line with the ambivalent content and relationship of the 'Album' and the 'Lexikon', Nazis do not appear in one's own families, 'Germans' and 'Nazis' are viewed as two entirely different groups and the Holocaust does not have a place within the German family memory. Just as Nazis are a separate group, so Jews are never integrated into intimate memories/the 'Album'.[15] This logic is extended in an interesting way in *Walk On Water:* While Axel's and Pia's family is in fact directly implicated in the Holocaust – the grandfather, Alfred Himmelmann, is described by Menachem as the man responsible for the murder of the Jews in a whole area of

Germany, including Menachem's and Eyal's mother's family – they are nevertheless not representative given the family's obvious wealth and their depiction as a disappearing 'old-fashioned' class.

Highly interesting in this context, however, is the representation of the neo-Nazis and drag queens at the Alexanderplatz subway station. After Eyal has arrived for a surprise visit in Berlin, he and Axel visit a gay bar and are on their way to the tracks in the *U-Bahn* (subway). After passing a group of neo-Nazis at the entrance they meet acquaintances of Axel. Axel's friends are in drag and from different ethnic/'racial' backgrounds, and they come to represent the shifts in German domestic policy at the turn of the millennium: The legalisation of gay marriage, the re-styling of Berlin in particular as a new-old glamorous capitol for non-mainstream lifestyles and so forth. In opposition, the neo-Nazis are framed as outsiders, loitering aim-lessly at the subway entrance, and Axel's and Pia's parents represent the past and dying values no longer in tune with the new Germany. In fact, in *Walk On Water* the new generation, who came into adulthood in the reunified Germany, closes the gaps in the contents of the 'Album' and the 'Lexikon' by integrating 'Jews' as well as 'Nazis' into both. The Holocaust begins to receive a place in family memory, (old) Nazis are no longer a different group from Germans, and Jews, or rather 'things Jewish', will no longer be a part of both through their absence but rather a renewed presence. A renewed (desire for) Jewish presence is alluded to in several sequences, for instance in the obvious knowledge Pia and Axel have about Israel, Jewish history, their familiarity with particular songs, and so on.

When Axel arrives at Tel Aviv Airport from Berlin, he wears a T-Shirt imprinted with the words 'The Miracle Worker', the very same shirt he also wears when leaving Israel. Several teleplays, Broadway plays and movies entitled *The Miracle Worker* are based on the autobiography *The Story Of My Life* by Helen Keller, first published in 1903.[16] The movie's link to Keller's famous account of her life without the senses of hearing and seeing seems particularly poignant considering the manifold references to water throughout the film. Not only do we move from the Bosphorus to Tel Aviv but the trope of water is overtly present in several scenes: after Eyal has picked up Axel from the airport, they drive to the kibbutz where Pia works only to find her outdoors, fishing knee-deep in a lake. We have not yet been introduced to the main protagonists' conversations about 'walking on water', and hence Axel tells his sister to be careful while she hurries out of the lake to great him.

In *The Miracle Worker*, water is at the centre of Helen's break-through to speech. The word 'water' is her first word spoken (as 'wah-wah') after she had lost sight and hearing as a small child. And her teacher Anne Sullivan is the 'miracle worker': she draws the letters into Helen's palm while letting her hear the sound of running water. In *Walk On Water,* it is due to the kindness and openness of the two siblings, Axel and Pia, that Eyal will finally be able to arrive at his own miracle. Eyal had told Axel, while at the Dead Sea, that he never cried, and that, in fact, he has 'a good excuse', namely a rare eye condition which prevents his eyes from producing tears. Eyal is the stereotype of the Israeli macho who will neither talk about his feelings nor shed a tear, yet, at the end of the film in Berlin in the villa at the Wannsee he is not only able to cry for the first time – in Axel's arms after Axel has killed his grandfather – but also to put his pain into words.

Axel invites Eyal to the family home, tellingly a large villa near Wannsee, precisely on his father's birthday. As Menachem had suspected, Axel's grandfather arrives for the 70th birthday of his son, Axel and Pia's father. Pia remains in Israel. Before Alfred Himmel-mann makes a surprise entrance at the birthday party, Axel had introduced Eyal, and later makes all the guests join him as he teaches them the Israeli folk dance he learned from Pia and her group at the kibbutz. Axel's parents leave little doubt about their dislike of Eyal – who they seem to think is their son's new lover. In any case, Himmelmann is dependent on a wheelchair and medical equipment and later, when he lies in bed, Eyal enters the room with the aim of killing him but cannot bring himself to do it as the old man lies helplessly sleeping before him. According to Lynley Shimat Lys,

> As Eyal stealthily enters the grandfather's room, holding a lethal hypodermic needle, he begins to realize that he has lost the emotional tolerance for killing. The impact of his wife's recent suicide finally hits him. He backs away, defeated.[17]

While it is indeed the case that Eyal has changed considerably by this point, the scene nevertheless can be read in a more specific way: Eyal's inability to kill Himmelmann not only contrasts with his earlier attitudes but may be triggered by the fact that the man is old, helpless, and his white beard and striped pyjama potentially resonate with popularised images of Himmelmann's victims in the Holocaust. Unnoticed by Eyal, Axel has been watching the scene from the doorway and enters the room. Eyal leaves, and Axel tenderly touches the cheeks of the old man before switching off the life saving machine at the bedside. The young generation, the new Germany thus relieves the Jews from having to perform the (symbolic) killing of the German (grand)father, the perpetrator. Shimat Lys notes,

> Eytan Fox examines painful currents hidden within Israeli and German society and the microcosm of defiance and dissonance in a single family's legacy to offer the possibility of redemption for second- and third-generation survivors in *Walk on Water*.[18]

Yet while Fox addresses the notions of victimhood, of perpetrator, of trauma and redemption, he does so in a way that precisely enables such a construction of traumatised generations on both the German and the Israeli side. Axel represents the generation which is able and willing to belatedly defeat the Nazis. Thus, Axel becomes Eyal's saviour, a point emphasised by Eyal crying in Axel's arms. Finally, the shell of the macho breaks up and he can admit to his emotions. He relates to Axel that Iris had committed suicide, that he feels he kills everything around him and that he 'just cannot kill anymore'. The end of the film sees Pia and Eyal living together in Israel and having a baby. At this point, Eyal returns to the notion of 'walking on water': After having looked after the baby during the night, Eyal is sleepless and writes an email to Axel, inviting him for a visit, and telling him about the dream he had: they would both be at Lake Kineret again and, finally, they would both be able to walk on water together.

   The connotations of the movie's title, *Walk on Water*, which, apart from pointing to the obvious significance of water for the narrative as well as the region, allude to the figure of Jesus Christ ('the saviour')[19] and thus, in the film's context of the trauma of the Holocaust, to constructions of 'something good' or, indeed, potential saviours to emerge out of catastrophe. Hyam Maccoby has noted on the function of the 'sacred executioner' in mythological history:

> Some good consequence will be seen to flow from the slaying: a city will be founded, or a nation will be inaugurated, or a famine will be stayed, or a people will be saved from the wrath of the gods, or a threatening enemy will be defeated. Such good consequences are exactly the results that were hoped for by the performance of human sacrifice.[20]

In fact, the sacrifice that is performed by Axel reverses post-Holocaust history: at long last the German character no longer leaves the punishment to the (descendant of) the victim, and thereby releases the Israeli from the militaristic masculinity he had to build for himself in response to the trauma of the Holocaust. The 'good consequence' that will 'flow from the slaying' is thus the inauguration of the new German nation taking responsibility for the past, and, moreover, the beginning of a new German-Jewish/Israeli chapter made literal in the birth of Pia's and Eyal's child.

In scholarly accounts discussing *Walk On Water,* the main focus has been on Zionist sexual politics, Israeli trauma, or on an equally shared trauma of 'second and third generation' thus construing a misleading German generational succession in relation to the Holocaust, analogous to the descendants of survivors. Most striking, however, is the movie's presentation of an idealised vision of redemption through a queered/feminised new generation/nation. Raz Yosef, for instance, convincingly argues that

> *Walk On Water* fails to listen to the trauma of the Other. The film does not take ethical responsibility for the Other's traumatic wound. Instead, it channels the trauma of the Other in favor of reconstructing the Israeli male heterosexual subjectivity. In this film, the Israeli subject indulges in a love affair with *himself,* dissimulating and recovering the lost object by identifying with him and inhabiting his place. This is an autoerotic fantasy of incorporation [...][21]

Yosef refers here to the Palestinian 'Other', and my reading of the movie supports his analysis. However, as has been argued in this chapter, while *Walk On Water* is concerned with Eyal's trauma, it is also invested in the suffering of another, more closely connected 'Other': the new German generation that has to come to terms with the Nazi perpetrator 'within the family'. In contrast to Yosef's argument, this paper suggests that it is not only Eyal who is traumatised and repairing his loss by rescuing (for instance in the subway scene) Axel and his queer friends who stand in for the new Germany. In *Walk On Water,* the German siblings' suffering and their emotional rescue of Eyal – and thus Israel – is equally at the heart of the narrative.

In conclusion, in *Walk On Water* Fox created interactions between German and Israeli characters which can be read as providing a discursive space for 'German suffering' in Israeli cinema. The film achieves this via constructions of a German second and third generation trauma but mainly, and most notably, through negotiating gendered and queered notions of nation as well as ethnicised notions of gender and queerness. The depicting of 'German suffering' and 'Germans as victims' is not only possible due to the introduction of a generalised notion of traumatised individuals but also inevitably linked to images of and debates about the Israeli and the new German nation-state and politics, and about gender/queerness. The main binary that is being construed, and thereby allows 'German suffering' to be present on screen, is the juxtaposition of machismo and nationalism versus open minded, queer lifestyle-multiculturalism. In short, we are confronted with the mutually exclusive pairing of the Israeli 'muscle-Jew' versus the 'effeminate', gent(i)le German whose emotional openness is redeeming. Ultimately, in *Walk On Water,* Germany is also suffering, but s/he is now gay and female, and women and queers appear as particularly qualified to serve as the (gent(i)le) therapist of the Israeli heteronormative macho.

Notes

[1] Quoted from *Don't Touch My Holocaust/ Al Tigu Li B'Shoah,* Dir. Asher Tlalim, Israel, 1994.

[2] Michael Heinlein discusses in this volume how a generationally transmitted trauma is being constructed in Germany via the invention of a collective of 'Kriegskinder'.

[3] Nicholas Baer, 'Points of Entanglement: The Overdetermination of German Space and Identity in *Lola + Bilidikid* and *Walk On Water'*, *TRANSIT,* 4:1 (2009), http://www.escholarship.org/uc/item/8q04k8v1 (accessed 28 February 2010).

[4] Jacques Derrida, *On Cosmopolitanism and Forgiveness,* London and New York: Routledge, 2001, p. 48.

[5] Raz Yosef reads this sequence in the sense of Eyal attempting to 'rescue' Axel from Palestinians (Rafik and his uncle, the 'greedy' shopkeeper). I would add that the encounter between Eyal and the siblings is embedded in this theme: Pia insisted on hiring a tour guide for Axel because she was worried about terrorist attacks. See Raz Yosef, 'Phantasmatic Losses: National Traumas, Masculinity, and Primal Scenes in Israeli Cinema – *Walk On Water'*, *Framework: The Journal of Cinema and Media,* 49:1 (2008), 93-105 (here: p. 101).

[6] *Walk on Water,* United King Films Ltd., 2004. All quotations from this DVD.

[7] Ibid., p. 166.

[8] Ibid.

[9] Jeffrey T. Richelson, 'The Mossad Imagined: The Israeli Secret Service in Film and Fiction', *International Journal of Intelligence and CounterIntelligence*, 20:1 (2007), 136-66 (here: p. 142).

[10] Ibid., pp. 142-3.

[11] Yosef, 'Phantasmatic Losses'. p. 98.

[12] Asher Tlalim's *Don't Touch My Holocaust* is an interesting negotiation of Israeli and Palestinian traumata and body politics but also in the context of the construction of German suffering from a transgenerational perpetrator trauma after the Holocaust. Dani Verete's *Here is Not There* (which is part of his shorts trilogy *Yellow Aphalt/Asfalt Zahov,* Israel 2000) construes the gendered nation and the common ground between a German woman and an Israeli man against the violence and 'backwardness' of the Bedouins. Here as in *Walk On Water*, the German female and gay characters, respectively, are depicted as victims (or potential victims) of not only their own history but moreover, due to their openness to 'the other', also of the always potentially dangerous Arabs.

[13] At this point, I shift Leslie Adelson's terms from her work in the context of post-1945 migrations and literature in Germany into a broader context. Adelson argues for replacing the notion 'encounter' with the term 'touch' in order to account for historical and cultural 'touching' rather than remaining within the framework of fixed and mutually exclusive group identities as implied in the term 'encounter'. See Leslie A. Adelson, 'Touching Tales of Turks, Germans, and Jews: Cultural Alterity, Historical Narrative, and Literary Riddles for the 1990s', *New German Critique*, No. 80 (2000), 93-124; and Adelson, *The Turkish Turn in Contemporary German Literature: Toward a New Critical Grammar of Migration*, New York: Palgrave Macmillan, 2005.

[14] Ella Shohat, 'Making the Silences Speak in Israeli Cinema', in: Esther Fuchs, ed., *Israeli Women's Studies: A Reader,* New Brunswick: Rutgers University Press, 2005, pp. 291-300 (here: p. 294).

[15] See Harald Welzer, Sabine Moller and Karoline Tschugnall, *'Opa war kein Nazi': Nationalsozialismus und Holocaust im Familiengedächtnis,* Frankfurt/M.: Fischer, 2002, pp. 9-10.

[16] I refer in the following to the Broadway play *The Miracle Workers* written by William Gibson and directed by Arthur Penn. See also Helen Keller, *The Story Of My Life*, New York: Simon & Schuster, 2005. One might also argue that the words 'The Miracle Worker' on Axel's T-Shirt echoes the famous term 'Wirtschaftswunder' ('economic miracle') proclaimed in 1950s and 1960s West Germany – and thus this could be another implicit 'point of entanglement' (Baer) with the otherwise invisible 'Turks' and, generally, labour migrants who contributed to the 'Wirtschaftswunder'.

[17] Lynley Shimat Lys, 'Visceral Holocaust: Film and the Haptic Representation of Jewish Trauma'. Paper given at Society for Cinema and Media Studies (SCMS) Conference, Chicago, IL (March 2007), p. 2. http://essaysandplays.weebly.com/uploads/5/3/3/7/53370/kedmashoahwalk_conference_paper.doc (accessed 28 Feb 2010).

[18] Ibid., p. 5.

[19] In the sequences showing Axel and Eyal at Lake Kineret and their attempts to 'walk on water' (balancing forward on stones partly under water), both men have their arms stretched out to the side, feet and legs close together while carefully moving into the lake. At first, only Axel tries to 'walk on water' while a wide-eyed Eyal in close-up is watching him both amused and in awe. Axel explains that there are miracles, and that one just has to believe in something in order to make it happen. The shots resonate both with crucifixion images and a miracle-performing messiah, and so further the redemptive narrative of the (queer German) saviour.

[20] Hyam Maccoby, *The Sacred Executioner: Human Sacrifice and the Legacy of Guilt*, Bath: Thames and Hudson, 1996, p. 8.

[21] Yosef, 'Phantasmatic Losses', p. 103.

List of Contributors

Suzanne Brown-Fleming is Director of Visiting Scholar Programs at the United States Holocaust Memorial Museum's Center for Advanced Holocaust Studies (CAHS) and a former Center Fellow (2000). She is the author of *The Holocaust and Catholic Conscience: Cardinal Aloisius Muench and the Guilt Question in Germany* (2006). She has published articles and entries in *New Catholic Encyclopedia*, *Religion in Eastern Europe*, *Holocaust and Genocide Studies*, and *Kirchliche Zeitgeschichte*. Her current research project, 'The Vatican-German Relationship Re-Examined, 1922-1939', is a study of the Vatican nunciature in Munich and Berlin during the Weimar Republic (1918-1933) and the period of Eugenio Pacelli's tenure as Secretary of State (1930-1939).

Bas von Benda-Beckmann holds a doctorate from Amsterdam University on German historiography of the Allied Bombings. He is currently working on a post-doc on history and memory of Communist resistance during the Second World War in the Netherlands. He has published on Thomas Mann, Günter Grass, German memory culture and the Allied bombings. His latest publications are: 'Geen familiegeheim. De herinnering aan de geallieerde bombardementen in recent onderzoek: een besprekingsartikel' (*Tijdschrift voor Geschiedenis* 122, 2009) and 'Eine deutsch-deutsche Katastrophe? Deutungsmuster des Bombenkriegs in der ost- und westdeutschen Geschichtswissenschaft', in: Jörg Arnold, Dietmar Süss and Malte Thiessen eds., *Luftkrieg. Erinnerungen in Deutschland und Europa* (2009).

Cathy S. Gelbin, is Senior Lecturer in German Studies at the University of Manchester. She specializes in German-Jewish culture, Holocaust Studies, gender and film. Before serving as Director of Research and Educational Programs at the Centre for German-Jewish Studies (Sussex University, 1998-2000), she was coordinator of the Holocaust video testimony project *Archiv der Erinnerung*, carried out at the Moses Mendelssohn Zentrum für europäisch-jüdische Studien (Universität Potsdam) under the aegis of Yale's Fortunoff Video Archive for Holocaust Testimonies. Her publications include *An Indelible Seal: Race, Hybridity and Identity in Elisabeth Langgässer's Writings* (2001), *Archiv der Erinnerung: Interviews mit Überlebenden* *der Shoah* (co-ed., 1998) and *Aufbrüche: Kulturelle Produktionen von Migrantinnen, Schwarzen und jüdischen Frauen in Deutschland* (co-ed., 1999). Her monograph *The Golem Returns: From German Romantic Literature to Global Jewish Culture* is forthcoming.

Christian Groh received his PhD in History from Heidelberg University in 2002 with a study on the reconstruction of local police forces in post-war Germany. Since 1989 he has worked as a historian at the Stadtarchiv Pforzheim, since 2006 as deputy head. He has published on local history, the history of police and memory culture.

Michael Heinlein teaches sociology at the Ludwig Maximilians University in Munich. His research focuses on memory, labour, globalisation, cosmopolitanisation and reflexive modernity. Empirically, he works on the memory of war children, trans-national memory spaces, the role of mediation in the development of collective memory, care practices, and the cosmopolitanisation of labour.

Jeffrey Luppes is currently a PhD candidate in the Department of Germanic Languages and Literatures at the University of Michigan. He is the recipient of two DAAD research grants and a university-wide fellowship. His general academic interests include post-WWII German political and cultural history and memory culture. More specifically, he is interested in discourses about and representations of German wartime suffering.

Bill Niven is Professor of Contemporary German History at the Nottingham Trent University. He is the author of *Facing the Nazi Past* (2001) and *The Buchenwald Child* (2007), and editor of *Germans as Victims* (2006). His most recent publications include an edited volume on *Memorialization in Germany since 1945* (2009, with Chloe Paver).

Helmut Schmitz is Associate Professor of German at the University of Warwick. He is the author of a monograph on Hanns-Josef Ortheil (1997) and of *On Their Own Terms. The Legacy of National Socialism in Post-1990 German Fiction* (2004) and has published widely on German cultural memory of National Socialism. His most recent publications include the edited volumes *A Nation of Victims? Representations of German Wartime Suffering from 1945 to the Present*

(2007), *Von der nationalen zur internationalen Literatur. Transkulturelle deutschsprachige Literatur und Kultur im Zeitalter globaler Migration* (2009) and *Autobiographie und historische Krisenerfahrung* (2010, with Heinz-Peter Preußer).

Annette Seidel-Arpacı is currently a visiting scholar at the Institute for Research on Women and Gender (IRWaG) at Columbia University. She studied at the Centre for Jewish Studies and the Centre for Cultural Analysis, Theory and History (CentreCATH) at the University of Leeds. From 2005-2008, Annette was the convenor of the AHRC-funded research project 'Discourses of German Wartime Suffering 1945-present' at Leeds. Her research focuses on the tensions between Holocaust memory and constructions of German 'victimhood', and on minority positionality in Germany today. Annette has published articles and book chapters on Migration, Pedagogy, and German Memory Culture, on the writings of Jewish-German authors Esther Dischereit and Maxim Biller, and W. G. Sebald's *Luftkrieg und Literatur*. She is currently working on a book on Holocaust memory, migration and alterity in reunited Germany.

Nicholas J. Steneck received his doctorate in history from The Ohio State University and is now Assistant Professor of History at Florida Southern College, Lakeland, Florida. His current research focuses on early-Cold War West German civil defence planning and its role in shaping personal and collective identity.

Krijn Thijs is an historian at the German Studies Center at the University of Amsterdam. He wrote his dissertation at the Centre for Contemporary Studies in Potsdam: *Drei Geschichten, eine Stadt. Die Berliner Stadtjubiläen 1937 und 1987* (2008). He has published on German and Dutch memory cultures and historiography, and co-edited *Duitsers als slachtoffers. Het einde van een taboe?* (2007). He is currently working on symbolic transformation from the 'old' to the 'new' Berlin in the 1980s and 1990s.

Index

rodopi

Orders@rodopi.nl—www.rodopi.nl

Trauma, Memory, and Narrative in South Africa

Interviews

Edited by
Ewald Mengel,
Michela Borzaga,
Karin Orantes

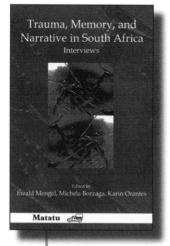

Twenty years after the fall of apartheid, South Africa is still struggling with its traumatic past. In this interdisciplinary collection of interviews, prominent South African novelists, psychologists, and academics reflect on the issues of trauma, memory, and narrative.

The authors André Brink, Maxine Case, Sindiwe Magona, Susan Mann, and Zoë Wicomb recount their personal experiences of writing about trauma, discussing its literary-aesthetic relevance and potential. The psychologists Don Foster, Ashraf Kagee, Pumla Gobodo—Madikizela, and Miriam Fredericks reflect on traditional Western conceptualizations of trauma and the need to extend and even re-write trauma theory from a postcolonial perspective. In the third part, Neville Alexander and Alex Boraine look back on the achievements and shortcomings of the Truth and Reconciliation Commission, describe the state of the nation, and underscore the need to relocate trauma structurally and historically. Annie Gagiano, Helen Moffett, Tlhalo Raditlhalo, and Chris van der Merwe show how trauma theory can open new horizons and create a new vocabulary for literary criticism by tackling issues of gender, representation, and genre.

All in all, these interviews provide fascinating insights into the present state of the South African soul, its current hopes and anxieties. Rather than claiming final answers to a complex and controversial issue, this volume aims at opening up debate and making a contribution to the already existing discussion about trauma in the South African context.

Amsterdam/New York, NY
2010. XIII, 256 pp.
(Matatu 38)
Bound €54,-/US$76,-
E-Book €54,-/US$76,-
ISBN: 978-90-420-3102-9
ISBN: 978-90-420-3103-6

USA/Canada:
248 East 44th Street, 2nd floor,
New York, NY 10017, USA.
Call Toll-free (US only): T: 1-800-225-3998
F: 1-800-853-3881

All other countries:
Tijnmuiden 7, 1046 AK Amsterdam, The Netherlands
Tel. +31-20-611 48 21 Fax +31-20-447 29 79
Please note that the exchange rate is subject to fluctuations

Theorie und Praxis der Kasualdichtung in der Frühen Neuzeit

Herausgegeben von
Andreas Keller, Elke Lösel,
Ulrike Wels und Volkhard Wels

rodopi

Orders@rodopi.nl—www.rodopi.nl

Gegenstand des Bandes ist das in der Forschung lange Zeit wenig beachtete, aber wichtige und extrem weite Feld der Kasualdichtung der Frühen Neuzeit. Die Kasualdichtung umfaßt als 'Gelegenheits'- oder anlaßgebundene Dichtung kleine Formen wie etwa Glückwunschgedichte, Trauergedichte, Reisegedichte oder Grabinschriften, aber auch 'große' Formen wie höfische Festspiele oder Ballette. Verhandelt werden in dem Band Fragen der Theorie, Poetik und Normierung von Kasualdichtung, sowohl aus historischer als auch moderner wissenschaftlicher Perspektive, genauso wie Überlegungen zur Gattungsspezifik (Lyrik, Drama, Schäferdichtung), zu sozialgeschichtlichen Aspekten (bürgerlicher Raum, Hof, Schule, Universität) und zu spezifisch regionalen Erscheinungsformen (Schlesien, Preußen, Bayern, Schweiz). Detaillierte Studien gelten etwa der Kasualdichtung von Wilhelm Ludwig Gleim, Anna Louisa Karsch, Andreas Tscherning, Andreas Gryphius, Johann Christian Günther, Johann Gottfried Schnabel, Heinrich Mühlpfort, Christian Gryphius, Christian Hoffmann von Hoffmannswaldau, Johann von Besser, Gottlieb Wilhelm Rabener und Siegmund von Birken. Die Beiträge umfassen damit den Zeitraum von ca. 1500 bis in die zweite Hälfte des 18. Jahrhunderts. Der Band, der sich vor allem an Germanisten, Historiker und Kunsthistoriker, die im Bereich der Frühen Neuzeit forschen, richtet, bildet den Stand der Forschung ab und stellt ein Kompendium neuerer Ansätze und Perspektiven dar.

Amsterdam/New York, NY
2010. II, 516 pp.
(Chloe 43)
Bound €104,-/US$146,-
E-Book €104,-/US$146,-
ISBN: 978-90-420-3104-3
ISBN: 978-90-420-3105-0

USA/Canada:
248 East 44th Street, 2nd floor,
New York, NY 10017, USA.
Call Toll-free (US only): T: 1-800-225-3998
F: 1-800-853-3881
All other countries:
Tijnmuiden 7, 1046 AK Amsterdam, The Netherlands
Tel. +31-20-611 48 21 Fax +31-20-447 29 79
Please note that the exchange rate is subject to fluctuations

A Companion to Heidegger's *Phenomenology of Religious Life*

Edited by
S.J. McGrath and
Andrzej Wierciński

In the academic year 1920–1921 at the University of Freiburg, Martin Heidegger gave a series of lectures on the phenomenological significance of the religious thought of St. Paul and St. Augustine. The publication of these lectures in 1995 settled a long disputed question, the decisive role played by Christian theology in the development of Heidegger's philosophy. The lectures present a special challenge to readers of Heidegger and theology alike. Experimenting with language and drawing upon a wide range of now obscure authors, Heidegger is finding his way to *Being and Time* through the labyrinth of his Catholic past and his increasing fascination with Protestant theology. *A Companion to Heidegger's Phenomenology of Religious Life* is written by an international team of Heidegger specialists.

Amsterdam/New York, NY
2010. XIX, 375 pp.
(Elementa 80)
Paper €80,-/US$112,-
E-Book €80,-/US$112,-
ISBN: 978-90-420-3080-0
ISBN: 978-90-420-3081-7

USA/Canada:
248 East 44th Street, 2nd floor,
New York, NY 10017, USA.
Call Toll-free (US only): T: 1-800-225-3998
F: 1-800-853-3881
All other countries:
Tijnmuiden 7, 1046 AK Amsterdam, The Netherlands
Tel. +31-20-611 48 21 Fax +31-20-447 29 79
Please note that the exchange rate is subject to fluctuations

rodopi
Orders @ rodopi.nl—www.rodopi.nl

rodopi

Orders@rodopi.nl—www.rodopi.nl

Shrinking Citizenship

Discursive Practices that Limit Democratic Participation in Latvian Politics

Edited by
Maria Golubeva
and Robert Gould

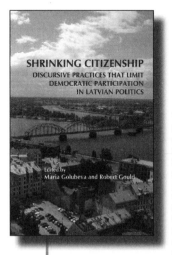

SHRINKING CITIZENSHIP
DISCURSIVE PRACTICES THAT LIMIT
DEMOCRATIC PARTICIPATION
IN LATVIAN POLITICS

Edited by
Maria Golubeva and Robert Gould

The book, based on research results from a three-year study of parliamentary and media debates in Latvia, analyses the discourses of Latvian politicians and the media about nation, citizenship, cultural diversity, history and the nation-state. This is the first large-scale study of political debates in a Baltic State from the perspective of Critical Discourse Analysis (CDA). Separate chapters, by researchers from Canada, Latvia, Lithuania and the UK, analyse the intersections between national identity construction, national mythmaking, concepts of citizenship, journalistic action, press ownership and questions of control of political and media discourses. All of these have impact on the fundamental questions of the relationship between individuals and the state. The authors conclude that even after the accession to the European Union in 2004, political pressures in Latvia, as also frequently on the political Right in other EU countries, promote ethnic membership as the guiding factor of state-building.

Amsterdam/New York, NY
2010. 197 pp.
(On the Boundary of Two
Worlds: Identity, Freedom,
and Moral Imagination
in the Baltics 26)
Paper €40,-/US$58,-
E-Book €40,-/US$58,-
ISBN: 978-90-420-3133-3
ISBN: 978-90-420-3134-0

USA/Canada:
248 East 44th Street, 2nd floor,
New York, NY 10017, USA.
Call Toll-free (US only): T: 1-800-225-3998
F: 1-800-853-3881
All other countries:
Tijnmuiden 7, 1046 AK Amsterdam, The Netherlands
Tel. +31-20-611 48 21 Fax +31-20-447 29 79
Please note that the exchange rate is subject to fluctuations

Rodopi

rodopi

Orders @ rodopi.nl—www.rodopi.nl

Weltanschauliche Orientierungsversuche im Exil / New Orientations of World View in Exile

Herausgeber
Reinhard Andress
Mitherausgeber
Evelyn Meyer und
Greg Divers

Amsterdamer Beiträge zur neueren Germanistik 76 2010

Weltanschauliche Orientierungsversuche im Exil
New Orientations of World View in Exile

Herausgeber
Reinhard Andress
Mitherausgeber
Evelyn Meyer and Greg Divers

Die Radikalität der Exilerfahrung führte viele ausgewanderte Intellektuelle, Schriftsteller und Künstler dazu, ihre Weltanschauung neu zu orientieren. Dies wirkte sich in vielfacher Hinsicht aus, u.a. philosophisch, psychologisch, sozial, politisch und religiös, und zeigte sich in epistolarischen, essayistischen, literararischen und anderen künstlerischen Formen. Dabei beschränkt sich das Exilphänomen keineswegs auf den Nationalsozialismus, sondern ist z.B. auch im Mittelalter aufzufinden. Der vorliegende Band geht den Strängen der exilbedingten Neuorientierungen nach, ausgehend von einer Tagung der North American Society for Exile Studies, die im Oktober 2008 an der Saint Louis University stattfand.

Amsterdam/New York, NY
2010. II, 371 pp.
(Amsterdamer Beiträge zur
Neueren Germanistik 76)
Bound €74,-/US$107,-
E-Book €74,-/US$107,-
ISBN: 978-90-420-3168-5
ISBN: 978-90-420-3169-2

USA/Canada:
248 East 44th Street, 2nd floor,
New York, NY 10017, USA.
Call Toll-free (US only): T: 1-800-225-3998
F: 1-800-853-3881

All other countries:
Tijnmuiden 7, 1046 AK Amsterdam, The Netherlands
Tel. +31-20-611 48 21 Fax +31-20-447 29 79
Please note that the exchange rate is subject to fluctuations

Rodopi

rodopi

Orders@rodopi.nl—www.rodopi.nl

Jean Potocki à nouveau

Études réunies et présentées par Émilie Klene avec la collaboration d'Emiliano Ranocchi et de Przemysław B. Witkowski

Suivies de la première version du Manuscrit trouvé à Saragosse, dans une édition modernisée de François Rosset et Dominique Triaire

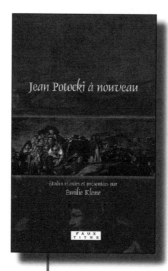

Cinquante-deux ans après la première édition partielle du *Manuscrit trouvé à Saragosse*, voici, réunis ici, les échos que l'œuvre de Jean Potocki suscite et éveille dans l'esprit et la conscience du XXIe siècle. Regards croisés qui vont s'efforcer d'interroger des textes dont on a le sentiment qu'ils recèlent beaucoup de choses à nous dire et qu'ils n'ont pas encore totalement livré leur mystère et leur secret. Ce volume présente également des documents inédits : le *Recueil Raisoné des plus anciennes notions historiques*, l'*Essai sur le déluge*, ainsi que la première version du *Manuscrit trouvé à Saragosse* (« version de 1794 »), dans une édition modernisée.

Amsterdam/New York,
NY 2010. 434 pp.
(Faux Titre 356)
Bound €87,-/US$126,-
E-Book €87,-/US$126,-
ISBN: 978-90-420-3162-3
ISBN: 978-90-420-3163-0

USA/Canada:
248 East 44th Street, 2nd floor,
New York, NY 10017, USA.
Call Toll-free (US only): T: 1-800-225-3998
F: 1-800-853-3881
All other countries:
Tijnmuiden 7, 1046 AK Amsterdam, The Netherlands
Tel. +31-20-611 48 21 Fax +31-20-447 29 79
Please note that the exchange rate is subject to fluctuations

Rodopi

Klabund.
Sämtliche Werke

Band I, Lyrik. Dritter Teil

Herausgegeben von Ramazan Şen

Verzeichnis & Register der abgedruckten Gedichte
*Verzeichnis der abgedruckten Gedichte, Band I, Erster
Teil _ Zweiter Teil _ Dritter Teil*
Band I Dritter Teil
Kleines Klabund-Buch
Lesebuch
Der Leierkastenmann
Der Neger
Wie Ich den Sommernachtstraum im Film Sehe
Einzelveröffentlichungen (1911–1928)
Postume Einzelveröffentlichungen
Unveröffentlichte Gedichte
Register

Amsterdam/New York, NY
2010. 366 pp. (Klabund –
Sämtliche Werke I,
Lyrik Teil 3)
Paper €73,-/US$106,-
E-Book €73,-/US$106,-
ISBN: 978-90-420-3145-6
ISBN: 978-90-420-3146-3
Band I-V:
ISBN: 978-90-420-0523-5

USA/Canada:
248 East 44th Street, 2nd floor,
New York, NY 10017, USA.
Call Toll-free (US only): T: 1-800-225-3998
F: 1-800-853-3881

All other countries:
Tijnmuiden 7, 1046 AK Amsterdam, The Netherlands
Tel. +31-20-611 48 21 Fax +31-20-447 29 79
Please note that the exchange rate is subject to fluctuations

rodopi

Orders@rodopi.nl–www.rodopi.nl

Imagology
Revisited

Waldemar Zacharasiewicz

rodopi

Orders@rodopi.nl–www.rodopi.nl

Imagology Revisited brings together in one volume essays written over a forty-year period on the perception and representation of foreign countries and peoples, the "other".

The book traces the emergence of national and ethnic stereotypes in the early modern age and studies their evolution and multiple functions in a wide range of texts from travelogues and diaries to novels, plays and poetry, produced between the 16th and 20th centuries.

The collection of essays, many of which are appearing in English for the first time, examines such phenomena as the mutual perception and misperception of Europeans and (North) Americans and the role of the theory of climate as a justification for stereotyped representations. It analyzes such national images as the hetero-stereotypes of Germans and Austrians in North American texts, and illuminates the depiction of the English abroad, as well as that of the Scots, the Jews and Italians in American literature.

The book is of interest to comparatists, to practitioners of cultural studies and cultural history, to scholars in the fields of ethnic and inter-cultural German studies and especially to Anglicists and Americanists.

Amsterdam/New York, NY
2010. VI, 571 pp.
(Studia Imagologica 17)
Bound €110,-/US$149,-
E-Book €110,-/US$149,-
ISBN: 978-90-420-3199-9
ISBN: 978-90-420-3200-2

USA/Canada:
248 East 44th Street, 2nd floor,
New York, NY 10017, USA.
Call Toll-free (US only): T: 1-800-225-3998
F: 1-800-853-3881

All other countries:
Tijnmuiden 7, 1046 AK Amsterdam, The Netherlands
Tel. +31-20-611 48 21 Fax +31-20-447 29 79
Please note that the exchange rate is subject to fluctuations

r o d o p i

Orders@rodopi.nl—www.rodopi.nl

Karl Philipp Moritz

Signaturen des Denkens

Herausgegeben von Anthony Krupp

Die Beiträge dieses Bandes zum vielfältigen Werk von Karl Philipp Moritz bringen neue Lesarten der für die 'Sattelzeit' um 1800 wichtigen Texte, vor allem seinen ästhetischen Schriften und dem psychologischen Roman *Anton Reiser*. Zudem bringt der Band Studien zu Moritz' Sprachschriften, zum ersten Mal zu seinen insgesamt vier Büchern für Kinder, auch zu seinen Reiseberichten, den *Andreas Hartknopf*-Romanen und der *Götterlehre*.

Der Einzelgänger Moritz bietet einen sehr eigenen Blick auf die geistesgeschichtlichen Probleme der Übergangszeit von Spätaufklärung zur Frühromantik.

This collection of 18 articles, in English and in German, on the diverse oeuvre of Karl Philipp Moritz provides new interpretations of texts widely recognized as significant to German letters around 1800 (Moritz's aesthetic writings and *Anton Reiser*). His writings on language receive welcome scrutiny, and contributors break ground on Moritz's particular classicism, his travelogues, and his use of the sermon. Furthermore, this is the first collection to examine all four of Moritz's books for children.

Readers interested in the transitional period of late Enlightenment and early Romanticism should profit from the study of this solitary walker and the signatures of his thought.

Amsterdam/New York, NY
2010. 314 pp.
(Amsterdamer Beiträge zur
Neueren Germanistik 77)
Bound €63,-/US$85,-
E-Book €63,-/US$85,-
ISBN: 978-90-420-3220-0
ISBN: 978-90-420-3221-7

USA/Canada:
248 East 44th Street, 2nd floor,
New York, NY 10017, USA.
Call Toll-free (US only): T: 1-800-225-3998
F: 1-800-853-3881
All other countries:
Tijnmuiden 7, 1046 AK Amsterdam, The Netherlands
Tel. +31-20-611 48 21 Fax +31-20-447 29 79
Please note that the exchange rate is subject to fluctuations

Soldiers of Memory

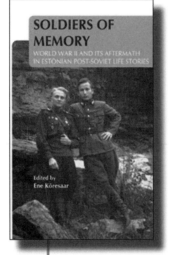

World War II and Its Aftermath in Estonian Post-Soviet Life Stories

Edited by
Ene Kõresaar

Soldiers of Memory explores the complexities and ambiguities of World War II experience from the Estonian veterans' point of view. Since the end of World War II, contesting veteran cultures have developed on the basis of different war experiences and search for recognition in the public arena of history. The book reflects on this process by combining witness accounts with their critical analysis from the aspect of post-Soviet remembrance culture and politics.

The first part of the book examines the persistent remembrance of World War II. Eight life stories of Estonian men are presented, revealing different war trajectories: mobilised between 1941 and 1944, the narrators served in the Red Army and its work battalions, fought against the Soviet Union in the Finnish Army, Waffen-SS, Luftwaffe, the German political police force and Wehrmacht, deserted from the Red Army, were held in German and Soviet prison and repatriation camps.

The second part of the book offers a critical analysis of the stories from a multidisciplinary point of view: what were the possible life trajectories for an Estonian soldier under Soviet and German occupations in the 1940s? How did the soldiers cope with the extreme conditions of the Soviet rear? How are the veterans' memories situated in terms of different memory regimes and what is their position in the post-Soviet Estonian society? What role does ethnic and generational identity play in the formation of veterans' war remembrance? How do individuals cope with war trauma and guilt in life stories?

Offering a wide range of empirical material and its critical analysis, *Soldiers of Memory* will be important for military, oral and cultural historians, sociologists, cultural psychologists, and anybody with an interest in the history of World War II, post/communism, and cultural construction of memory in contemporary Eastern European societies.

Amsterdam/New York, NY
2011. VIII, 441 pp.
(On the Boundary of Two Worlds: Identity, Freedom, and Moral Imagination in the Baltics 27)
Bound €90,-/US$122,-
E-Book €90,-/US$122,-
ISBN: 978-90-420-3243-9
ISBN: 978-90-420-3244-6

USA/Canada:
248 East 44th Street, 2nd floor,
New York, NY 10017, USA.
Call Toll-free (US only): T: 1-800-225-3998
F: 1-800-853-3881

All other countries:
Tijnmuiden 7, 1046 AK Amsterdam, The Netherlands
Tel. +31-20-611 48 21 Fax +31-20-447 29 79
Please note that the exchange rate is subject to fluctuations

Orders @ rodopi.nl

rodopi.nl–www.rodopi.nl